ANGELS
ANGELS
ANGELS

EMBRACED BY THE LIGHT...OR...
EMBRACED BY THE DARKNESS?

PHIL PHILLIPS

ANGELS
ANGELS
ANGELS

EMBRACED BY THE LIGHT...OR...
EMBRACED BY THE DARKNESS?

PHIL PHILLIPS

STARBURST PUBLISHERS

P.O. Box 4123, Lancaster, Pennsylvania 17604

To schedule Author appearances write:
Author Appearances, Starburst Promotions, P.O. Box 4123
Lancaster, Pennsylvania 17604 or call (717) 293-0939

Credits:
Cover art by Kerne Erickson
Unless otherwise stated all Scripture references are from the
New King James Version of the Bible.

ANGELS, ANGELS, ANGELS

First Printing, October 1994

ISBN: 0-914984-65-9
Library of Congress Catalog Number 94-67444
Printed in the United States of America

Contents

1   Angels: Everywhere, All the Time, But Especially Now   7

THE TRUTH ABOUT ANGELS—What the Bible Has to Say   14

2   What the Bible Says and Doesn't Say About Angels   15

3   Four Key Questions People Ask About Angels   42

4   The Messages of Angels   54

5   Jesus and Angels: A Portrait of Angelic Involvement with Mankind   70

6   Angels Through the Ages and Around the World   82

7   What is *Not* Ours to Know   90

THE LIES ABOUT ANGELS—What the New Age Teaches   93

8   Angels: The Latest Hijacking by the New Age Movement   94

9   Attempts at Conjuring Angels   113

10   How Angels Fit into the New Age Agenda   135

11   The Great Emphasis on "Experience"   157

12   The Subtlety of Deceit   167

FALLEN ANGELS—Two Takes on Ancient Foes   170

13   Angels, Demons, and Demons in Disguise   171

ANGELS AND THE AFTERLIFE   191

14   Embraced by the Light, or Embraced by the Darkness?   192

15   Death and Near-Death Experiences: When Are We Really Out of the Body?   216

16   Heaven and Hell   247

ANGEL ENCOUNTERS   270

17   What About Angelic Encounters?   271

18   Blurring Lines: How to Test the Spirits?   285

Reference Notes   305

Bibliography   312

1

Angels:
Everywhere, All the Time,
But Especially Now

Bless the Lord, you His angels,
Who excel in strength, who do His word,
Heeding the voice of His word.
Bless the Lord, all you His hosts,
You ministers of His, who do His pleasure.
                                                   Psalm 103:20,21

ANGELS, angels, angels.

They're everywhere.

They certainly aren't just for Christmas anymore.

There was a time when we only made angels in snowdrifts, baked cookies in the shape of angels, topped Christmas trees with angel ornaments, or dressed our children in white sheets so they might be angels in Christmas pageants. No longer. Angels are now a year-round and highly profitable business phenomenon.

There are angels-only boutique and stores, and many stores now have "angel departments."

Angels are the topic of newsletters.

Entire sections of book stores are devoted to angels.

Calendars and date books have angels as their themes.

Harvard Divinity School has a course on angels. Boston College has two such courses.

Tour companies have begun to specialize in conferences on angels and nature spirits, held in such places as Hawaii, Ireland, and England.

Weekend conferences, angel workshops, and even "angel class workbooks" are readily found, especially in the Northwest and Northeast regions of the United States.

We have long sung about angels in Christmas carols—"Hark, the herald angels sing. Glory to the newborn King." We have also sung about them in Gospel songs. The refrain to a familiar Fanny J. Crosby song speaks of "angels descending, bring from above, echoes of mercy, whispers of love."

But an estimate has been made that one in every ten popular songs also refers to angels in some form. That may have been even more true in the 1950s with songs such as "Teen Angel," "Earth Angel," "Johnny Angel," "Angel Eyes," and "I'm Living Right Next Door to an Angel" at the top of the charts.

Movies have featured angels, both old and new. Classics such as "Angel on My Shoulder," "The Bishop's Wife," and "It's a Wonderful Life" had angel themes. In the summer of 1994, one could find "Angels in the Outfield" at "Angel Stadium," helping the "Anaheim Angels" baseball team.

In 1993, First Lady Hillary Rodham Clinton made angels the theme of the White House Christmas tree.

A Media Phenomenon

You can hardly watch television these days without some mention of angels. One of the highest-rated television series in recent years was "Highway to Heaven," featuring an angel as its hero. Today, angels are the frequent topic of talk shows. They appear often as an element in advertisements and commercials.

An NBC television special on angels aired in May 1994. *Angels: The Mysterious Messengers*, scored such a ratings success that it was rebroadcast in July. After the first airing, some 17,000 people called in to request a tape of the show. A book by the same title was released by Ballantine in August and several other angel specials are planned by NBC in the fall of 1994. The vice-president of direct sales for Ballantine, Jon Conti, told *Publisher's Weekly* "our accounts reported 300%–500% increases in sales of angel titles after the May 24th NBC special."[1]

One of the foremost writers about angels is Sophie Burnham. Her book, *A Book of Angels,* has had thirty-six printings, with more than 700,000 books in print. *Where Angels Walk* was on the best-seller list for eighteen weeks, and had 500,000 copies in print after fifteen printings. *Angel Letters* has had twelve printings and 245,000 copies in print. While these books have made the top of the secular bookselling charts, other books on angels have been regulars on *Publisher's Weekly* Religion Bestseller lists, as well as on lists published by the Christian Booksellers Association.

The popularity of angels does not seem to wane.

Paintings and sculptures of angels have been displayed in major museums and galleries around the world for centuries. Many of these depict Bible scenes. But today, angels have moved beyond being players in Bible stories to being symbols of beauty, grace, strength, mercy, wisdom, hope, innocence, peace, truth, and guardianship.

Angels are a part of our vocabulary, our conversations.

We eat angel food cake and delicate angel hair pasta. We put angel fish in our aquariums.

We have named a city for angels—Los Angeles, as well as the longest uninterrupted waterfall in the world, Angel Falls in Venezuela.

We say that a person who barely scrapes by does so "on a wing and a prayer."

We say that children "look like angels" when they are asleep, that people with beautiful voices "sing like angels," and that those who help others are "angels of mercy."

Not Only a Bible-Related Idea

Angels seem to have a role in the folklore of many cultures, including many that do not draw the basis of their belief system from the Bible.

To the Balinese, angels are depicted as winged mermaids.

To the Viking they are called "valkyries."

The Greeks called them "horae," the Persians "freshta," and the Hindus "apsaras."

In Malasia, freckles are called angel kisses.

But Are They Real?

Apparently we not only talk and sing about angels, paint them, study them, and tell stories about them . . . but we actually believe in them.

A 1993 Time magazine poll indicated that 69 percent of Americans believe in angels, while only 25 percent said they did not.

The young, especially, seem to have a *growing* belief in angels. A Gallup Youth Survey conducted in the fall of 1992 found that 75 percent of American teenagers ages thirteen to seventeen believe in angels. This figure was up from 64 percent in 1978. During the intervening years, teen belief in other supernatural and paranormal events declined.

What exactly do we believe about them?

When a Time magazine poll asked five hundred Americans which description best described the angels a person believed in, the answers broke down as follows:

- Higher spiritual beings created by God with special powers to act as his agents on earth 55%
- The spirits of people who have died 15%
- An important religious idea but merely symbolic 18%
- Figments of the imagination 7%

In the same poll, subjects were asked if they had ever felt an angelic presence in their lives. Some 32 percent said yes and 35 percent said no. About a third, apparently, were unsure—maybe so, maybe not.

When asked if they believed in the existence of fallen angels, or devils, 49 percent said yes, and 45 percent said no.

What we can conclude from polls such as these is that although angels are very popular, we attach very different meanings and beliefs to them.

Increased Rate of Experience

What we can also conclude is that the rate of interest in angels has increased dramatically in the last decade. Literally thousands of accounts of activities of angels have been recorded in recent months and years.

And that calls us to ask several questions:
- Why this great interest in angels?
- Why an apparent increase in angel activity?
- Why are people apparently more willing to talk about their experiences with angels?
- What types of angels are being depicted?
- Is today's representation of angels the same as that in the Bible?

I strongly believe that the Lord God wants us to be informed about the supernatural realm, and that He also wants us to have accurate information. That is the number-one reason for this book.

At the outset, I feel a need to let you know these three things: First, *I believe in angels.*

I believe they are real, not because so many people today are having experiences with them, but because the Word of God, the Holy Bible, tells us they are real. I believe the Lord is much more pleased when we rely on His Word for our perception of reality than on even the most reliable eye-witness accounts of human beings. Because the Bible tells of the existence of angels, I would believe they were real even if nobody in today's world claimed to have seen one or been helped by one.

This is not to say that I dismiss every experience I hear about angels.

Quite the contrary.

I believe many people today are having bona fide experiences with elect angels of God. Angels are active in human affairs, and periodically, they reveal themselves to some people.

My concern regarding angel experiences is not that people are having them, but what kinds of experiences people are having, and what the outcome of those experiences tends to be in their lives.

Second, *I am not anti-angel when it comes to angel art or artifacts.*

For some time, my wife Cynthia and I have been searching for a particular design of gold-framed mirror. We spotted one early in our marriage that had on it what Cynthia terms "gold baby angels," and we've been looking for one like it to hang over our fireplace.

We also decorate our Christmas tree each year with angel ornaments. And Cynthia would like to have an angel painted on the
wall of one of our daughter's bedrooms.

Why?

Certainly *not* because we are worshipping angels or attempting to conjure their presence. We simply like angels as artwork
and artifacts, just as other people might like flowers or land-
scapes. They represent to us a symbol that is associated with our
faith . . . a symbol that reminds us of God's presence, protection
and provision for us . . . a symbol that we find personally appealing and beautiful.

Many of the paintings and sculptures of angels through the
ages are exquisite works of art. Many of these depict Bible stories.
In like manner, the angels we have in our home remind us of what
the Bible says about angels.

Third, *I am strongly opposed to the lies that I perceive
to be spreading rampantly about angels.*

What many people don't seem to realize today is that the angels who are flying about in our culture aren't angels linked to
Christianity!

Just as with the word "peace" in the 1960s and the sign of the
rainbow in the 1980s, angels are a Christian symbol that has been
hijacked by the New Age movement.

As we began the research for this book, Cynthia and I went to
two major bookstores in the area in which we live. In both cases,
we asked a clerk, "Can you tell us where we might find information about angels?"

And in both cases the clerk responded, "Oh, they're in the
New Age section."

Between the two stores, we walked out with more than $500
worth of books about angels. More than ninety percent of them
presented New Age thinking, including a couple of books that
had apparently been misfiled in the general "religion" section.

Much of the information being circulated in books, movies,
and at seminars flies directly in the face of God's Word.

And Christians need to know not only what is being said, but
who is saying it and why.

Beginning with the Truth

My greatest temptation is to dive headlong into what the New Age writers are saying about angels—and also about the afterlife, which is often so closely related to the existence of angels—but I believe the better place to begin is with the Truth. Once we know what God's Word has to say about angels, it is much easier to sort out what is simply man's idea, and what is straight from the devil's pit.

Therefore, let us begin with the Truth and explore what the Bible has to say about these awesome, Heaven-sent ministering spirits. Some of what you read may surprise you!

The Truth About Angels—

What the Bible Has to Say

2

What the Bible Says and Doesn't Say About Angels

ANGELS are mentioned more than three hundred times in the Scriptures.

The writers of both the Old and New Testaments do not explain the origin of angels. They simply assume their existence. The "good angels" of Heaven are called "elect angels" in the Scriptures (1 Timothy 5:21).

Their appearance is recorded:

- 32 times in the first five books of the Bible
- 37 times in the books that detail the development of the kingdom of Israel (Joshua, Judges, 1 and 2 Samuel, 1 and 2 Kings, 1 and 2 Chronicles)
- in the oldest book of the Bible, Job
- frequently in the Psalms
- by all of the major prophets except Jeremiah
- by the minor prophets Hosea and Zechariah

The Old Testament writers did not feel it necessary to offer formal proof that angels exist. They simply assumed them to exist and to be involved with men at the directive of God.

The Gospels of the New Testament are filled with references to angels. They are mentioned six times in the Book of Acts. Paul wrote of angels in many of the epistles attributed to him and James and Peter also referred to them. The book of Revelation alone has at least 65 references to angels. Among those many references, angels are seen by John:

- in relationship to the book with seven seals (Revelation 5:2-5)
- standing on the four corners of the earth, holding back the four winds of the earth (Revelation 7:1)
- ascending from the east having the seal of the living God (Revelation 7:2-3)

In the Life of Jesus

The angels were very active in the life of Jesus. From what He said and taught about them, it seems fairly obvious that Jesus believed what most Jews in that day believed—that angels are real, they are present all around us, and that angels are assigned to individual human beings. Jesus is recorded as saying:

- those who confess His name, He will confess before the angels, and those who deny Him, He will deny before the angels (Luke 12:8-9)
- the angels rejoice when a sinner repents (Luke 15:10)
- angels see the face of the Father and therefore, we should not despise "one of these little ones" (Matthew 18:10)
- the reapers of the harvest at the end of the age are angels (Matthew 13:39)
- when Jesus returns, He will come "in the glory of His Father with the holy angels" (Mark 8:38)
- angels escort saints to God's presence at the time of their death (Luke 16:22)
- He had the authority to call many legions of angels to his aid (Matthew 26:53)

Highly Active

To the surprise of many, angels are *not* readily associated with harps, music, or halos in the Scriptures. They do not lazily look out their heavenly windows on human affairs, or sit passively on clouds. These elements have, in the main, been added by artists through the ages.

Angels in the Scriptures are very active. They are in continual worship around the throne of God. (See Revelation 5:11-12 and Isaiah 6:3.) They are also active in the affairs of men.

A Personality Profile of the Heavenly Host

Do angels have personality?

Yes.

Personality is not defined by who man is, but by who God is. God is the originator of all personality. He is the archtype of all personality in the creatures He has made, including angels. We know from Scripture that angels have these major aspects to their personality: intelligence, emotion, and will. We'll take a look at each in turn.

Personality Trait #1: Intelligence

Angels desire to learn, communicate with speech, and have a revelatory knowledge of God's plan for the world. (See Matthew 28:5, Revelation 10:5-6, 17:1-18.)

The wise woman of Tekoa in 2 Samuel 14:20 refers to the king as "Wise, according to the wisdom of the angel of God, to know everything that is in the earth."

What is it that angels know?

Perhaps the chief thing that angels know is the nature of God. They have a vital, intimate, face-to-face relationship with God. They dwell in His presence, surround His throne, and worship Him continually. The elect angels of Heaven obey His commandments completely, and in that, they know God's desires and right judgments.

The prophet Micaiah also reported seeing angels: *I saw the Lord sitting on His throne, and all the host of heaven standing by, on His right hand and on His left* (1 Kings 22:19).

The elect angels also know the reality and nature of the fallen angels. They observed Lucifer's rebellion and the fall of Lucifer and those who rebelled against him to the earth. They know how to counteract these demons in a way that no human being can grasp fully. They are not only able to discern the devil's traps and snares, but they are one hundred percent capable of defeating the devil and his demons at every turn. They know that hell has been created for Lucifer, the rebellious evil angels, and all whom they entice to join them.

Angels also know about mankind. Whether you theologically place the creation of angels prior to the creation of the earth or on the fourth day of creation, angels were created prior to man. They know our very origin. They witnessed the creation of man and know God's purposes for mankind. They saw the fall of man in the Garden of Eden. They have observed man all through history.

Angels know God's plan. They were witnesses to the birth, crucifixion, resurrection, and ascension of Jesus Christ. They know of His second coming (as stated in Acts 1:10-11). They know God's purpose is to save men and women from their sins. In 1 Peter 1:10-12 we are told that the angels long to know about salvation even more than they do. Angels, of course, have no need for salvation, but they apparently long for the closeness of relationship that a restored relationship brings to mankind. Angels know of the ministry and purpose of the church.

The important thing to note is that . . .

*Angels **have** intelligence. They aren't "just ideas of God" or "God thoughts," as many in the New Age movement would have you believe.*

Personality Trait #2: Emotions

Angels worship God with deep awe and humble reverence. They express joy at God's creation. They ascribe to Jesus' "blessing, honor, and glory," indicating that they know something of the emotions attendant with blessing, honor, and glory. (See Isaiah 6:3, Job 38:7, Revelation 5:13.) They fall on their faces and cry out in loud voices as they worship—both indicators, at least in human experience, of deep-felt emotion.

As noted above, angels are creatures of worship. In Revelation we find that worship is their *primary* function and role. John writes in Revelation 5:11-12:

> *Then I looked, and I heard the voice of many angels around the throne, the living creatures, and the elders; and the number of them was ten thousand time ten thousand, and thousands of thousands, saying with a loud voice:*
> *Worthy is the Lamb who was slain*
> *To receive power and riches and wisdom,*
> *And strength and honor and glory and blessing!*

In Revelation 7:11-12 we find the description of a similar scene:

*All the angels stood around the throne and the elders and
the four living creatures, and fell on their faces before the
throne and worshiped God, saying:*
"Amen! Blessing and glory and wisdom,
Thanksgiving and honor and power and might,
Be to our God forever and ever. Amen."

It stands to reason, therefore, that angels would be most comfortable in settings where God is being worshiped. Numerous men and women of God have noted the presence of angels in places of worship, or have noted their appearance during times of worship.

It is important to note:

Angels **show** *emotion as they worship. Angels aren't just
"feelings" of love, kindness, and generosity, as some in the New
Age movement would have you believe.*

Furthermore:

Angels worship **God alone.** *They are not devoted to human
exaltation or deification, and they do not praise men.*

Personality Trait #3: Will

Angels have an ability to choose and to follow through on their choices. (See Hebrews 1:6 and Isaiah 14:12-15.)

Does this mean that angels have free will?

Yes, at least to a degree.

The implication drawn from the Bible is that in order for Lucifer to rebel, and for other angels to join in the rebellion, angels must have been capable of making a decision for or against God.

The implication of the Scriptures, however, is also that angels have "limited" free will. They have only one choice—to obey God or to disobey God. Human beings also face this choice, but in addition, human beings face a myriad of choices every day about *how* they will live their lives and to what extent they will participate in the ongoing creative processes of God. When angels choose for God, their loyalty is one hundred percent. They then carry out only God's orders, and they do so explicitly without interjecting their own will.

Lucifer's "Will."—The prophet Isaiah records five "I will" statements made by Lucifer:

- *I will ascend into heaven*
- *I will exalt my throne above the stars of God*
- *I will sit on the mount of the congregation on the farthest sides of the north*
- *I will ascend above the heights of the clouds*
- *I will be like the Most High* (Isaiah 14:12-13).

God responded with some "I will" statements of His own, as recorded in Ezekiel 28:16-18:

- *I cast you as a profane thing out of the mountain of God*
- *I destroyed you . . . from the midst of the fiery stones*
- *I cast you to the ground*
- *I laid you before kings, that they might gaze at you*
- *I brought fire from your midst; it devoured you*
- *I turned you to ashes upon the earth*

Lucifer's desire was to replace God. God's response was to remove Lucifer and destroy him.

That is a sobering thought for any person who seeks to put his or her own desires, will, and plans above those ordained by God.

It is important to note that . . .

*Angels **exercise** their will to obey God, and then they **manifest** God's will. Angels do not replace human will, take over human will, or manifest themselves through human will or as the result of human will . . . as many in the New Age movement will tell you.*

Although Similar in Personality— Not All Angels Are Alike in Function

The Hebrew understanding of angels includes the concept of "emanation." In very simple terms, this means that God sends out messengers from His eternal throneroom who embody His presence in a particular situation–His presence, including, of course, both His will and His power. Thus, angels have the same power as if the Father Almighty was present in physical, tangible form in a particular setting.

They are *not* God, however. Rather, they are sent from God to bear the fullness of His being into a situation or circumstance.

Consider, as an analogy, what would happen if you sent a registered letter, signed and notarized in the most authentic and legal means possible, authorizing a particular action to take place regarding a piece of property you owned a thousand miles away. You cannot be physically present on the scene, but your letter finds its way to the location and on the basis of its contents, your will is carried out. The person receiving the letter makes very few distinctions between you and the letter. What the letter conveys is clearly your intent. Action is taken on the letter just as if you were present, verbally making your desire known.

In many ways, angels are God's "letters of intent" sent out in tangible, physical form to carry out God's will.

And just like letters are written for various purposes and with different tones of voice, so the angels vary in their purpose, function, and style.

The Organization of Angels

The biblical concept is that angels are very well ordered, and that they may be arranged in a hierarchy. Some claim that angels are not in a hierarchy to each other, but rather, all of them report directly to God and they are arranged in different categories, all of which are equal.

The apostle Paul wrote to the Colossians about various angelic orders: thrones, dominions, principalities, and powers (Colossians 1:15-16). The same categories are used by him in referring to evil angelic hosts. His list should not be inferred, however, to be a hierarchy.

During the Middle Ages, Christian theologians developed an elaborate scheme for angels. Much of the writings of that time are based on the work of a fifth century theologian named Dionysius. He divided Heaven into nine choirs of angels, each with its own role. The highest angels were the seraphim and cherubim, those closest to God in nature. Their role was strictly to worship God. Other ranks of angels and their roles were:

- thrones—justice
- dominions—ordered life in heaven
- powers—protected mankind from evil
- principalities—welfare of nations

- archangels and angels—guides and messengers for individual human beings.

Various theologians through the centuries have developed their own hierarchies. Below are two such lists:

St. Ambrose	Billy Graham
Seraphim	Archangels
Cherubim	Angels
Dominations	Seraphim
Thrones	Cherubim
Principalities	Principalities
Potentates (Powers)	Authorities
Virtues	Powers
Archangels	Thrones
Angels	Might
	Dominion

The Bible gives a fairly clear description of only four main types of angels: cherubim, seraphim, archangels, and personal angels.

Cherubim Are "Guard" Angels

The cherubim are "guard" angels, or the angels who "cover" an area, a people, or a situation.

They are the first angels to be mentioned in the Bible. Their appearance is recorded in Genesis 3, after man and woman had sinned and God had driven them from the garden of Eden. In this instance, angels are set to guard the tree of life. The Scriptures tell us:

So He drove out the man; and He placed cherubim at the east of the garden of Eden, and a flaming sword which turned every way, to guard the way to the tree of life (Genesis 3:24).

A traditional Christian teaching has been that these angels guarded Eden so that man might not return and eat of the Tree of Life. If he had done so, man would have been "forever" left in his fallen state.

The actual Hebrew word for Cherubim is "Keruh," which has been translated by some scholars as meaning "one who intercedes" and by others as "knowledge." This leads to an interesting possibility. Could it be that God set His divine messengers of Knowledge at the gate to Eden to guard man against returning to a *full* knowledge of good and evil? Adam and Eve only "partook" of the fruit, indicating that they did not eat all of the tree's fruit. Had they eaten more, would they have known even more of evil? It may be that the very reason we do not see angels and demons regularly is that we simply could not stand a *full* knowledge of the warfare that exists between good and evil, or between angels and demons.

Cherubim are traditionally presented as large winged guards, with drawn swords or spears.

Guarding the Presence of God

Cherubim are also pictured as those angels which guard the holy presence of God. We see this in Isaiah 37:16 when Hezekiah proclaims, *O Lord of hosts, God of Israel, the One who dwells between the cherubim, You are God.*

Cherubim were a part of God's design for the ark of the covenant: *You shall make a mercy seat of pure gold; two and a half cubits shall be its length and a cubit and a half its width. And you shall make two cherubim of gold; of hammered work you shall make them at the two ends of the mercy seat. Make one cherub at one end, and the other cherub at the other end; you shall make the cherubim at the two ends of it of one piece with the mercy seat. And the cherubim shall stretch out their wings above, covering the mercy seat with their wings, and they shall face one another; the faces of the cherubim shall be toward the mercy seat. You shall put the mercy seat on top of the ark* (Exodus 25:17-21).

The children of Israel had long envisioned the Lord as riding the winds in the midst of angels. The mercy seat was designed to symbolize the presence of God between two worshiping angels. These angels were not graven images intended to be worshiped, but rather, symbols that placed the unseen Lord at the center of all worship.

We have this same imagery at the time of the Resurrection. When Mary looks into the empty tomb, she *saw two angels in white sitting, one at the head and the other at the feet, where the body of Jesus had lain* (John 20:12). The empty tomb became the new Mercy Seat!

The prophet Ezekiel described the cherubim in close association with *the glory of the God of Israel* (Ezekiel 12:22) and John described them as *living creatures* who continually *give glory and honor and thanks to Him who sits on the throne* in Revelation 4. (See especially vs. 9.)

Baby Angels?

Angels are frequently referred to as "cherubs." They are depicted as baby angels. That is not a Bible picture. The Bible picture of a cherub is a creature of great strength, majesty, and power.

The idea that cherubim are "babies," came from Roman folklore. It was from English folklore that cherubim took on the image of cupid-like creatures.

Lucifer: Chief Cherub

The chief cherub was once Lucifer. Ezekiel 28:11–19 describes him this way:

> You were the seal of perfection, full of wisdom and perfect in beauty. You were in Eden, the garden of God; every precious stone was your covering: the sardius, topaz, and diamond, beryl, onyx, and jasper, sapphire, turquoise, and emerald with gold. The workmanship of your timbrels and pipes was prepared for you on the day you were created. You were the anointed cherub who covers; I established you; You were on the holy mountain of God; You walked back and forth in the midst of fiery stones. You were perfect in your ways from the day you were created, till iniquity was found in you. By the abundance of your trading you became filled with violence within, and you sinned; therefore I cast you as a profane thing out of the mountain of God, and I destroyed you, O covering cherub, from the midst of the fiery stones. Your heart was lifted up because of your beauty; you corrupted your wisdom for the sake of your splendor; I cast you to the ground, I laid you before kings, that they might gaze at you. You defiled your sanctuaries by the multitude of your iniquities, by the iniquity of your trading; therefore I brought fire from your midst; it devoured you, and I turned you to ashes upon the earth in the sight of all who saw you. All who knew you among the peoples are astonished at you; you have become a horror, and shall be no more forever.

Nancy Gray points out in her book, *The Angelic Army*, that an "anointed cherub" is one with outstretched wings, or an angelic being intent on "expanding" his power.[1] Ezekiel indicates that Lucifer was cast out of Heaven because of an abundance of trading, which indicates a desire to expand his authority and God-given boundaries.

The prophet Isaiah tells a similar story:

> *How you are fallen from heaven, O Lucifer, son of the morning! How you are cut down to the ground, you who weakened the nations! For you have said in your heart: "I will ascend into heaven, I will exalt my throne above the stars of God; I will also sit on the mount of the congregation on the farthest sides of the north; I will ascend above the heights of the clouds, I will be like the Most high." Yet you shall be brought down to Sheol, to the lowest depths of the Pit* (Isaiah 13:12–15).

From these accounts, we can conclude that Lucifer had the ability to "cover" the wealth of the earth with his wings, but that this did not suffice Lucifer's desire for grandeur. He coveted Heaven itself.

Seraphim Are Radiantly Ablaze

The word seraphim literally means "fiery" or "burning." The name may indicate the color of these angels: a shining copper color. It was the seraphim who brought a live coal and placed it on the lips of the prophet Isaiah to cleanse them. (See Isaiah 6:6–7.)

The seraphim are a very high-ranking order of angels. They are described only by the prophet Isaiah:

> *In the year that King Uzziah died, I saw the Lord sitting on a throne, high and lifted up, and the train of His robe filled the temple. Above it stood seraphim; each one had six wings: with two he covered his face, with two he covered his feet, and with two he flew. And one cried to another and said: "Holy, holy, holy is the Lord of hosts; the whole earth is full of His glory!" And the posts of the door were shaken by the voice of him who cried out, and the house was filled with smoke* (Isaiah 6:1–4).

A few verses later Isaiah tells us that one of the seraphim "flew" to him with a live coal taken from the altar and he touched

Isaiah's mouth with it, saying, *Behold, this has touched your lips; Your iniquity is taken away, and your sin purged* (Isaiah 6:6-7).

This should not be construed to say that the angel himself forgave Isaiah's sins, but rather, that the angel was announcing a "fact of Heaven." He was declaring reality to Isaiah.

James Russell Lowell regarded the shining glow of angels as the result of their having seen God, much the same way that Moses' face was radiant after he encountered the presence of the Almighty on Sinai. Lowell wrote:

> But all God's angels come to us disguised:
> Sorrow and sickness, poverty and death,
> One after other lift their frowning masks,
> And we behold the Seraph's face beneath,
> All radiant with the glory and the calm
> Of having looked upon the front of God.[2]

Archangels Are "Chief Princes"

Archangels are considered to be the "chief princes of heaven." They have always been thought to be fairly limited in number.

Traditionally, the Church has recognized four archangels: Michael, Gabriel, Raphael, and Uriel. Jewish traditional literature also refers to four archangels. Some Christian literature through the ages has named seven archangels, and some today speculate there may be twelve. New Age writers have assigned archangels to each spoke of the zodiac, each planet, each season, each day of the moon cycle, each day of the week, each hour of the day, and each point of the compass.

The Bible does not give the number of archangels.

Only two archangels are mentioned in the Bible by name: Michael and Gabriel.

Michael

Mentioned by name in Daniel 10:12-14:

> *Then he said to me, "Do not fear, Daniel, for from the first day that you set your heart to understand, and to humble yourself before your God, your words were heard; and I have come because of your words. But the prince of the kingdom of Persia withstood me twenty-one days; and behold, Michael, one of the chief princes, came to help me, for I had been left alone there with the kins of Persia. Now I have*

come to make you understand what will happen to your
people in the latter days, for the vision refers to many days
yet to come. "

Michael is specifically described as an *archangel* in Jude 9:
Yet Michael the archangel, in contending with the devil,
when he disputed about the body of Moses, dared not bring
against him a reviling accusation, but said, "The Lord
rebuke you!"

The name Michael literally means "who is like God?" He is
always pictured as warring or fighting. And He seems to have a
special concern for the children of God, as seen in Daniel 12:1:
At that time Michael shall stand up, the great prince who
stands watch over the sons of your people; and there shall
be a time of trouble, such as never was since there was a
nation, even to that time, and at that time your people shall
be delivered.

In the Dead Sea Scrolls, Michael is referred to as the "Prince
of Light." In Jewish traditional writings, of the seventy angel-
princes set over the seventy nations, Michael is the protector of
Israel and the chief of the angel-princes. In the Apocryphal book
of 2 Enoch, Michael is called "general" and "great captain." In
other Jewish legends, it is Michael who spoke out of the burning
bush and who carried the tablets to Moses on Mount Sinai.

Gabriel

Gabriel literally means "hero of God" is the angel of annuncia-
tion, heavenly mercy, resurrection, and revelation. In Jewish traditional writings, he is the chief of the angelic guards and the
keeper of the celestial treasury. He is the angel who told the virgin
Mary that she would bear the Son of God.

Raphael

Raphael is identified as an archangel in apocryphal writings,
not in the traditional canon of the Holy Bible. He is associated in
the Apocrypha with prayer, love, joy, light, providence, and healing. In the book of Enoch, he is "set over all the diseases and all
the wounds of the children of men." In the book of Tobit, he is the
guardian, guide, matchmaker, teacher, healer, and companion to
Tobias and his family.

The Hebrew word "rapha" means "healer." It is often translated doctor or surgeon. The Hebrew concept of healing, however, is one of wholeness. Rapha refers to that which makes whole. Raphael is traditionally associated in Church lore with healing, but his alleged identity should perhaps be much broader than that to include his ability to convey to people the spiritual wisdom and power they need to pursue wholeness.

Uriel

In addition to Michael, Gabriel, and Raphael, a fourth archangel has been identified in Christian literature as Uriel, or in some texts, Phanuel. The name Uriel means "Fire of God" and both traditional Jewish and Christian writings name Uriel as one of the two angels placed at the entrance of Eden to guard the way to the tree of life. He is usually associated with light, illumination, and interpretation. Again, like Raphael, he is not mentioned by name in the Bible.

Another Angel

There is another angel mentioned by name in the Bible, although he is not classified as an archangel. He is considered to be "the angel of the bottomless pit, whose name in Hebrew is Abaddon, and in Greek, Apollyon" (Revelation 9:11). He is king over hideous creatures who have the "power to hurt men five months" (Revelation 9:10).

"But," you may say, "I know the names of a lot of angels."

You are probably thinking of the angels in *Paradise Lost*. It is there that we find the most thorough listing of angels in any piece of literature. Besides Satan, Milton speaks of Beelzebub, Moloch, Chemosh, Baalim, Ashtaroth, Astoreth, Azazel, Mammon, Thammuz, Dagon, Rimmon, and Belial as being in hell with Satan. Also there in hell are the pagan gods Osiris, Iris, Orus, the Golden Calf, and the Greek gods.

Six angels are mentioned as fighting beside Satan but they are not listed in hell: Adramelec, Asmadai, Ariel, Arioc, Ramiel, Nisroc. The good angels are named by Milton as Uriel, Gabriel, Michael, Raphael, Uzziel, Ithuriel, Zephon, and Abdiel.

Singular vs. Plural Names

As far as we know, Michael and Gabriel have singular names in the Bible.

By contrast, Lucifer—whom theologians have assumed for centuries was also an archangel before his fall—has many names. This multitude of names is apparently necessary to describe the many facets of his evil character. He is called Satan, the devil, the old serpent, the great dragon, the accuser, the deceiver, the destroyer, the tempter, and a "murderer from the beginning."

This diversity of names stands in sharp contrast to Michael and Gabriel, whose apparent purity of motive and devotion has no deviance or variation.

Angels, as a whole, have several names in the Bible. King Nebuchadnezzar referred to angelic beings in his visions as "a watcher, a holy one" and as "holy ones." (See Daniel 4:13, 17, 23.)

Personal or "Guardian" Angels

While the cherubim guard the things of God, the Bible also seems to speak of personal angels who guard each person.

Many English-speaking children have recited the poem below as a bedtime prayer:

Matthew, Mark, Luke, and John
Bless the bed that I lie on.
Four corners to my bed,
Four angels there be spread:
One at the head, one at the feet,
And two to guard me while I sleep.

Do you believe that *you* have a guardian angel—one who watches over you not only sleeping, but twenty-four hours a day?

Nearly half of all Americans seem to think they have one. In a Time magazine poll conducted in 1993, some 46 percent of those polled said they believed they had their own guardian angel. Only 21 percent of those polled said they did not.

The Bible seems to support the idea of a guardian angel, at least for children. In Matthew 18:10 Jesus is recorded as telling His disciples: *Take heed that you do not despise one of these little ones, for I say to you that in heaven their angels always see the face of My Father who is in heaven.*

Guardian angels seem to play two roles in their relationship with human individuals.

Rescue and Protection

Psalm 34:7 tells us that "the angel of the Lord encamps all around those who fear Him, and delivers them."

Psalm 91:11 reiterates this role for angels:

For He shall give his angels charge over you, to keep you in all your ways. In their hands they shall bear you up, lest you dash your foot against a stone. You shall tread upon the lion and the cobra, the young lion and the serpent you shall trample under foot.

The angels of the Lord have a charge to protect us and keep us safe. They are like a buffer zone between us and the enemy who would seek to destroy us.

Note, however, that this protection is limited. It doesn't apply to all people. In Psalm 92 the protection regarding angels is prefaced by these verses:

He who dwells in the secret place of the Most High shall abide under the shadow of the Almighty. I will say of the Lord, "He is my refuge and my fortress; my God, in Him I will trust." (vss. 1-2)

and,

Because you have made the Lord, who is my refuge, even the Most high, your dwelling place, no evil shall befall you. (vss. 9-10)

The protecting power of angels is reserved for those who have put their total trust in the Lord and who see God as their refuge.

Tobias 5:21 (Apocrypha) describes the "guardian" work of angels this way: "For a good angel will go with him, his journey will be successful, and he will come home safe and sound."

Jacob apparently believed he had a guardian angel. Shortly before his death, he blessed Joseph, saying:

God, before whom my fathers Abraham and Isaac walked, the God who has fed me all my life long to this day, the Angel who has redeemed me from all evil, bless the lads (Genesis 48:15-16).

Note that the word "redeem" in this instance refers to being spared or saved from natural disaster; it does not imply a spiritual ability to forgive sins.

Escorts at Death

A second major function of guardian angels seems to be that they escort us into the presence of God at the time of our death.

Jesus told a parable about a sick beggar named Lazarus who was laid at the gate of a rich man, desiring only to be fed the crumbs that fell under the rich man's table. Jesus said, *So it was that the beggar died, and was carried by the angels to Abraham's bosom.* (Luke 16:22).

The implication of this verse is that angels are there to escort us to the hereafter at the time of our death.

A beautiful poem about the ministering work of angels is that of Adelaid A. Procter:

> Angels of light, spread your bright wings and keep
> Near me at morn:
> Nor in the starry even, nor midnight deep,
> Leave me forlorn.
> From all dark spirits of unholy power
> Guard my weak heart,
> Circle around me in each perilous hour,
> And take my part.
> From all foreboding thoughts and dangerous fears,
> Keep me secure;
> Teach me to hope, and through the bitterest tears
> Still to endure.
> If lonely in the road so fair and wide
> My feet should stray,
> Then through a rougher, safer pathway guide
> me day by day.
> Should my heart faint at its unequal strife,
> O still be near!
> Shadow the perilous sweetness of this life
> With holy fear.
> Then leave me not alone in this bleak world,
> Where'er I roam,
> And at the end, with your bright wings unfurled,
> O take me home!

Bible Accounts of Angelic Deliverance

Although the function of "deliverance" is not directly attributed to guardian angels in many places in the Bible, the Bible is filled with stories of individual deliverance, as well as deliverance for the people of God as a group.

Daniel credited an angel with shutting the lion's mouths in the dungeon in which he had been thrown. (See Daniel 6:22.)

Another of the foremost accounts of deliverance by angels is found in Exodus 14, where the *angel of God, who went before the camp of Israel, moved and went behind them; and the pillar of cloud went from before them and stood behind them. So it came between the camp of the Egyptians and the camp of Israel. Thus it was a cloud and darkness to the one, and it gave light by night to the other, so that the one did not come near the other all that night* (Exodus14:19-20).

In this account we find an angel to be the agent that causes the Egyptians to be blinded to the whereabouts of God's people, while at the same time, God's people have light. As a result, the children of Israel are spared in the night, to face the crossing of the Red Sea the next day on dry ground.

This delivering power is described by the prophet Isaiah in this way:

"For He said, 'Surely they are My people,
Children who will not lie.'
So He became their Savior.
In all their affliction He was afflicted,
And the Angel of his Presence saved them;
In His love and in His pity He redeemed them;
And He bore them and carried them
All the days of old." (Isaiah 63:8-9)

As 2 Peter 2:11 tells us, "they are great in power and might."

Peter's Deliverance

Prisons are certainly no match for angels. In Acts 5:18 we read how the apostles were put in the common prison and "at night an angel of the Lord opened the prison doors and brought them out, and said, 'Go, stand in the temple and speak to the people all the words of this life.'"

One of the most profound examples of rescue in the Scriptures is Peter's deliverance from prison as recorded in Acts 12:5-11:

Peter was therefore kept in prison, but constant prayer was offered to God for him by the church. And when Herod was about to bring him out, that night Peter was sleeping, bound with two chains between two soldiers; and the guards before the door were keeping the prison. Now behold, an angel of the Lord stood by him, and a light shone in the prison; and he struck Peter on the side and raised him up, saying, "Arise quickly!" And his chains fell off his hands. Then the angel said to him, "Gird yourself and tie on your sandals;" and so he did. And he said to him, "Put on your garment and follow me." So he went out and followed him, and did not know that what was done by the angel was real, but thought he was seeing a vision. When they were past the first and second guard posts, they came to the iron gate that leads to the city, which opened to them of its own accord; and they went out and went down one street, and immediately the angel departed from him. And when Peter had come to himself, he said, "Now I know for certain that the Lord has sent His angel, and has delivered me from the hand of Herod and from all the expectation of the Jewish people."

I'd like to call your attention to several facts related to this story of angelic deliverance.

First, *while Peter was in prison, the saints in Jerusalem were in constant, earnest prayer for him.* In fact, they had established a twenty-four hour prayer meeting in his behalf.

Second, *the angel apparently had no difficulty overcoming all the obstacles to Peter's deliverance.* He had no problem causing the guards to sleep through Peter's escape. He also had no difficulty dealing with shackles and iron gates. Angels apparently have authority over the laws of nature when they are given a job to do by God.

Third, *the angel did not do what Peter was capable of doing.* He didn't lift Peter up, dress him, or put on his sandals. Angels don't do for human beings what human beings are able to do for themselves.

Fourth, *the angel apparently was given an order to "get Peter out of prison." His was a mission of deliverance, not a mission to deliver a message.* In such an instance, the angel apparently had the prerogative to tell Peter specific things to do *as they were needed* in order for the angel to accomplish the mission on which he had been sent by God.

The angel speaks strictly in a "command" tense. He tells Peter precisely what to do and he wastes no words. When we take the words of angels as a whole in the Scripture, we find that they have great economy of words. Most of what they speak to men is in the form of proclamations, announcements, or commands. They engage in very little dialog.

It is easy to infer from this that the orders given to angels from God's throne are much in the same tenor—angels receive commands, proclamations, and announcements. God does not have a familial, congenial, chatty relationship with His angels. They are His servants, subject to His commands, always ready to carry out His orders.

Our relationship with God, however, is defined in much different terms in the Scriptures. We are to consider God as our heavenly Father. We were created out of God's desire for fellowship and loving communication.

Fifth, *Peter responded primarily to the deliverance he experienced, not to the fact that an angel had appeared to him.* We can learn a great deal from Peter's response to his angelic deliverer. He did not perceive that the angel had delivered him merely from prison, but rather, that *God* had delivered him from the "hand of Herod." Peter regarded his deliverance as a sure sign that he was to live and to continue to preach and lead the Church. He saw his deliverance as benefiting the Church.

Martyrdom was *expected* in the early Church. These apostles had seen their perfect, guileless Lord Jesus crucified and resurrected to new life. They expected no less in their own lives than to die in proclaiming the Gospel and rise to newness of life in Him. What a far cry from many today, who expect deliverance and who regard martyrdom as a "failure" of faith.

Peter openly acknowledged that it was the Lord who had delivered him and that is what he proclaimed to those gathered at the house of Mary. (See Acts 12:17.) He did not give praise to the angel, but to the Lord.

Sixth, *as in the case of so many others in the Scriptures, Peter was not fully aware of the angel's presence or activity until he "came to himself" out on the streets near the prison.* Until that time, his encounter with the angel had seemed like a dream to him.

Thrones or Wheels?

There are those who believe the angels closest to the throne of God have no form at all. Rather, they appear as pure, raw energy, great sweeping balls of fire swirling almost like supernovas. These angelic forms are generally called Wheels or Thrones.

These wheels or thrones have been called by some as the "chariots of God." Psalm 68:17 seems to agree with this approach: *The chariots of God are twenty thousand, even thousands of thousands; The Lord is among them as in Sinai, in the Holy Place.*

Is There A Death Angel?

The Bible speaks in a number of places of the "destroyer" or the "angel of death." (See 1 Corinthians 10:10 and Exodus 12:23 as examples.)

Who controls this angel?

Jesus said clearly, *The thief does not come except to steal, and to kill, and to destroy. I have come that they may have life, and that they may have it more abundantly* (John 10:10). In Hebrews 2:14 we read, *that through death (on the Cross) He (Jesus) might destroy him who had the power of death, that is, the devil, and release those who through fear of death were all their lifetime subject to bondage.*

The Bible position is clearly that the devil presently has the power of death. It is his very nature to kill, steal, and destroy.

Have you ever seen a nature film about lions who stalk prey in the wilds of Africa? They target the weak, young, or sick animals who are more easily frightened by their roar, and who allow themselves to become paralyzed by fear. When that happens, the terrorized and weak animal is rendered completely incapable of staying with the herd. Once separated, the lions move in for the kill.

When a person separates himself from God and from the household of faith, he is in a very vulnerable position. He is alone, away from the fellowship that can protect him and give wise counsel to his life. He is easy prey for the enemy.

When the devil sees an entire group of people who have hardened their hearts against God and are steadfast in their rebellion against Him, it is his very nature to kill them while he has his chance. He is the "destroyer." The destroying angels are actually demonic powers of death at his command.

God allows them to do their work because to intervene otherwise would be to countermand His own laws of justice.

God is loving, absolutely perfect, and He extends his mercy freely. But those who refuse to enter into a relationship with God cannot know His love, justice, or mercy. What is the opposite? Hate, wrath, indignation, trouble, evil.

Consider for a moment a person who resides within the walls of a city ruled by the most benevolent king who has ever lived. Outside the city walls, however, is a dark forest, filled with all manner of savagery and terror. The person who chooses to reside within the city walls has all that he needs. However, should that person choose *not* to live within the city, he would be subject to the evils of the dark forest. The king cannot protect him there because he has allowed someone else to have jurisdiction over the forest. There are those who would say that the king of the city "caused" the person who leaves the city to experience evil, but the truth of the matter is that the person has made a choice to live outside the city walls. In making that choice, he has made a choice *for* evil and he is subject to its forces.

The Death Angel and the Assyrians

One of the most powerful displays of angelic power against God's enemies is recorded in Isaiah 36–37. King Hezekiah and the tribes of Judah were the target of Sennacherib, the king of Assyria. Sennacherib sent Rabshakeh, one of his most trusted men, to Hezekiah to demand his surrender. Rabshakeh made his demands in the most insulting manner, including insults about the Lord. He said, *Who among all the gods of these lands have delivered their countries from my hand, that the Lord should deliver Jerusalem from my hand?* (Isaiah 36:20).

When King Hezekiah heard the words of Rabshakeh he tore his clothes, covered himself with sackcloth, and went into the house of the Lord. He called upon Isaiah to pray.

Again Rabshakeh made his taunting threats and demanded surrender. Hezekiah took his demands and spread them before the
Lord in the house of the Lord and prayed. Isaiah came to the king,
saying:

> *Thus says the Lord God of Israel, "Because you have prayed
> to Me against Sennacherib king of Assyria, this is the word
> which the Lord has spoken concerning him" and Isaiah
> gave a long prophecy about the defeat of the Assyrians. He
> said specifically concerning the king of Assyria, "He shall
> not come into this city, nor shoot an arrow there. Nor come
> before it with shield, nor build a siege mound against it. By
> the way that he came, by the same shall he return; and he
> shall not come into this city . . . for I will defend this city to
> save it for My own sake and for My servant David's sake"*
> (Isaiah 37:33-35).

And then we read these words:

> *The angel of the Lord went out, and killed in the camp of
> the Assyrians one hundred and eighty-five thousand; and
> when people arose early in the morning, there were the
> corpses—all dead* (Isaiah 37:36).

In the wake of this destruction, the king of Assyria returned
home by way of Nineveh and while there, two of his own sons
killed him.

The Final Destruction

God will use angels to signal the start of the final harvest, according to the Book of Revelation:

> *Then I looked and behold, a white cloud, and on the cloud
> sat One like the Son of Man, having on His head a golden
> crown, and in His hand a sharp sickle. And another angel
> came out of the temple, crying with a loud voice to Him who
> sat on the cloud, "Thrust in Your sickle and reap, for the
> time has come for You to reap, for the harvest of the earth is
> ripe." So He who sat on the cloud thrust in His sickle on the
> earth, and the earth was reaped* (Revelation 14:14-16).

Angels are used to carry out God's commands related to destruction. In Revelation 14:17-19, angels are directed to take part
in the final destruction of the wicked:

> *Another angel came out of the temple which is in heaven,
> he also having a sharp sickle. And another angel came out*

from the altar, who had power over fire, and he cried with a loud cry to him who had the sharp sickle, saying, "Thrust in your sharp sickle and gather the clusters of the vine of the earth, for her grapes are fully ripe." So the angel thrust his sickle into the earth and gathered the vine of the earth, and threw it into the great winepress of the wrath of God.

The Old Testament understanding is that God sends "angels of destruction" to defeat the enemies of God. The New Testament understanding is that God allows "angels of destruction" to defeat those who have made themselves enemies of God. The net result is the same for the enemies, of course! It's simply a matter of interpretation as to the one who ultimately has caused the destruction.

The real point is this: we must never allow ourselves to become enemies of God. In so doing, we are putting ourselves beyond the reach of God's benevolent angels, and at the same time, we are putting ourselves directly into the line of fire of the destroyer.

Limitations of Angels

For all of their great power, angels have limitations. Those limitations include:

Space—Angels cannot be more than one place at a time. An angel must move spatially from one location to another, and this involves the lapse of time and sometimes, delay. (See Daniel 9:21–23 and 10:10–14.)

Power—Angels are limited also in power. They have limited authority, sometimes struggle, and sometimes stand in need of assistance. (See Job 1:12, 2:6, Revelation 12:7, Daniel 10:13.)

Knowledge—Angels are limited in their intellect. They do not, for example, know the hour of Christ's return, and they desire to know more about human salvation. (See Matthew 24:36 and 1 Peter 1:11–12.)

Holiness—Angels are not absolutely holy since some fell into sin and bondage. (Isaiah 14:12, Revelation 12:3-4)

Communication About Man—They do not accuse men or speak evil of people. (2 Peters 2:11). That is the work of the accuser of the brethren, the devil himself.

Influence Over Man's Will—Although angels might proclaim the Gospel, they do not have the convicting power of the Holy Spirit.

Neither do angels lead or guide us into a new truth or a new insight that gives specific direction to our lives. This is also the work of the Holy Spirit, who is called the Spirit of Truth. (See John 16:13.) Angels declare the Word of God and the Will of God, but they do not give any instructions or guidance that is apart or separate from God's directives to them.

In other words, angels do not provide us ongoing daily advice. Their realm of proclamation is in the absolutes of God's Word.

We have no record in God's Word that the Lord dispatches His angels to give practical daily advice to men and women. The message of Gabriel to Mary was that she would bear the Son of God. This was an event of history-changing proportions. It was a one-time proclamation that impacted all of eternity. Angels did not come to Mary to tell her when to change the diapers of Jesus or when to give Him a bath!

Angels are not available to us as our personal slaves, nor are they available for daily consultation or conversation.

All of these limitations stem from and point toward this one inescapable and vital fact about angels . . . .

Angels Are Created Beings

Angels are a part of God's creation. They are not God, they are not divine. They are creatures, not Creator.

In the Bible account of Creation, we find no mention of angels. The Bible tells us that at the outset of Creation, *the earth was without form, and void; and darkness was on the face of the deep. And the Spirit of God was hovering over the face of the waters*(Genesis 1:1-2).

When were angels created?

The understanding of most Bible writers seems to be that they were created as a part of the firmament called heaven. (Genesis 1:8). Throughout the Scriptures, angels are part of the Creation. They are never on equal footing with the Trinity.

Nehemiah 9:6 states:

You alone are the Lord God;
You have made heaven,
The heaven of heavens, with all their host,
The earth and everything on it,
The seas and all that is in them,
And you preserve them all.
The host of heaven worships You.

Also these words are found in the Book of Psalms pointing toward the fact that angels are a part of the creation. They are clearly associated with the creation of the skies:

Praise the Lord from the heavens;
Praise Him in the heights!
Praise him, all His angels;
Praise Him, all His hosts!
Praise Him, sun and moon;
Praise Him, all you stars of light!
Praise him, you heavens of heavens,
And you waters above the heavens! (Psalm 148:1-4).

Others contend that angels were created before the earth. In Job, angels are called the "sons of God" who were present at the creation of the earth:

Where were you when I laid the foundations of
the earth? When the morning stars sang together
and all the sons of God shouted for joy? (Job 38:4,7).

God clearly warned against worshiping the things of the skies in both the Old and New Testaments. We are to worship the Creator, never the creation. (See Romans 1:24-25.)

During the New Testament time, however, a number of Jewish sects worshiped angels as an expression of the Deity.

Both the apostles Paul and John, however, warned against worship of angels. Paul even said that when a person worships angels, they are cheating themselves of the true spiritual nourishment that comes from worshiping God.

Let no one cheat you of your reward, taking delight in false
humility and worship of angels, intruding into those things
which he has not seen, vainly puffed up by his fleshly mind,
and not holding fast to the Head, from whom all the body,
nourished and knit together by joints and ligaments, grows
with the increase that is from God (Colossians 2:18).

John wrote in Revelation 19:10 about his attempt to worship one of the angelic messengers:

> *I fell at his feet to worship him. But he said to me, "See that you do not do that! I am your fellow servant, and of your brethren who have the testimony of Jesus. Worship God! For the testimony of Jesus is the spirit of prophecy."*

Consider what happened to Herod when he allowed his subjects to worship him in place of God. He was struck by an angelic being precisely because *he did not give glory to God* and was subsequently *eaten by worms and died.* (See Acts 12:22–23.) This is a classic example of a person who has exalted himself above God and who gives no value to God in his life. He is open prey for destruction.

As author Charlie Shedd has said, "angels are not looking for publicity or visibility. Apparently all they have in mind is to get their job done."[3] Angels do not do anything that does not reflect glory back to God.

In fact, that is the image the Bible presents—that they surround the throne of God, their wings outstretched, so that the glory of God is reflected back onto God, rather than be absorbed by the angels. The light they bear is a reflection of His glory, it is not a glory the angels claim for themselves.

While we may respect and revere angels as messengers and servants of the Lord God, we are never to give them homage or worship them. Our worship belongs to God alone—Father, Son, and Holy Spirit.

3

Four Key Questions
People Ask About Angels

THE Bible doesn't answer all of our questions about angels.
There is a great deal of mystery surrounding these messengers
from Heaven. The Bible does provide answers, however, to four of
the key questions people often ask:

- How many angels are there?
- What do angels look like?
- Why don't the angels help everybody?
- Do people become angels when they die?

We'll take a look at each of these questions, again from a biblical point of view.

Question #1: How Many Angels Are There?

Angels are innumerable. We do not know how many angels
have been created by God but the writer to the Hebrews referred
to an *innumerable company of angels* in the heavenly Jerusalem
(Hebrews 12:22).

When Jacob returned to the Land of Promise, we read that *the
angel of God met him.* Jacob named the place Mahanaim, which
means "two bands" (Genesis 32:1-2). Apparently Jacob perceived
that God had sent two bands of angels to meet him.

Jesus said that He had at least seventy-two thousand angels at
His personal command, should He desire to call them. In Matthew
26:53, Jesus told the disciples who attempted to protect Him and

keep Him from being arrested in the Garden of Gethsemane, "Put your sword in its place, for all who take the sword will perish by the sword. Or do you think that I cannot now pray to My Father, and He will provide Me with more than twelve legions of angels? How then could the Scriptures be fulfilled, that it must happen thus?"

A legion in those days was composed of six thousand men. Twelve legions would be seventy-two thousand.

Jesus was clearly stating that He had the *power* to destroy those who had come to arrest Him. He *could* have averted His own crucifixion. But, out of obedience to Father God, He was *willing* to suffer what lay before Him.

Daniel, in his vision of God in His throneroom, stated that *a thousand thousands ministered to Him; ten thousand times ten thousand stood before Him* (Daniel 7:10). Ten thousand times ten thousand is a one hundred million! We don't know if Daniel is being literal or speaking symbolically. Either way, a vast number of angels are at God's immediate command.

Bildad The Shuhite, a supposed "friend" of Job, wrote of the angels, *Is there any number of His armies?* (Job 25:3). John saw angels around the throne, including living creatures and the elders, numbering *ten thousand times ten thousand, and thousands of thousands* (Revelation 5:11).

Certainly the conclusion about the number of angels must be that they are sufficient in number to do God's will. Otherwise, God would create more of them!

Heavenly Hosts

Even though one angel has enormous power, certainly far more power than any individual person has ever had, in the Scriptures we frequently find that God sends "hosts" of angels to help His people.

As Joshua approached Jericho, he lifted his eyes and saw that "a Man stood opposite him with His sword drawn in His hand." And Joshua went to Him and said to Him, "Are You for us or for our adversaries?" So He said, "No, but as Commander of the army of the Lord I have now come." And Joshua fell on his face to the earth and worshiped, and said to Him, "What does my Lord say to His servant?" Then the Commander of the Lord's army said to Joshua, "Take your sandal off your foot, for the place you stand is holy" (Joshua 5:13-15). God sent an *army* of angels to help Joshua. He did the same for Elisha.

Elisha and his servant had taken refuge in Dothan. Meanwhile, the invading king of Syria was upset that the king of Israel always seemed to know his next move. In seeking to discover the identity of the "informer," his servants told him that the prophet Elisha was the one who was advising the king of his every move. Thus, the king of Syria sent a great army to Dothan, with horses and chariots, and they surrounded the city. Elisha's servant saw them and came to Elisha saying:

> *Alas, my master! What shall we do? And Elisha answered, Do not fear, for those who are with us are more than those who are with them. And Elisha prayed and said, Lord, I pray, open his eyes that he may see. Then the Lord opened the eyes of the young man, and he saw. And behold, the mountain was full of horses and chariots of fire all around Elisha.* (See 2 Kings 6:15-17.)

Question #2: What Do Angels Look Like?

Angels are spirit beings. (See Psalm 104:4.) This means that angels might be considered to have an "essence"—an identity that lasts beyond a particular task or moment. Specific angels or demons are recorded in Scripture as having a "name," which indicates they have an identity unique to themselves.

They are not, however, tied to a material body such as the type man has. Angels do not have sexual identity or human desires and appetites. Angels are immortal, so their bodies are not subject to sickness and death.

Because they are spirit beings, angels are:

invisible—Angels only take on a form visible to human beings on rare occasions, and only when God commands them to do so for a very specific reason. Angels traditionally were said to assume bodies only when a body was needed to carry out a task.

immortal—Angels never get sick or die. (See Luke 20:36.)

We have no indication whatsoever in the Scriptures that angels will ever become obsolete or no longer needed. They exist even at the close of the age, and the assumption must be that they will continue on into eternity.

do not marry—Jesus stated so in Matthew 22:30. We do not know if they are both male and female. The Scriptures do not say. Generally speaking, Bible angels appear to be male. The only possible reference to angels being female is in Zechariah 5:9 where we read that Zechariah raised his eyes *and looked, and there were two women, coming with the wind in their wings; for they had wings like the wings of a stork, and they lifted up the basket between earth and heaven.*

What we do know is that they have no commitment to anyone or anything other than God. Although they may be "assigned" to individuals as guardian angels or "sent" to individuals with specific messages, their sole loyalty and line of authority is to God.

Do Angels Have Wings?

The earliest depictions of angels show them with wings. The earliest angels in the Bible, however, do not.

Many times the gods of the ancient world are also given wings. In Babylon, for example, the winged bull-men were among the pantheon of gods they worshiped. The angels in Bali are depicted as winged mermaids. The angels on Jacob's ladder, although they are often shown in artistic renditions as having wings, seem to ascend and descend as mortal human beings would take stairs. Jacob does not describe them as having wings.

Highly Diverse in Appearance

Angelic beings apparently have a great deal of diversity in their appearance. Ezekiel described cherubim as being in the form of man, but with four faces and four wings. Their legs were straight, but their feet had soles like calve's feet, and they sparkled like polished bronze. Under their wings they had human-like hands. One of the four faces was like a man, one like a lion, one like an ox, and one like an eagle.

Other angelic beings seen by Ezekiel had two wings, which covered their bodies. They flew in a straight-ahead fashion. Some had wheels beside them, gleaming with rims full of eyes. The wheels also had four faces: cherub, man, lion, and eagle.

Daniel had a vision of an angelic being that appeared as a man clothed in linen, girded with gold, a body like beryl, his face like lightning, his eyes like flaming torches, his arms like the gleam of burnished bronze, and his voice like the noise of a multitude.

Isaiah saw angelic beings with six wings—two covering the face, two covering the feet, and two with which they flew.

John saw living creatures full of eyes in front and behind, each living creature taking on a different identity: lion, ox, man, eagle. These beings had six wings, full of eyes all round and within, and they sang continually.

John also described an angel wrapped in a cloud with a rainbow over his head, his face like the sun, and his legs like pillars of fire. He had a scroll in his hand, and stood with one foot on the sea, the other on the land, and cried out with a voice that sounded like a lion roaring, or the sound of seven thunders.

In spite of this diversity in the Bible, the most common representation of angels is that they are human-like in form. Virtually all of the Bible writers who claimed to have visited with angelic beings directly—that is, not in a vision—saw them in human-like form, capable of walking and talking in a way understood by human beings.

Awesome!

In spite of the wide variety of forms angels take, the universal image is one of "awesomeness." Angels give a powerful, radiant appearance in many instances. Their apparent sudden appearance and disappearance is sometimes seen as disconcerting.

Perhaps it is because angels have such an awesome, powerful presence that the first words they seem to speak repeatedly to mankind in the Scriptures are these: "Fear not."

Those were the first words the angel spoke to the shepherds watching their flocks by night outside Bethlehem:

And behold, an angel of the Lord stood before them, and the glory of the Lord shone around them, and they were greatly afraid. Then the angel said to them, "Do not be afraid" (Luke 2:9–10).

In spite of what many people think of them, shepherds were among the bravest men in the ancient world. They regularly had to fend off wild beasts who sought to steal sheep from their flocks; they often engaged in hand-to-hand combat with these animals. The appearance of an angel, however, sent them into paralytic shock.

Question #3: Why Don't Angels Help Everyone?

Why don't guardian angels "guard" us from all harm?

Apparently they are limited in their ability to assist us because of *our own level of trust in the Lord* and *our own sin.* We have no example in the Scriptures of angels assisting those who doubt God's Word or who refuse to put their trust in God.

Hebrews 1:14 tells us that ministering spirits minister *for those who will inherit salvation.*

In Psalm 78 we find a recapped history of the children of Israel and how the Israelites strayed from God, *for their heart was not steadfast with Him, nor were they faithful in His covenant* (vs.37). It was only the extended and compassionate mercy of God that kept the Israelites alive, in the opinion of the psalmist. When it came to those who overtly rejected God and claimed another in His place—the Egyptians who worshiped Pharaoh as god—the mercy of God did not apply. "Angels of destruction" swept over the Egyptians repeatedly. (See Psalm 78:49.) The understanding of the psalmist is that God's mercy extends to those who are called by His name and who place their confidence squarely in Him, but that those who rebel against or reject the Lord put themselves into a position of potential destruction.

Does this mean that all people who die before the fullness of their days are in a position of rebellion against God?

Does it mean that those who experience accidents are temporarily or permanently out of God's will?

No, definitely not.

We live in a fallen world and even righteous people are the victims of the sin of others, both in our present generation and in past generations.

In the opinion of New Testament writers, the issue is also related to submission. All of us are under authority of some type, and when we rebel against that authority and refuse to submit to it, we become open prey for the ultimate rebel, Satan himself. In

1 Corinthians 11:10, the apostle Paul points out that a woman in ministry *ought to have a symbol of authority on her head, because of the angels.* The understanding of most theologians is that a person who is not in the proper line of authority for ministry has opened herself (or himself) up to the influence of evil angels.

In sum, angels have no basis on which to assist those who are mired in their own sinfulness, or who are victims of the sin of others. They cannot forgive sin, or overlook it. They are subject to God's absolute laws regarding obedience and justice. However, angels do obey any and every command that comes from the throne of God. When we ask God's protection for ourselves and our children, in full confidence of God's Word and with faith that God will act on our behalf, we can know that the Lord activates His angels on our behalf. We can trust Him to forgive us and to remove all vestiges of sin from our lives—including the influence of the sin of others—and to keep us pure before Him. In that state, we are God's prized possession, whether we live or die. We are His to claim as His own. It is His prerogative to assign angels to protect and preserve us. We cannot require that, demand that, or expect that. But we can know with assurance that when our sins are forgiven and our trust is in the Lord, we are in a position for angels to be dispatched to us should that be God's plan.

In other words, we cannot insist or insure ourselves in any way that angels *will* come to assist us. But we can, through receiving God's forgiveness of us and turning from sin, put ourselves into a position where the enemy angels (demons) will have no hold over us and where God's angels can help us if God dispatches them to us.

What About Innocent Children?

What about babies and young children? Why do their guardian angels sometimes seem to fail at their jobs?

Again, the fact may reside in sin—in this case, the sin of the parents or grandparents or great-grandparents. The consequences of unrepented sin, according to the Bible, extend to the fourth generation. We can reverse that curse through faith in the Lord Jesus Christ, but those who are unrepentant are subject to its consequences in their lives, even if they know nothing of the past sins of their fathers.

When the Jews at the time of Jesus' trial before Pilate cried, *His blood be on us and on our children,* they were well aware of the consequences of their saying. (See Matthew 27:25.) We have no record of that statement being reversed on a universal scale, only as individuals repent and ask for God's mercy.

We Can Limit Angel Activity

The Bible gives several other ways in which we can limit the activity of the elect angels . . . .

We tie the hands of our angels by refusing to fulfill the vows we make before God. The Book of Ecclesiastes gives a warning along these lines. It says:

> *When you make a vow to God, do not delay to pay it; for He has no pleasure in fools. Pay what you have vowed—better not to vow than to vow and not pay.*
>
> *Do not let your mouth cause your flesh to sin, nor say before the messenger of God (in many translations, angel) that it was an error. Why should God be angry at your excuse and destroy the work of your hands?* (Ecclesiastes 5:6).

We limit angels when we purposefully break the laws of society, or purposefully attempt to defy natural law. We find very few instances of angels helping those who break natural or societal law as an act of their will. By contrast, stories of angelic intervention are quite common in *accidental* events.

We can limit angels by our own greed, or by seeking to have our own way. Jesus taught, *Whoever seeks to save his life will lose it, and whoever loses his life will preserve it* (Luke 17:33). Jesus is speaking directly to the root of pride, which seeks to amass for the individual great power, fame, and wealth. The person who is seeking his own benefit as a top priority, rather than the kingdom of God, limits the aid of angels in his life. (See Matthew 6:33.)

The same holds true for those who pursue their own course of action, rather than follow the will of God. Angels apparently have no authority to help us complete our own agendas—only the agenda of God!

A great example of this is found in Numbers 22-24 with the story of Balaam. Balaam was considered by all to be a great prophet—what he blessed was blessed and what he cursed was cursed. Balak, the son of the king of Moab, sought out Balaam to come and curse the Israelites. The Lord said to him, *You shall not go with them; you shall not curse the people, for they are blessed* (Numbers 22:12). Balaam sent that word from the Lord back to Balak.

Balak responded with an offer of great honor and riches. Balaam invited the bearers of this message to spend the night while he consulted the Lord. The Lord said to Balaam that if the men came to call him, he should rise and go with them, but only speak what the Lord told him to speak. Balaam, however, didn't wait for their wake-up call. He rose in the morning and saddled his donkey and went. This angered the Lord and *the Angel of the Lord took His stand in the way as an adversary against him.* (Numbers 22:22). Balaam's donkey, however, was more spiritual than Balaam at this point. He saw the Angel standing in the path, with His drawn sword in his hand, and he refused to go forward. Eventually Balaam also saw the Angel of the Lord with his drawn sword and Balaam bowed his head and fell flat on his face. The Lord gave him a second chance at obedience and Balaam did, indeed, obey.

We limit angels when we fail to adhere to God's Word, or to place our trust in God. Roy H. Hicks states this well in his book, *Guardian Angels:*

"Angels are not going to close doors we so carelessly leave open. Angels are not going to clean germs from our unkept houses. Angels are not going to sit by your swimming pool to guard your little one from falling in. If we insist on driving carelessly, angels cannot do their work of protection. Angels cannot protect a child from wandering away if parents become too involved in their own interests."

Psalm 91 includes a great promise about angels, but notice the way in which this passage begins.

Because you have made the Lord, who is my refuge,
Even the Most high, your dwelling place,
No evil shall befall you,
Nor shall any plague come near your dwelling;
For He shall give His angels charge over you,

To keep you in all your ways.
In their hands they shall bear you up,
Lest you dash your foot against a stone.
You shall tread upon the lion and the cobra,
The young lion and the serpent you shall trample
underfoot (Psalm 91:9-13).

The psalmist says that because they have made the Lord their dwelling place, no evil will befall them! Once again we must conclude that there are limitations and stipulations regarding the protective power of angels, and most of those relate to *our own response to the Lord.*

In sum, the angels have no role in helping mankind disobey.

Question #4: Do People Become Angels When They Die?

Do human beings die and become angels?

That's the opinion of many people today.

But that is not what the Scriptures teach.

One of the passages often referenced regarding this is Hebrews 2:7—*You have made him (mankind) a little lower than the angels.*

Those who believe that human beings "become" angels see man as being elevated in rank upon death.

The writer to the Hebrews, who is actually quoting Psalm 8:5, is referring to man's state while man is on earth. On earth, mankind has less power, less mobility, and less wisdom than angels.

There are many things that man experiences, however, that angels cannot experience. Angels have never experienced the frailty of flesh as we know it, nor have they experienced the healing power of God. They have never known the pain of sin and guilt, nor the joy of salvation. They have never known what it means to be separated from God, nor the deep sweetness of reunion with God.

Furthermore, angels have no knowledge of what it means to be filled with God's Holy Spirit, nor to operate with the Spirit functioning from within an individual human being's personality and soul. It is as we bear the fullness of the holy Spirit in our beings that we are to oversee the "works" of God's hands, both the natural and supernatural works.

Our relationship with God the Father is as his children, not as his servants.

Upon our death, we enter into an even fuller relationship with the Father. The Scriptures say that we are His "heirs." It is for us that heaven is being created.

To become an angel upon death would be a demotion, not a promotion! Would any child of a King desire to become a slave? Would an heir choose to become a servant?

Set Apart

The Bible refers to angels as holy. To be holy means to be "set apart." Angels are set apart from the rest of the created order, including man, by their capacity to behold the Lord's face continually. Jesus referred to them specifically as *holy angels* in Mark 8:38.

There is no indication in Scripture that man and angels are of the same created order now, or that they ever will be.

Men Will Judge Angels

The Bible also states that one day man will judge the angels. First Corinthians 6:1-3 tells us:

> *Dare any of you, having a matter against another, go to law before the unrighteous, and not before the saints? Do you not know that the saints will judge the world? And if the world will be judged by you, are you unworthy to judge the smallest matters? Do you not know that we shall judge angels? How much more things that pertain to this life?*

The realm now overseen by angels will one day belong to the saints of God. Daniel 7:18,27 looks ahead to that day:

> *But the saints of the Most High shall receive the kingdom and possess the kingdom forever, even forever and ever. . . Then the kingdom and dominion, and the greatness of the kingdoms under the whole heaven, shall be given to the people, the saints of the Most High.*

It may be that our judgment of angels is not related to their past behavior, but rather, that we will be "ordering" angels toward activities in eternity. We may very well become repositioned in God's order of command so that we are above angels and they receive commands from us and report to us. That power, however, is *not* something we have today. Nor is it an established fact of Heaven. It is simply a possible interpretation of the word "judge."

Answers about Angels Require Faith

In general terms, what we can conclude about angels is that there are a lot of them . . . with a wide variety of appearances . . . who assist righteous man in numerous ways but who are not available to help man disobey or sin . . . and who are distinctly separate from man—above us at present but subject to our judgment in eternity.

We may wonder why God hasn't told us more.

As with most imponderable questions in the Bible, our conclusion about angels must be, "God apparently didn't think we needed to know more."

A knowledge of angels is apparently not considered vital to our life on this earth. Angels apparently have little to do with our faith, our relationship with Jesus, or our access to our Heavenly Father. They are *not* the Holy Spirit. Nothing about them is a sacrament.

We can have faith that the Lord is in control of our lives, and at His discretion, He will employ His holy angels to do His bidding on our behalf.

That may not be all that we would *like* to know, but it apparently is what God desires for us to know in this present age.

Furthermore, to seek to know what God has not revealed in His Word puts a person on dangerous ground.

4

The Messages of Angels

THE word "angel" comes from the Greek word *angelos*, which means messenger. The Hebrew word is *malakh*, which also means messenger. Other Bible words for angels—both Hebrew and Aramaic—have been translated as "the mighty," "sons of God," "ministers," and "servants."

Saint Augustine differentiated between the nature of angels and the "office," or work, of angels. He said:

> "Angels are spirits, but it is not because they are spirits that they are angels. They become angels when they are sent. For the name angel refers to their office, not their nature. You ask the name of this nature, it is spirit; you ask its office, it is that of an angel, which is a messenger."[1]

It is in the function or office of "speaking," or "giving messages," that we find a number of angels at work.

We need to note at the outset that this word *angelos* can refer to both human beings and spirit beings in the Greek. A pastor or a human message-bearer might be called *angelos*. Some of the references in the Book of Revelation may be to pastors, or to human messengers. This is especially true for chapters two and three, which are about messages being carried to specific congregations in the early Church.

Later in Revelation, however, the messages are more clearly linked to spirit-being messengers. Angels fill the role of:

preaching—The angels in Revelation 14:6–7 have a definite preaching mission:

*Then I saw another angel flying in the midst of heaven,
having the everlasting gospel to preach to those who dwell
on the earth—to every nation, tribe, tongue, and people—
saying with a loud voice, "Fear God and give glory to Him,
for the hour of His judgment has come; and worship Him
who made heaven and earth, the sea and springs of water."*

Up to that time in the last days, however, we have no mention
of angels preaching directly to men and women.

An acquaintance of mine recently thanked a member of the
United States Passport Office for her help in expediting her passport. She said to the woman quite casually, "You're an angel!"

The woman quickly replied, "No, I'm better than an angel. I
can share the Gospel of Jesus Christ."

She's right!

warning—In Revelation 14:9-11, angels give a warning to
those who receive the mark of the beast:

*If anyone worships the beast and his image, and receives
his mark on his forehead or on his hand, he himself shall
also drink of the wine of the wrath of God, which is poured
out full strength into the cup of His indignation. He shall be
tormented with fire and brimstone in the presence of the
holy angels and in the presence of the Lamb. And the smoke
of their torment ascends forever and ever; and they have no
rest day or night, who worship the beast and his image, and
whoever receives the mark of his name.*

announcing—On a number of occasions, angels in the Bible
issue announcementsor proclamations, both to individuals and to
all mankind. In Revelation 14:8, it is an angel that announces:

*Babylon is fallen, is fallen, that great city, because she has
made all nations drink of the wine of the wrath of her
fornication.*

interpreting—In a number of places in God's Word we find
angels filling the role of interpreter. As John begins his *Revelation
of Jesus Christ*, he tells us that Jesus *sent and signified it by His
angel to His servant John, who bore witness to the word of God,
and to the testimony of Jesus Christ, to all things that he saw*
(Revelation 1:1). Later in Revelation we read how an angel interprets

the mystery of the woman and the beast with seven heads and ten horns to John (Revelation 17:7).

An angel also interpreted the visions that Zechariah received from the Lord. (Zechariah 1:18–19) Perhaps nowhere in the Scriptures are angels are more closely linked to prophecy than in the book of Zechariah. In only thirteen chapters, angels are mentioned twenty times, with frequent reference to *the angel who talked with me.* (See Zechariah 2:3 and 4:1 as examples.)

Daniel is told twice that Gabriel has come to give him understanding. In Daniel 9:21–23, we read:

> *While I was speaking in prayer, the man Gabriel, whom I had seen in the vision at the beginning, being caused to fly swiftly, reached me about the time of the evening offering. And he informed me, and talked with me, and said, "O Daniel, I have now come forth to give you skill to understand. At the beginning of your supplications the command went out, and I have come to tell you, for you are greatly beloved; therefore consider the matter, and understand the vision."*

Gabriel proceeds to give the meaning of Daniel's vision regarding seventy weeks.

Messengers with Specific Messages

Repeatedly in the Scriptures we find passages in which angels came to individuals with specific messages. A number of them were to Abraham and his family members.

Hagar

One of these messages was given to Hagar, Sarah's maidservant. Sarah had given Hagar to Abraham so that he might have an heir, and when Hagar discovered she was pregnant, she began to show disrespect to Sarah. Sarah, in turn, dealt harshly with Hagar and Hagar fled.

Now the Angel of the Lord found her (Hagar) by a spring of water in the wilderness, by the spring on the way to Shur. And He said, "Hagar, Sarai's maid, where have you come from and where are you going?"

She said, "I am fleeing from the presence of my mistress Sarai."

The Angel of the Lord said to her, "Return to your mistress, and submit yourself under her hand." Then the Angel of the Lord said to her, "I will multiply your descendants exceedingly, so that they shall not be counted for multitude." And the angel of the Lord said to her:

> *Behold, you are with child,*
> *And you shall bear a son.*
> *You shall call his name Ishmael,*
> *Because the Lord has heard your affliction.*
> *He shall be a wild man;*
> *His hand shall be against every man,*
> *And every man's hand against him.*
> *And he shall dwell in the presence of his*
> *brethren* (Genesis 16:7-13).

On the surface, we might conclude that we need to retract our statement that God does not send angels to assist those who will be disobedient. But that isn't the case here. God is *not* sending his angels to help those who are rebellious or outside His redemption. Hagar is a part of Abraham's family. She is carrying Abraham's child and God has made a covenant with Abraham regarding his offspring. The Lord is not honoring Hagar's rebellion with an angelic visit; the purpose of this visit is to restore Hagar to Abraham's house. It is primarily for *Abraham's sake* that the angel appears to Hagar.

Notice, too, that the message the angel gives to Hagar is not necessarily a very good one. He gives Hagar the promise that her descendants will be numerous, and he also gives Hagar the name for her child, but he goes on to describe a child who is "a wild man."

New Age writers would have us believe that angels always give us messages about ourselves and our loved ones that are kind, generous, and loving. That is certainly not the case in Hagar's life. The angel tells her that she is going to bear a son who will be nothing but trouble!

This is not the only encounter that Hagar had with an angel. The next time came after Ishmael had scoffed at Isaac and Abraham had sent Hagar and Ishmael away. They wandered in the Wilderness of Beersheba until all of their water was gone.

> *Then the angel of God called to Hagar out of heaven, and said to her, "What ails you Hagar? Fear not, for God has heard the voice of the lad where he is. Arise, lift up the lad*

*and hold him with your hand, for I will make him a great
nation." Then God opened her eyes, and she saw a well of
water* (Genesis 21:17-19).

This time Hagar did not see an angel. She only heard his voice.
God remained true to his original promise to Hagar prior to Ishmael's birth.

About Isaac

An angel stayed Abraham's hand from killing Isaac. After lay-
ing out the wood, Abraham bound Isaac and placed him on the
altar, over the wood. Then, as he picked up the knife to slay his
son:

*"the Angel of the Lord called to him from heaven and said,
'Abraham, Abraham!' So he said, 'Here I am.' And He said,
'Do not lay your hand on the lad, or do anything to him; for
now I know that you fear God, since you have not withheld
your son, your only son, from Me'"* (Genesis 22:11-12).

Jewish commentators tend to see this as a very basic tenet of
Judaism, that God does not want killing done in His name—which
was a practice previously common throughout the ancient world.
That an angel would convey such an important lesson only adds
to the power and authority given to the angelic order.

In Genesis 24:7 we read that Abraham sent his servant to find
a wife for Isaac with this statement: *He (the Lord) will send His
angel before you, and you shall take a wife for my son from
there.*

Lot

Angels played a major role in saving the life of Lot, Abraham's
nephew. In Genesis 19 we read how two angels went to Sodom
and admonished Lot, his wife, and his daughters to get out of the
city before the Lord destroyed it. In this passage we see a limitation of angels regarding the human will. Although these angels
had been authorized by God to speak words of deliverance to Lot
and his family, they could not over-ride the will of Lot's wife—they
could not keep her from turning back to the city.

Jacob

Abraham's grandson, Jacob, had an encounter of a different
type. In a dream, he saw a ladder reaching into Heaven, *and there*

the angels of God were ascending and descending on it (Genesis 28:12). This dream of angels caused Jacob to build an altar and make a vow, *If God will be with me, and keep me in this way that I am going, and give me bread to eat and clothing to put on, so that I come back to my father's house in peace, then the Lord shall be my God. And this stone which I have set as a pillar shall be God's house, and of all that You give me I will sure give a tenth to You* (Genesis28:20-22).

Moses and Joshua

Many Jewish commentators believe the burning bush of Exodus 3 is a type of angelic visitation. Moses certainly had experiences with the angel of destruction as he prepared to lead the Israelites out of Egypt.

Joshua, Moses' assistant for many years in the wilderness, had an encounter with the Angel of the Lord prior to the battle for Jericho.

When you read this account in Joshua 5:13-15, you'll note that Joshua fell on his face before the Captain of the Lord's army, but then the Angel of the Lord told Joshua to take off his sandals. It's impossible to fall prostrate before someone and take off your sandals at the same time. The angel, in effect, was saying, "This is hallowed ground and a divinely ordained moment and message from God, but I am not to be worshiped."

The message that the angel went on to give was the complete battle plan for Jericho.

The angelic messenger to Joshua made no pretense that the message was his own. It was clearly a message from God Almighty. In fact, it is recorded as a message in which "the Lord said."

Gideon

A number of characteristics of angels are revealed in Gideon's account with the Angel of the Lord:

> *Now the Angel of the Lord came and sat under the terebinth tree which was in Ophrah, which belonged to Joash the Abiezrite, while his son Gideon threshed wheat in the winepress, in order to hide it from the Midianites. And the Angel of the Lord appeared to him, and said to him, "The Lord is with you, you mighty man of valor!"*
>
> *Gideon said to Him, "O my lord, if the Lord is with us, why then has all this happened to us? And where are all His*

miracles which are fathers told us about, saying, 'Did not the Lord bring us up from Egypt?' But now the Lord has forsaken us and delivered us into the hands of the Midianites."

Then the Lord turned to him and said, "Go in this might of yours and you shall save Israel from the hand of the Midianites. Have I not sent you?"

So he said to Him, "O my Lord, how can I save Israel? Indeed my clan is the weakest in Manasseh, and I am the least in my father's house."

And the Lord said to him, "Surely I will be with you, and you shall defeat the Midianites as one man."

Then he said to Him, "If now I have found favor in Your sight, then show me a sign that it is You who talk with me. Do not depart from here, I pray, until I come to You and bring out my offering and set it before You."

And he said, "I will wait until you come back."

Then Gideon went in and prepared a young goat, and unleavened bread from an ephah of flour. The meat he put in a basket, and he put the broth in a pot; and he brought them out to Him under the terebinth tree and presented them. The Angel of God said to him, "Take the meat and the unleavened bread and lay them on this rock, and pour out the broth." And he did so.

Then the Angel of the Lord put out the end of the staff that was in His hand, and touched the meat and the unleavened bread; and fire rose out of the rock and consumed the meat and the unleavened bread. And the Angel of the Lord departed out of his sight.

Now Gideon perceived that He was the Angel of the Lord. So Gideon said, "Alas, O Lord God! For I have seen the Angel of the Lord face to face" (Judges 6:11–22).

As in other places in Scripture:

- we see that the angel was capable of "acting" like a man—he sat under the tree, wielded a staff, and was capable of conversing with Gideon.
- we see that the angel refuses to eat of the offering brought to him, but rather, directs that it be made a sacrifice to the Lord.

- the angel does not depart from the basics of his message, in spite of Gideon's protests. He sticks by his claim that the Lord is with Gideon and Gideon *is* a man of *valor*, which is a term assuming that Gideon will save his people.

- Gideon only recognizes that he has experienced an encounter with an angel after the angel departs.

- we see that the angel is so closely aligned with both the presence and will of God that Gideon perceives that he has actually seen the Lord face to face.

The work of the Lord in Gideon's life was not limited to his encounter with the angel. Later the Lord speaks to his heart in a direct manner the very specific instructions he has for Gideon. There is no mention of an angel.

Angels Give Birth Announcements

A number of the messages given by angels in the Bible have to do with the birth of children. One of the most detailed is the appearance of an angel to the wife of Manoah regarding the birth of her son Samson. This account has within it several important points to consider so I am going to give you the entire account:

Now there was a certain man from Zorah, of the family of the Danites, whose name was Manoah; and his wife was barren and had no children. And the Angel of the Lord appeared to the woman and said to her, "Indeed now, you are barren and have borne no children, but you shall conceive and bear a son. Now therefore, please be careful not to drink wine or similar drink, and not to eat anything unclean. For behold, you shall conceive and bear a son. And no razor shall come upon his head, for the child shall be a Nazirite to God from the womb; and he shall begin to deliver Israel out of the hand of the Philistines."

So the woman came and told her husband, saying, "A man of God came to me, and His countenance was like the countenance of the Angel of God, very awesome; but I did not ask Him where He was from, and He did not tell me His name. And He said to me, 'Behold, you shall conceive and bear a son. Now drink no wine or similar drink, nor eat anything unclean, for the child shall be a Nazirite to God from the womb to the day of his death.'"

Then Manoah prayed to the Lord, and said, "O my Lord, please let the Man of God whom You sent come to us again and teach us what we shall do for the child which will be born."

And God listened to the voice of Manoah, and the Angel of God came to the woman again as she was sitting in the field; but Manoah her husband was not with her. Then the woman ran in haste and told her husband, and said to him, "Look, the Man who came to me the other day has just now appeared to me!"

So Manoah arose and followed his wife. When he came to the Man he said to Him, "Are You the Man who spoke to this woman?"

And He said, "I am."

Manoah said, "Now let Your words come to pass! What will be the boy's rule of life, and his work?"

So the Angel of the Lord said to Manoah, "Of all that I said to the woman let her be careful. She may not eat anything that comes from the vine, nor may she drink wine or similar drink, nor eat anything unclean. All that I commanded her let her observe."

Then Manoah said to the Angel of the Lord, "Please let us detain You, and we will prepare a young goat for You."

And the Angel of the Lord said to Manoah, "Though you detain Me, I will not eat your food. But if you offer a burnt offering, you must offer it to the Lord." (For Manoah did not know He was the Angel of the Lord.)

Then Manoah said to the Angel of the Lord, "What is Your name, that when Your words come to pass we may honor You?"

And the Angel of the Lord said to him, "Why do you ask My name, seeing it is wonderful?"

So Manoah took the young goat with the grain offering, and offered it upon the rock to the Lord. And He did a wondrous thing while Manoah and his wife looked on—it happened as the flame went up toward the heaven from the altar—the Angel of the Lord ascended in the flame of the altar! When Manoah and his wife saw this, they fell on their faces to the ground. When the Angel of the Lord appeared no more to

*Manoah and his wife, then Manoah knew that He was the
angel of the Lord* (Judges 13:2-21).

This passage reveals eight distinct things about the character
and nature of angels.

(1) *The angel appeared as a man.* In fact, it seems obvious
from this account that neither Manoah nor his wife recognized
him immediately as an angel, even though his countenance was
angelic and "very awesome." This description of angels is consistent throughout the Scriptures. Only once in the Bible are angels
given a *possible* feminine description. New Age writers and artists, by contrast, often feature angels as feminine, with flowing
skirts and delicate features.

(2) *The angel re-appeared to Manoah and his wife after
Manoah prayed to the Lord and requested his appearance.*
Manoah did not pray to the angel or do anything in himself to
conjure up the angel's appearance.

Note that it was forbidden in the culture for a woman to be
addressed by a man who wasn't her husband. This is perhaps why
the Lord answered Manoah's request that the "man" reappear. Manoah wanted to hear, and is given an opportunity to hear, the message directly.

(3) *The angel's message remains succinct and consistent.* He does not elaborate, give reasons, or go beyond what he
has been authorized to say. Manoah asks about the child. The angel repeats only what he has been authorized to say to the woman.

(4) *The angel may appear to be a man, but he is not of
human flesh and blood.* He does not eat. He is not of this earth
in his origin.

(5) *The angel does not have a name of his own, at least
not that he is willing to share with man.* Manoah is eager to
honor the messenger of these good tidings by naming his son in
his honor, but the angel responds only, "Why do you ask My name,
seeing it is wonderful?" Another possible translation of this word
wonderful is "secret." Angels have no reason to be known to us
by name.

Keep in mind that names bore great power in the thinking of
the ancient world. If you knew the name of something or someone

you had a certain amount of control over that person. You had an understanding of their identity, their origin, their homeland, and even their character (since children were often named in response to the parent's intuitive understanding of the nature of the child.) An angel, however, has only a heavenly origin and homeland; his character and identity is totally subsumed by the nature of God. A human being has no control over an angel, and therefore, no need to know his name.

(6) *The angel refuses to take any reward for having delivered his message.* When Manoah offers him a young goat as a meal, the angel replies that Manoah should offer it to the Lord instead as a burnt offering.

(7) *Manoah and his wife only knew they had encountered an angel after he was gone.* The fullness of the experience came about *after* it was over, and certainly the message given was fully confirmed when Samson was born. In Hebrews 13:2 we have these words of advice: *Do not forget to entertain strangers, for by so doing some have unwittingly entertained angels.* That was certainly true for Manoah and his wife.

(8) *The angel is intimately linked with an act of worship to God.* The angel disappears from their sight in the flame of the sacrifice that Manoah makes. This sacrifice was the highest form of worship possible by Manoah. Another way of looking at this passage is to conclude that the angel ascended back into heaven in the blaze of their worship! The expression of worship belongs clearly to God, not to the angel.

Angelic Messages in the New Testament

Do angels speak to men directly in the New Testament?

Yes, but as is the Old Testament, they speak at God's initiative, not man's.

Philip

In Acts 8, an angel spoke to Philip, *Arise and go toward the south along the road which goes down from Jerusalem to Gaza* (Acts 8:16).

Cornelius

In Acts 10, an angel spoke to Cornelius, a God-fearing Roman centurion. He spoke Cornelius' name in a vision and then said,

*Your prayers and your alms have come up for a memorial be-
fore God. Now send men to Joppa, and send for Simon whose
surname is Peter. He is lodging with Simon, a tanner, whose
house is by the sea. He will tell you what you must do* (vss.4-6).

Paul

In Acts 27, an angel spoke to Paul, who was being tossed about
on a stormy sea with a shipload of sailors. He said to them:

*Men, you should have listened to me, and not have sailed
from Crete and incurred this disaster and loss. And now I
urge you to take heart, for there will be no loss of life
among you, but only of the ship. For there stood by me this
night an angel of the God to whom I belong and whom I
serve, saying, "Do not be afraid, Paul; you must be brought
before Caesar; and indeed God has granted you all those
who sail with you."*

Note that each one of these messages was very specific, complete with detailed instructions. The encounter with Cornelius concludes, "And when the angel who spoke to him had departed . . . ."

Angels give their messages, and then they depart. It is up to
the human beings who receive their messages to act upon them
or to believe them. Rarely do we have a true "conversation" between men and angels. More commonly, angels give their messages and leave fairly abruptly.

This does not mean that the messages given by angels are cold-
hearted. On the contrary, the angelic messages to both Cornelius
and Paul include words of great encouragement. It simply means
that the angels do not linger or develop an ongoing relationship
with these men of God, and indeed, that is true for all angelic
appearances in the Scriptures.

Once angels have issued their messages, they do not linger on
the earth, but return to Heaven.

The heavenly host at the time of Jesus' birth went back into
Heaven after they had sung their great song of praise and proclamation. (See Luke 2:15.)

The angels that appeared to Gideon and Manoah both "ascended" or disappeared in the flame and smoke of sacrificial of-
ferings.

In sum, the messages that angels deliver are always more important than the angels themselves.

Limited Angel Activity in the Apostles' Lives

You may feel like asking, "Why don't the apostles have more encounters with angels than they do?"

One of the main reasons may be that the apostles had direct access to Jesus. They had very little need of angelic intervention because they were led daily by the Holy Spirit.

Jesus told His disciples:

Whoever confesses Me before men, him the Son of Man also will confess before the angels of God. But he who denies Me before men will be denied before the angels of God (Luke 12:8-9).

Another translation of the word "confess" in this passage might be "covenant." The confession of Jesus we make is tantamount to a covenant, and in turn, the confession of Jesus to the angels bears the same weight as a covenant. It is binding and sure. What we say about Jesus is repeated by Jesus to the angels.

This communication works in two ways. If we confess Jesus positively before men, then the message Jesus gives to the angels is a positive one. On the other hand, if we deny Jesus, the words of Jesus to the angels are ones of denial.

The implications of this are profound.

When We Confess Christ as Lord

I believe when we confess Christ as Lord it *activates* the heavenly host in a positive manner. They, in turn, move toward us. When we deny Jesus, the heavenly host moves away from us.

The most important conclusion we can draw from Luke 12:8-9 is that *we* don't have direct communication with angels.

We do not pray to them.

We do not order them into battle.

We do not make requests of them.

The angels are subject to the power and authority of Father, Son, and Holy Spirit.

Psalm 103:20-21 reinforces this truth: *Bless the Lord, you His angels, who excel in strength, who do His word, heeding the voice of His word.*

Angels and the Holy Spirit

Perhaps the most basic difference between the holy angels and the Holy Spirit is that the Holy Spirit indwells us and works within us. Angels are always external to mankind.

The ministry of the Holy Spirit is to help us live godly lives—to discern right from wrong, to bring the Word of God to our remembrance, to empower us to be bold witnesses of the Gospel, to flow through us to bring wonderful gifts to others, and to bear fruit that is of the highest morality and ethical nature. (See Galatians 5:22–23.) The Holy Spirit enables us to be God's people.

Angels, by contrast, do not enable us, but rather, they assist us in doing what God has called us to do—both individually and corporately. *Angels are accompanying allies, not indwelling authority.*

Invitation to a Direct Encounter

Note specifically that at no time in teaching His disciples to pray does Jesus instruct His followers to request a supernatural experience or to ask for visitations from angels, visions, dreams, or other so-called "spiritual experiences."

Rather, He invites His disciples to come directly into the throne room of their heavenly Father and to worship the Father and ask Him to meet their needs.

Jesus invites us also to have a direct encounter and relationship with the Father.

There are those who seem to think that having a vision of Jesus or an angelic visitation is a more direct encounter than the one they can experience in prayer. Not so, according to God's Word. The most direct encounter a person can have with God is an encounter in prayer.

The fact that Jesus invites us to have this intimate and personal relationship with the Father is even more profound when we consider that it was the understanding of the ancient Hebrews was that a person could not have a *direct* encounter with God and live. The Almighty was simply too awesome, too powerful, too majestic, too wonderful, too wise, too everything to be experienced by mankind in a direct way.

In some ways, I find it regrettable that we have lost sight of some of this overwhelmingly awesome nature of God. Our privilege at having a direct relationship with God is taken casually far too often, in my opinion. Some people seem to lose sight of the fact that God is the Almighty King of the Universe. Yes, He has drawn near to us in the form of His beloved Son, Jesus Christ. Yes, through Christ we have direct access to God. But God is not on our level and we will never be on His level! He is above all. The prophet Isaiah recorded these words of the Lord, *My thoughts are not your thoughts, nor are your ways My ways, says the Lord; For as the heavens are higher than the earth, so are My ways higher than your ways, and My thoughts than your thoughts* (Isaiah 55:8-9).

Those who truly think themselves to be on a chummy, chatty basis with God are deceived. God certainly hears our prayers and desires to have an intimate, deep relationship with us, but He is not our pal or buddy. He is the Lord God who created the Universe. He is worthy to be worshiped, praised, adored, and obeyed.

He is our Creator. We are His creation.

He is our Author and Finisher. We are the work of His hands.

He is our Savior and Redeemer. Without him we are nothing.

Throughout the Bible we find man's response to God as one of holy fear, or perhaps better translated for our times, "awesome awe." The person who truly stands in God's presence does so with stunned silence, overwhelmed by God's majesty and overcome by God's presence.

The ancient people had a much clearer understanding of the awesomeness of God.

Moses encountered the Lord by means of a burning bush in the desert regions of Horeb, but Moses never thought that the burning bush *was* God. He was always very clear on the fact that God *called to him from the midst of the bush* (Exodus 3:4). He certainly recognized God's voice, but He made no claim at having seen God's visage.

On Sinai, Moses appealed to God,

"Please, show me Your glory." And the Lord responded to him, *"I will make all My goodness pass before you, and I will proclaim the name of the Lord before you. I will be*

gracious to whom I will be gracious, and I will have
compassion on whom I will have compassion." But He said,
"You cannot see My face; for no man shall see Me, and live."
And the Lord told Moses to stand in the cleft of a rock and
that He would cover Moses with His hand so that Moses
would see His back, but not his face. (See Exodus 33:18–23.)

The glory of the Lord is something we cannot know fully, and
which we will not see, until we are with the Lord in Heaven. It is
only then, when we are removed from the finite constraints of
time, space, and our physical bodies that we will *begin* to be capable of grasping His infinite being.

The word used repeatedly to describe the Lord in the Scriptures is Holy. God dwells in the Holy of Holies. He is the Most
Holy. As stated earlier, to be holy literally means to be set apart.
The Lord is apart from us, even though He has chosen to draw
very close to us.

In this light, the encounters of angels in the Bible are much
more understandable. God is desiring to communicate with His
people. Angels are His messengers. They are His representatives,
the ones to whom He has delegated what He desires to communicate to His chosen servants.

Angels are sent by God to serve us, to be an aid to us, but they
always hearken to God's voice, not ours. It is the will of God that
they are committed to perform, not our will.

5

Jesus and Angels: A Portrait of Angelic Involvement with Mankind

Aₙgₑₗₛ in the New Testament are nearly always associated with moments of high glory. In the Gospels, these moments of glory are focused on Jesus Christ.

Angels appear at virtually every major experience in the life of Jesus, beginning with His birth . . . .

Angels at Jesus' Birth

Angelic visitations surrounding the birth of Jesus involved experiences not only directly related to His mother, but to His father, cousin's father, and nearby shepherds.

Zacharias

In the case of Zacharias and Elizabeth, the parents of Jesus' cousin John the Baptist, the angel did not come first to a woman to foretell a birth—as with Hagar or Samson's mother—but to her husband, Zacharias. While Zacharias was serving as a priest before God, burning incense in the temple of the Lord:

> Then an angel of the Lord appeared to him, standing on the right side of the altar of incense. And when Zacharias saw him, he was troubled, and fear fell upon him.
>
> But the angel said to him, "Do not be afraid, Zacharias, for your prayer is heard; and your wife Elizabeth will bear you a son, and you shall call his name John. And you will have

joy and gladness, and many will rejoice at his birth. For he
will be great in the sight of the Lord, and shall drink neither
wine nor strong drink. He will also be filled with the Holy
Spirit, even from his mother's womb. And he will turn
many of the children of Israel to the Lord their God. He will
also go before Him in the spirit and power of Elijah, 'to turn
the hearts of the fathers to the children,' and the disobedient
to the wisdom of the just, to make ready a people prepared
for the Lord."

And Zacharias said to the angel, "How shall I know this?
For I am an old man, and my wife is well advanced in years."

And the angel answered and said to him, "I am Gabriel,
who stands in the presence of God, and was sent to speak to
you and bring you these glad tidings. But behold, you will
be mute and not able to speak until the day these things
take place, because you did not believe my words which will
be fulfilled in their own time" (Luke 1:11-20).

Note two things about this visitation.

First, *as in so many other instances, the angel visitation*
was linked with a time of worship. Zacharias was engaged in
the highest form of worship possible at that time—the burning of
incense outside the veil of the Holy of Holies in the Temple.

Second, *the angel says that he has appeared because the*
Lord has heard the prayer of Zacharias. The angel has clearly
come as the result of the Lord's initiative. His opening line is, *Do*
not be afraid, Zacharias, for your prayer is heard (vs 13).

In this case Gabriel identifies himself by name for a very specific purpose: he wants Zacharias to know that he is the angel
who stands in the presence of God. Zacharias will not be able to
utter Gabriel's name for many months, but during those months,
he certainly can ponder the full nature of his angelic visitor. No
doubt he was able to help Mary later in identifying the angel who
visited her since we have no mention that Gabriel identified himself by name to Mary.

Why did Gabriel cause Zacharias to be mute? Gabriel says that
it is because Zacharias did not believe his words. Gabriel knew
that the words he spoke were not his own, but the words of the
Lord God. *Those who do not believe God's words have no*

authority to speak God's words. That is such an important statement that I hope you will read it again. Should you be visited by
an angel of the Lord, believe what that angel says to be true!

Consider what Gabriel's options must have been in that moment when he encountered Zacharias' unbelief. If Gabriel had
taken no action, Zacharias may well have continued to doubt both
his appearance and his message. That doubt may have clouded the
very birth of John the Baptist, or made it impossible.

Or, Gabriel could have taken action to reinforce his own message. In being unable to speak, Zacharias was *forced* to face fully
what had happened to him: he had been visited by a messenger
from God. He was put into a position of having to take even more
seriously the message the angel had given to him. No doubt as
Zacharias pondered this message and messenger in the months of
silence ahead, the truth of the message became even clearer in his
heart and mind. He no doubt was better prepared to be a father to
the forerunner of Christ Jesus!

Mary

Gabriel's visit to a young woman named Mary in Nazareth was
also profound, perhaps the most profound appearance of an angel
in all of history:

> *Now in the sixth month the angel Gabriel was sent by God
> to a city of Galilee named Nazareth, to a virgin betrothed to
> a man whose name was Joseph, of the house of David. The
> virgin's name was Mary. And having come in, the angel
> said to her, "Rejoice, highly favored one, the Lord is with
> you; blessed are you among women!"*
>
> *But when she saw him, she was troubled at his saying, and
> considered what manner of greeting this was. Then the angel
> said to her, "Do not be afraid, Mary, for you have found
> favor with God. And behold, you will conceived in your
> womb and bring forth a Son, and shall call His name JESUS.
> He will be great, and will be called the Son of the Highest;
> and the Lord God will give Him the throne of His father
> David. And He will reign over the house of Jacob forever,
> and of His kingdom there will be no end."*
>
> *Then Mary said to the angel, "How can this be, since I do
> not know a man?"*

*And the angel answered and said to her, "The Holy Spirit
will come upon you, and the power of the Highest will
overshadow you; therefore, also, that Holy One who is to be
born will be called the Son of God. Now indeed, Elizabeth
your relative has also conceived a son in her old age; and
this is now the sixth month for her who was called barren.
For with God nothing will be impossible."
Then Mary said, "Behold the maidservant of the Lord! Let it
be to me according to your word." And the angel departed
from her* (Luke 1:26–38).

Gabriel's opening words to Mary are much the same as those
he had spoken to Zacharias: "Do not be afraid, Mary." In this case,
however, it is not Mary's prayers that are being answered, but her
pure and virtuous life that is being recognized. The angel says,
"You have found favor with God."

Mary questions how she will conceive. Some might say, "She
doubted Gabriel just as Zacharias did. Why wasn't she struck mute
also?" Upon closer reading, it is evident that Zacharias questioned
whether Gabriel was speaking the truth to him. He asked for a
corroborating sign. "How shall I know this?" Zacharias asked. He
didn't believe Gabriel at face value.

Mary, on the other hand, believed Gabriel but she couldn't
understand the mechanics of how she might conceive without a
man. She was not questioning whether what Gabriel said was
true, but rather, how what he said would come to pass.

There's a big difference in questioning *how* God is going to
fulfill His promises to you, and in questioning *whether* God has
made those promises!

Finally, note that Zacharias, Elizabeth, and Mary, are all said to
be in right standing with God. Elizabeth and Zacharias are identified as being *righteous before God, walking in all the commandments and ordinances of the Lord blameless* and Mary is said to
have *found favor with God* (Luke 1:6, 30).

Joseph

The angel of the Lord appeared to Joseph in a dream saying,
*Joseph, son of David, do not be afraid to take to you Mary your
wife, for that which is conceived in her is of the Holy Spirit. And*

she will bring forth a Son, and you shall call his name Jesus, for He will save His people from their sins (Matthew 1:20–21).

Later, it was an angel of the Lord who appeared to Joseph in a dream advising him to take Mary and Jesus and flee into Egypt (Matthew 2:13).

Angelic Ministry in the Wilderness

Jesus had angels minister to Him after His temptation by Satan in the wilderness. (Matthew 4:11)

Satan knew, of course, the power of Jesus to call upon the angels. Even during the temptation time in the wilderness, the devil acknowledged that God had given Jesus charge over them, so that *in their hands they shall bear you up, lest you dash your foot against a stone* (Luke 4:11). Jesus doesn't deny Satan's claim, but rather says, *You shall not tempt the Lord your God* (Luke 4:12).

Those very angels did come to Jesus at the close of the devil's temptations to aid Him.

Again, we find evidence in this that angels do not do for us what we are able to do for ourselves. We are to resist the temptations of the devil at every turn. Resisting him in head-on temptation is not the job of our angels. Protecting us from his blind-side assaults more accurately describes their role in our lives.

Just how then did the angels help Jesus? We are given no specific details, but we can draw some clues, perhaps, from the way in which an angel came and ministered to Elijah as he sat *a day's journey into the wilderness* (1 Kings 19:4).

Elijah had been running to escape the threat of Jezebel, and there in the wilderness, under a broom tree, he laid down and prayed that he might die. In utter exhaustion, he fell asleep and *suddenly an angel touched him, and said to him, "Arise and eat." Then he looked, and there by his head was a cake baked on coals, and a jar of water. So he ate and drank, and lay down again. And the angel of the Lord came back the second time, and touched him, and said, 'Arise and eat, because the journey is too great for you.' So he arose, and ate and drank; and he went in the strength of that food forty days and forty nights as far as Horeb, the mountain of God* (1 Kings 19:5–8).

The angel was an agent of refreshment to Elijah, and we can assume that the angels who ministered to Jesus after His wilderness experience also provided both physical and spiritual refreshment to Him.

Angels at the Time of Jesus' Death

An angel ministered to Jesus, "strengthening Him," as Jesus prayed in the Garden of Gethsemane prior to his arrest and subsequent crucifixion. (Luke 22:43)

Angels guarded the body of Jesus in the tomb where He was laid after His death on the Cross. (John 20:12)

Resurrection

At the Resurrection, it was the angel of the Lord who descended from Heaven and *rolled back the stone from the door, and sat on it. His countenance was like lightning, and his clothing as white as snow. And the guards shook for fear of him, and became like dead men* (Matthew 28:2).

Note that even though the Roman guards fainted in the sight of this majestic angel, the women followers of Jesus did not. The angel said to Mary Magdalene and the other Mary as they came to the tomb, *Do not be afraid, for I know that you seek Jesus who was crucified. He is not here; for He is risen, as He said, Come, see the place where the Lord lay. And go quickly and tell His disciples that He is risen from the dead, and indeed He is going before you into Galilee; there you will see Him. Behold, I have told you* (Matthew 28:5-7).

Angels Speak at the Ascension

Angels were also present as Jesus ascended into Heaven in the presence of His disciples:

> *And while they looked steadfastly toward heaven as He went up, behold, two men stood by them in white apparel, who also said, "Men of Galilee, why do you stand gazing up into heaven? This same Jesus, who was taken up from you into heaven, will so come in like manner as you saw Him go into heaven"* (Acts 1:10-11).

When Angels Appear—and When They Don't

As you review the life of Christ, it is interesting to note when angels appear, and when they don't. Angels foretell, announce, and witness the birth of Christ. The Bible tells us that angels are assigned to every person, especially to children.

One of the truths we might draw from this for our own lives is that angels are present at our birth, and that they also sing with joy at our arrival on earth. They are an expression of God's love and blessing to us—an acknowledgement that God is pleased with the birth of every child.

Do you know of someone today who is suffering from low self-esteem? Encourage that person with the news that the Lord was pleased with their birth, and even sent an angel to the scene on their behalf.

We can also note that angels do not appear during the active years of Jesus' ministry. They do not heal people for Jesus, prepare sermons for Him, or help Him raise the dead. They do not help Jesus walk on water or change water into wine. In fact, during the active years of ministry, angels are nowhere to be seen. Now, this does not mean that they weren't active "behind the scenes." But they are not visible to those who witnessed Jesus at work, and Jesus gives them no mention as being involved with or directly responsible for His work among the people.

Jesus doesn't preach a sermon about angels, tell people to put their trust in angels, or pray to angels. He doesn't teach about them extensively or invite people to get in touch with their own angels.

You may say, "Well, that's because Jesus was divine."

Jesus was also fully human. And if any human being ever needed divine intervention, or could have used the help of angels in accomplishing His day-to-day ministry, it would have been Jesus. And yet the Heavenly Father apparently expects Jesus to accomplish His mission in the same way He expects us to accomplish ours—through *faith and obedience*. As the old Gospel song tells us, we are to "trust and obey, for there's no other way."

Angels appear at Jesus' death, resurrection, and ascension *mostly* to encourage the witnesses to these events. With the exception of the angelic visit in the Garden of Gethsemane, these angels are not on the scene for Jesus' benefit, but for the benefit of His followers.

Was Jesus an Angel?

Through the ages many people have put forth the idea that Jesus was not actually human, but rather, a spirit being—an angel. That opinion has been classified as heresy by the Church on repeated occasions.

One of the reasons for this opinion is that Jesus was, indeed, the foremost messenger of God. In the purest sense of the Greek word *angelos*, Jesus was the Great Messenger. Jesus is referred to in Revelation 10 as the "mighty angel." We see this as Jesus because the description of Him is identical to that in the first chapter of Revelation. In this reference, angel may be taken quite literally to mean "messenger." Jesus is the greatest Messenger of God's love that the world has ever known!

Because they are so clearly associated with God's will and God's presence, angels are sometimes named in a way that makes it sound as if the Lord is actually present on the scene. A number of Bible people call the angels they see the Angel of the Lord. On this basis, some Bible scholars refer to several Old Testament references to angels as a manifestation of "the pre-incarnate Christ."

These visits are called a "theophany" or a "Christophany" by theologians. These are appearances in which we simply do not know if God himself was appearing in a human-like form, or whether the being that appeared was an angel.

Perhaps the foremost occurrence of this is in Genesis 18, which begins, *then the Lord appeared to him (Abraham) by the terebinth trees of Mamre.* The story proceeds to describe three men who come to visit Abraham. One of the men seems to be more important in appearance and demeanor than the other two. They announce to Abraham that Sarah will have a son. As they leave, two of the men walk toward Sodom, but *Abraham still stood before the Lord.*

The Lord tells Abraham of His plan to destroy Sodom. Abraham barters with the Lord until the Lord agrees not to destroy Sodom if ten righteous people are found within the city. The Lord agrees to this and then we read, *So the Lord went His way as soon*

as He had finished speaking with Abraham; and Abraham re-
turned to his place (vs.33).

Was this a visit by an angel or a visit by the Lord Himself in
human visage? The Scriptures are not definitive.

Another example of a possible Christophany is in Exodus 23.
The Lord said to the children of Israel as they wandered in the
wilderness, preparing to enter the Land of Promise:

> *Behold, I send an Angel before you to keep you in the way*
> *and to bring you into the place which I have prepared.*
> *Beware of Him and obey His voice; do not provoke Him, for*
> *He will not pardon your transgressions; for My name is in*
> *Him. But if you indeed obey His voice and do all that I*
> *speak, then I will be an enemy to your enemies, and a*
> *adversary to your adversaries. For My Angel will go before*
> *you and bring you in to the Amorites and the Hittites and*
> *the Perizzites and the Canaanites and the Hivites and the*
> *Jebusites; and I will cut them off* (Exodus 23:20-23).

In this passage, the angel makes the way for the Children of
Israel. Jesus called Himself the "Way." However, the Lord clearly
says that this angel in Exodus will *not* pardon the transgressions
of the people. The angel is clearly not capable of exercising that
authority. His orders are set: to lead the people into the Land of
Promise and to be an enemy to those who are the enemies of God.
As long as the Children of Israel willingly and obediently follow
him and do not "provoke him," the angel will carry out his orders.
If they do not, he cannot. The angel clearly has no leeway in what
he will do and not do; he has no will of his own to amend God's
directive.

The message is clear that when God speaks to man through an
angel, there is no room for negotiating with the angel.

Differences Between Jesus and the Angels

Jesus differs from the angels on a number of points. Angels,
including the Angel of the Lord, have no recorded birth, nor
death. Jesus had both.

Angels in the Bible appear to people, but do not develop ongoing relationships with the men and women they visit. Jesus had
deep relationships with human beings.

Jesus and angels are of completely different origin. Jesus was "begotten" of the Father, a human being completely filled with God's presence and spirit from the moment of His conception. Jesus had a will and mind of His own. As a human being, He had a free will with which to embrace or deny His divine calling and purpose on the earth. Angels, on the other hand, are beings created by God expressly to carry out God's will or to convey God's message. They are agents of Heaven, not bound to this earth by any physical fleshly form. Jesus had a free will to obey or disobey the will of the Father in His life, right up to the Cross!

The differences between Jesus and the angels are clearly outlined in Hebrews 1–14. Several key truths are presented in just the first four verses:

> *God, who at various times and in various ways spoke in time past to the fathers by the prophets, has in these last days spoken to us by His Son, whom He has appointed heir of all things, through whom also He made the worlds; who being the brightness of His glory and the express image of His person, and upholding all things by the word of His power, when He had by Himself purged our sins, sat down at the right hand of the Majesty on high, having become so much better than the angels, as He has by inheritance obtained a more excellent name than they.*

In this passage, we find several ways in which Jesus is far *superior* to angels:

- Jesus is heir of all things. The Bible never speaks of any inheritance given to angels.
- Jesus participated in the creation. The angels may do God's bidding, but they are never given "creative" power.
- Jesus "upholds all things by the word of His power."
- The angels speak only those messages given to them by God to speak. Their word does not hold together the created order.
- Jesus purged our sins. He alone is our Redeemer. This role is never given to angels in God's Word.
- Jesus is seated at the right hand of the Father. Angels may surround the throne of God, but they are never seated on

either the right or left hand of God—those places are reserved for those who are truly a part of the Godhead.

The writer concludes simply that Jesus is much better than the angels and has a more excellent name than they! The writer to the Hebrews continues:

For to which of the angels did He say:

"You are My Son, Today I have begotten You?And again: I will be to Him a Father and He shall be to Me a son?" But when He again brings the firstborn into the world, He says: Let all the angels of God worship Him. And of the angels He says: "Who makes his angels spirits and His ministers a flame of fire."

But to the Son He says:

"Your throne, O God, is forever and ever; A scepter of righteousness is the scepter of Your Kingdom. You have loved righteousness and hated lawlessness; therefore God, Your God, has anointed You with the oil of gladness more than Your companions."

And:

"You, Lord, in the beginning laid the foundation of the earth, and the heavens are the work of Your hands. They will perish, but You remain; and they will all grow old like a garment; like a cloak You will fold them up, and they will be changed, but You are the same, and Your years will not fall."But to which of the angels has he ever said:

"Sit at My right hand, till I make Your enemies Your footstool?"

Are they not all ministering spirits sent forth to minister for those who will inherit salvation? (Hebrews 1:5-14).

This passage points out two more distinctions between Jesus and angels.

- Jesus is the Son of God, first-born and only begotten. (See John 3:16.) Angels are created beings, just as you and I.
- Jesus is to be worshiped by angels and by men.
  Angels are to give worship, not receive it!

God Alone is Worthy of Worship

One of the main conclusions we can draw about angels at work in the life of Jesus is that the angels worship Jesus. He doesn't worship them.

Furthermore, we as human beings are to worship God—Father, Son, and Holy Spirit—and God alone. We are not to give homage to angels.

We are to give Jesus first place in our lives. That place does not belong to any human being, nor to any angel.

There is something special and wonderful about the will-full worship that we human beings give to Christ Jesus. Christina Rossetti wrote,

"Angels and archangels may have gathered there,
Cherubim and seraphim thronged the air;
But his mother only, in her maiden bliss,
Worshiped the beloved with a kiss."[1]

We do not replace the worship of angels before the throne of God. Neither do they replace ours. If anything, we join with the angels in worship of God—but in a distinctly human way!

6

Angels Through the Ages and Around the World

ANGELS are universal, it seems, to the major religions of the world.

Jews and Christians have strong belief in angels.

Muslims also call for belief in angels. There are angels in Buddhism, Hinduism, and Zoroastrianism. Angels can be found in ancient Egyptian tombs, on Assyrian murals, and in Sumerian carvings.

Just as in Judaism and Christianity, angels in these other religions serve as messengers.

The Earliest Mention of Angels

The earliest mention of angels in ancient religions comes from Mesopotamia. The Mesopotamians believed that a divine power created the world and then communicated with the world's inhabitants through spirit messengers, or angels. The angels traveled on a pathway between heaven and earth.

One of the earliest angelic forms was found in the city of Ur in the Euphrates Valley, about 140 miles from Babylon. Archaeologists found a stele that depicts a winged figure pouring the "water of life" into the king's cup. Some scholars believe it is the earliest known representation of an angel, from a civilization that existed between 4000 and 2500 years B.C.

Angels in Islam

According to the Koran, the holy book of Islam, angels were created before man but upon man's creation, angels were required to bow down before man. This, say the Muslims, is what prompted Lucifer's rebellion.

The angel Gabriel is quoted in the Koran as saying to Mohammed, "We do not descend from heaven save at the bidding of your Lord." The Koran also says, "The angels sing the praise of their Lord and ask forgiveness for those on earth."

Muslims believe that angels will testify for or against people on the Day of Judgment, and that angels are present in every mosque to record the prayers of the faithful.

The Native Indian Approach to Angels

In the native Indian religions, totems are roughly equivalent to the Judeo-Christian concept of angels. They embody spirit guides or helpers and their purpose is to help the spiritual development of a person They provide a source of spiritual and psychic power. Unlike the traditional concept of a guardian angel, who is assigned to a person at birth, totems may change during a person's life depending on their needs and growth.

From the Indian perspective, people get sick when they are out of touch with their totems. It is a "healer's" job, then, to waft the totem back toward the person, sometimes by fanning a feather, blowing breath, or smoking a substance and blowing the smoke toward the person.

Jewish Belief in Angels is Ancient

Angels are a part of ancient Jewish tradition. In addition to the Bible, angels appear in the Talmud and Midrash, as well as the Dead Sea Scrolls. Following the publication of *Zohar*, considered to be the classic of medieval Jewish mystic writings, demons, imps, and devils appeared quite frequently in Jewish folklore.

Jewish folklore maintains that Michael taught agriculture to Adam and that angels taught Moses the healing arts.

The Jewish prayer book, the *Siddur*, clearly states that the angels offer homage to God in hymns of praise that they constantly sing. The daily morning service has a prayer from Nehemiah 9:6:

You alone are the Lord;
You made heaven,
The heaven of heavens, with all their host,
The earth and everything on it,
The seas and all that is in them,
And You preserve them all.
The host of heaven worships You

In many Jewish prayer books, one of the prayers preceeding the Sabbath eve meal pleads: "I beg you, O King, who is the King of Kings, bid your angels, the angels who minister to you, to consider me with compassion and to bless me as they enter my home on our holy day."[1]

A vital part of every Jewish prayer service is the prayer of sanctification, the *Kedushah*. Several versions of this prayer exist, but virtually all include the words of angels recorded in Isaiah 6:3— *Holy, holy, holy is the Lord of hosts; the whole earth is full of His glory!* (This same verse, of course, is also a key part of the eucharistic services of the mainline Christian denominations.)

Rosh Hashana Prayers

One of the most powerful prayers associated with Rosh Hashana, the beginning of the Jewish new year, includes a description of the "day of awe and dread:"

A great shofar is sounded. A still small voice is heard. The angels hurry to and fro. Fear and trembling seize them, and they cry out: Lo, the day of Judgment! to arraign the heavenly host in judgment, for in Your sight not even they are pure. All mortals, too, are caused by You to pass before you as a flock of sheep. As a shepherd counts his herd and makes each sheep pass beneath his staff, so do You record and number and take account of every living soul, setting a limit to every creature's life and passing sentence upon all of them.

This idea that angels must undergo divine judgment underscores the belief that angels have the ability to make decisions and rebel if they so will.

The sounding of the shofar, the official trumpet, is intended to confound and confuse Satan, who is regarded as having control over the airwaves above the earth.

On both Rosh Hashana and Yom Kippur, the day of atonement, a prayer called the *Hineni* is said, in which the cantor leads the congregation in pleading to God that He will "rebuke Satan and keep him from blocking the ascent of my prayers." The prayer also states:

> May it be your will, God of Abraham, God of Isaac and God of Jacob, the great, mighty and revered, the God supreme over all . . . that all the angels who are assigned to prayers convey my prayer before the throne of your glory and spread it before you. (I ask this) for the sake of all the righteous, the pure and the upright and for the sake of the glory of your name which is mighty and awesome. For you heed the prayer of your people Israel with compassion.

Angels, thus, are perceived to be the "carriers" of prayer to heaven, as well as the conveyors of some of God's answers back to the earth.

Some modern Jewish writers have now concluded that prayers themselves are angels—that a prayer uttered to God sprouts wings and flies heavenward. Like many in the New Age movement, they have eliminated the difference between messenger and message. The message has become the messenger.

Other Jewish writers regard angels as "symbols of forces that operate within every one of us. Some are forces for good, some for evil; some are healing and protective, some destructive."[2] They are considered metaphors for the most basic human drives and emotions, such as love, hate, envy, lust, charity, greed, fear, hope, and so forth.

The Jewish perspective is generally this: God doesn't need angels. We mortals do. When we think of having a "gathering of angels" in us, the chasm between man and God is somehow narrowed.

In his book, *A Gathering of Angels,* Morris Margolies describes a teaching he received during childhood which he apparently considers to be characteristic of his own view on angels:

> "My first schoolteacher provided his eight-year-old students with a commentary on this passage (Genesis 3) that I remember to this day. He compared us to innocents in the Garden of Eden, and assured us we would not be responsible for our actions—even if we misbehaved—until we were bar-mitsvah at the age of

thirteen. But he warned us that after we became adults under
Jewish law, every one of our sins would create a devil or
demon who would hound us at every turn. The serpents who
would frighten us would be serpents of our own making, and
they would poison our lives. On the other hand, he insisted
that each of our good deeds would create a guardian angel at
our sides to take us through fires and storms and sickness and
heartache. The more good deeds, the more guardian angels.
He was teaching us, at a very early age, that we create our
own company, a very sophisticated lesson that has held up
well over the many years of though I've given the subject".[3]

This idea that angels are created by the deeds of man, according to the nature of the deed, is considered quite standard Kabbal-
istic teaching within Judaism.

The Kabbalah is a collection of secret teachings associated
with Jewish mystics in Europe. The Hebrew root of the word, *kbl*,
means "to receive." The teachings are considered sacred, but very
complex and difficult to interpret. One of the major texts appeared in the twelfth and thirteenth centuries. It is called the
"Book of Brightness," or the *Zohar*. The Kabbalah is considered
to be "the guide on the path to God, taken through a series of
heavenly halls with angelic assistance. It is filled with long descriptions of how to make the safe journey up through a tree of
angels. It requires secret passwords to overcome the demons on
the way."[4]

Centuries of Angels in Christianity

Through the centuries the angels associated with Christianity
have actually changed very little in function and identity from the
Bible perspective.

An angel has been found painted in the catacombs of Rome
which dates back to around A.D. 300.

Angels, however, are *not* mentioned in any of the major Christian creeds, such as the Nicene or Apostle's.

St. Augustine seemed to believe in the will of angels to make
choices. He wrote about the fall of the rebellious angels that "good
and bad angels have arisen, not from a difference in their nature
and origin . . . but from a difference in their wills and desires . . .
While some steadfastly continued in that which was the common

good of all, namely, in God Himself, and in His eternity, truth, and love; others . . . became proud, deceived, envious."[5]

An early Greek theologian, Origen, believed that angels were not only subject to birth and death, but they evolved over repeated lifetimes. Origen also believed that a person has two guardian angels: one good and one bad. The fairly popular concept of a person having a demon sitting on one shoulder and an angel on the other originated centuries ago!

St. Thomas Aquinas believed that angels are not capable of reason, and only had one brief moment of free will at the time they came into existence.

Some of those who have attempted a syllabus of angels are Pseudo-Dionysius, Pope Gregory the Great, Saint Ambrose, the Sibylline Oracles, and Clement of Alexandria.

In the Middle Ages

Medieval theologians believed angels filled a gap between God and humankind. Angels were described as moving freely between Heaven and earth. In fact, Christian theologians in medieval times theorized that the angels were the force behind the movement of the stars, the growth of plants, and the reproduction of animals and mankind. They were depicted always as doing God's bidding, with the net effect of easing man's spiritual journey.

During the twelfth and thirteenth centuries, Europe underwent an era of "angel fever" that is not unlike what we are seeing today in America. Angels were thought to govern the planets, seasons, months, days, and hours. Spells and incantations abounded to conjure up both angels and demons.

By the fourteenth century, those who focused their primary spiritual attention on angels conjectured that there were 301,655,722 angels hovering at the borders of the universe. Some 133,306,668 of these were considered to be fallen angels. Every blade of grass was thought to have its own guardian angel, whose sole job was to coax it to grow.

The Reformation and After

The Protestant Reformation signaled a decline in up-to-then universal understanding about angels. The "reformers" believed that man had direct communication with God and had no need for angels to intervene.

In the nineteenth century, John Wesley, founder of Methodism, wrote that the angels serve mankind "in a thousand ways . . . They may assist us in our searching after truth, remove many doubts and difficulties . . . they may warn us of evil in disguise, and place what is good in a clear strong light. They may gently move our will to embrace what is good, and to fly from that which is evil."[6] He also stated that angels "no doubt clearly discern all our words and actions, if not all our thoughts too; for it is hard to think these walls of flesh and blood can intercept the view of an angelic being."[7]

Angels seemed to lie somewhat "dormant" in the Protestant denominations until the 1970s.

The publication of Billy Graham's book, *Angels: God's Secret Agents* (1975) became a national best seller, with 2.6 million copies in print. Billy Graham advocated that angels are sent to help complete the will of the Ruler of the Universe and fulfill His judgment. (Psalm 103:19–21)

In many ways, it's surprising that evangelical Christians hadn't paid more attention to angels prior to that time. Anyone who believes in the literal interpretation of the Bible certainly must see angels as central figures in numerous Bible stories. They are also the manifestation of a merciful God—at least a God who is merciful to His children. The 1970s were a time when God's mercy and blessings became emphasized perhaps as never before.

No Agreement on Function

While all religions through the ages seem to have a *belief* in the existence of angels as divine messengers, there is no universally accepted opinion regarding many of their traits and features. The various religions do *not* give angels the same names, rankings, or jobs.

Metatron, for example, is said to hold the rank of the highest of angels according to Jewish mysticism. He is considered to be both the tallest angel and the one who occupies the throne next to God. In a number of sources, he is thought to be the prophet Enoch, who was taken up to Heaven and transformed into an angel of fire, given thirty-six pairs of wings, and assigned the position of celestial scribe. He is also thought by Jewish mystics to be the angel who wrestled with Jacob, the one who kept Abraham from sacrificing Isaac, and the one who led the Children of Israel through the wilderness.

Moroni is considered the angel of the Latter-Day Saints, an indigenous American angel.

Israfel is an Islamic angel who supposedly served for three years as a companion to Mohammed.

Melchizedek, whom the Bible describes as the ruler of Salem (later, Jerusalem), is considered in Phoenician mythology to be Sydik, an angelic being as opposed to a flesh-and-blood person. He is called the father of the seven Angels of the Divine Presence. He is thought to have given God's covenant to Abraham and to have introduced the concept of salvation through pure faith.

The fact that various religions do not hold universal opinion about the origin of angels or their relationship to man is a vitally important concept to keep in mind as we explore New Age teachings in the coming chapters.

7

What is *Not* Ours to Know

WE know a great deal about angels from God's Word. We know that angels:

- are real
- are spirit beings
- have intelligence, emotions, and limited free will
- have different functions or "orders"
- serve to protect, deliver from harm, give messages, and escort the righteous at their death
- are opposed to God's enemies, including Satan and his demons
- are innumerable
- take on many different appearances
- are *not* omnipresent, omnipotent, omniscient, and can be thwarted by our sin and lack of faith in God
- are *not* to be worshiped
- are not the ones to whom we should address prayer
- do not do for man what man can do for himself
- refuse to take rewards from man
- always do God's bidding, not man's

The angels as depicted in God's Word have four great qualities. *Angels are powerful, fearless warriors.* Most of those who encounter them stand in awe of their majesty and power. They fight to win, and they win their fights.

Bible angels cause people to reevaluate their lives. They issue challenges that cause those who encounter them to readjust their priorities, prepare for major changes, or take drastic lifechanging action. The people who see angels in the Bible always take action in response to the angel visit. But, they do not preach about the visit, exalt the visit, or claim to be special because of the visit.

Angels in the Bible are created by God and for God. They are creatures of worship, first and foremost. Their appearances to men are often linked to worship, and in many ways, bring about God's purposes which only serves to further the worship of God. They are creatures whose sole activity is to reflect back to God the glory of God.

Angels minister to God's people. Angels speak mostly to the righteous, although they do occasionally speak to the unrighteous, as in the case of King Nebuchadnezzar. They *help*, however, only the righteous—those who know and serve God.

Very often, the people who receive the help of angels are ones who have special needs, and do not have sufficient human strength or human allies to assist them.

The work of angels is summarized in Psalm 103:20–21 which says:

> *Bless the Lord, you His angels, who excel in strength, who do His word, heeding the voice of His word. Bless the Lord, all you His hosts, you ministers of His, who do His pleasure.*

This verse states clearly that angels are strong.

They carry out God's words.

They listen only to the voice of the Lord.

They minister praise and worship to the Lord.

They exist totally for His pleasure.

What Is *Not* Told to Us

For all that we know about angels, there is a great deal that we do not know.

We do not know how they "move" or seem to "appear from nowhere." We do not know all the details of their relationship with God. We do not know all of the activity in which they engage in the spiritual realm.

God apparently intends for it to be that way.

God has secrets. They are a part of His mystery and majesty. They are also a part of His faithfulness and trustworthiness. (Otherwise, we would be reluctant to tell God our own secrets.)

God is omniscient and omnipresent. He sees the beginning from the ending, and He knows what man is capable of knowing, as well as what man needs to know in order to live a righteous life on this earth.

God's foremost gift to us is a gift of faith. The Scriptures tell us that every person has been given a "measure" of faith. We all are capable of believing and trusting God. (See Romans 12:3.)

We are to live in that faith, and quite bluntly, we are to let God's secrets be God's secrets.

Those who seek to unlock or uncover the secret things of God are, by definition of the word, occultists. The occult literally refers to the "secret things of God." When we attempt to engage in certain activities with the hope that we will uncover God's secrets, we are on dangerous ground. It is then that we are most susceptible to the devil's lies and deceit.

Our purpose as human beings is clearly in the "seen" and "known" world. We are to live practical, down-to-earth lives that are marked by work, obedience to God's laws, good relationships with our fellow man, and continual faith in and worship of the Almighty.

When we seek out what is not ours to know, we begin to walk in shadows, not light.

The Lies About Angels—

What the New Age Teaches

8

Angels: The Latest Hijacking by the New Age Movement

CONSIDER these three quotes about angels:

"God made us angels of energy, encased in solids—currents of life dazzling through a material bulb of flesh."
—Paramahansa Yogananda[1]

"They are celestial visitants, flying on spiritual, not material, pinions. Angels are pure thoughts of God, winged with Truth and Love, no matter what their individualism may be."
—Mary Baker Eddy[2]

"Becoming an angel is to transcend our own limits, to unbury the Truth of all things, and to be swept into Perfection."
—Karen Goldman[3]

These three quotes represent three prominent New-Age opinions regarding angels:

- We are evolving into angels.
- Angels help us in that evolution process.
- Angel help is given in a variety of "angelic" ways. Thus, Angels are really various ideas and feelings resident in mankind.

Let's take a look at each of these beliefs in more detail . . . .

Belief #1: We are evolving into angels.

The belief that people are evolving into angels has its root in the Theosophical Society, which was founded in 1875 in the wake of Darwin's theory of the origin of the species and the natural evolution of man. The Theosophists contend that all world relig-ions have common truths that transcend potential differences. The society was founded on the belief that man's evolution has both physical and spiritual components. One of their core teach-ings is that "masters" lead the way of societal spiritual evolution. These masters are either spirit beings or fortunate men who are more highly evolved than the rest of the human race.

The spiritual evolution of the human race, of course, is seen as something that man can assist through mind-expansion tech-niques. It is a part of "self-actualization."

Self-actualization and self-realization are terms that are used frequently by New Age proponents. They are not exclusively New Age terms, but they appear frequently in the New Age literature because the New Age philosophy advocates that a person can reach deep within to discover their inner goodness.

The Current Awakening of Angels

One New Age writer has referred to the present time as "the great reawakening to the angels."

Why now?

Alma Daniel, Timothy Wyllie, and Andrew Ramer, authors of *Ask Your Angels*, will tell you that it is because of reorganization within the angel ranks. The angels themselves presently are "evolving" and have been told to have more frequent contact with mankind. Gabriel, for example, is said to have been the Angel of Revelation in the past, but now that man is coming closer to the angels, Gabriel has less need for revelation. Therefore, Gabriel is now evolving into the Angel of Relationship.[4]

Another reason cited by the same author trio, is that we are living at the end of the Age of Secrets, a time in which secret traditions are now being shared openly all over the planet. They see the current resurgence of interest in angels as a third wave of angelic visitations—the first occurring in Bible times, and the sec-ond in the medieval period (mostly to saints and seers). According to them, this third wave began in the middle of the nineteenth century. The angels supposedly began to make themselves known to a number of artists, scientists, and saints, such as the Spanish nun Theresa of Avila, the German Protestant mystic Jacob Boehme,

Jewish sages Moses Cordovero and Isaac Luria, the Swedish scientist Emanual Swedenborg, and Mother Ann Less of the Shaker community in America.

Their third reason, however—one that is central to the former two—is that we human beings have finally evolved in our consciousness to the place where we are ready to perceive angels and to interact with them on a regular basis.

Daniel tells us, "We're moving into a higher level of consciousness now, which is God consciousness . . . the second coming of Christ will be as a woman . . . . What that really means is that the feminine Christ consciousness is coming down now, into each one of us. It is the feminine principle that is being returned to the earth. The feminine principle represents the nurturer, the guardian, and the caretaker. We need a return of this energy because we've been dominated by a patriarchy."[5]

Belief #2: Angels help us evolve.

Whether angels are spirit beings or already-evolved humans, angels help us evolve. In other words, there are some who have already evolved, and they reach down to help the rest of us rise up to their level.

This belief stems from a more basic belief that angels are "loving friends" to man. They reside, very specifically, next to man's heart.

It is the Sufis, the mystics of the Islamic world, who were the first to put an emphasis on man's meeting and interacting with angels in this manner. They regarded angels as the companions of the heart. It is in Sufi writings that angels are first regarded as being part of the human soul or Higher Self.

Other mystic religions, including spiritualism and the New Age, see guardian angels as "spirit guides." These spirits come alongside man and ultimately reside within man in order to show man the way he should go. In ancient times, these spirit guides were perceived to be assigned to each person in male-female pairs. In today's New Age thinking, these spirit guides may be one or many, and may be either male or female.

Rosemary Ellen Guiley writes,

"We view angels as always with us—they never desert us, no matter how poorly we perform. And even though they do not

always save us from catastrophe, they stand ready as a source
of strength to help us through all our trials. We seem to have a
great, collective hunger for spiritual guidance that is personal
and intimate, a hunger that is not being met through
conventional religion. Angels are our personal companions,
our guides, our protectors."[6]

It's true, of course, that we human beings do long for an intimate and personal relationship with God. But that hunger is not
satisfied by angels. It is satisfied only by a personal relationship
with Jesus Christ and the indwelling of the Holy Spirit!

Indian Spirit Guides

In various pagan religions, notably those of the American Indians, shamans or "spirit guides" are featured prominently. Are
these spirit guides actually angels?

They are like the angels who appear in the Bible in this regard:
they often appear as human men.

They are *unlike* angels in that shamans nearly always walk beside a person to guide their way, or help a person at a task. Angels
in the Bible appear to convey a message or engage in a direct act
of deliverance, rather than to assist a particular person with an
ordinary task or decision.

Shamans, or spirit guides, are also capable of taking the form
of creatures, very often birds. Sophy Burnham tells in her book *A
Book of Angels*, about people who supposedly have conversed
with angels who appeared in the form of crows, a swan, or a great
white dog.[7] Others claim to have seen angels in butterflies.

A Different Vibration

New Age writers believe that angers exist on a "slightly finer
vibrational frequency from the one to which our physical senses are
tuned." They can perceive us, but we can't perceive them. They
are androgynous citizens of an "inner space" whose responsibilities
include the harmonious organization of the inhabited universe.[8]

They supposedly work with our souls, in conjunction with
Universal Mind, to help us raise our sights and spirits by reminding
us of the truth, beauty, and goodness that exist within everything.

Omnipresent

Angels in New Age literature are capable of existing in several places at one time. In order for them to be seen in one place and time, they must slow themselves down, something only they can do.

Nature Spirits

The cousins of angels are regarded, at least by some New Age writers, to be "nature spirits" such as devas, elves, fairies, trolls, gnomes, sylphs, and so forth. These are proclaimed to oversee the living, growing things on the earth and are considered to be responsible for configuring flocks of birds and schools of fish. We supposedly connect with the nature spirits whenever we tend plants, hug trees, walk through a nature preserve, or eat anything that has been grown.

Many Colors

Some New Age writers say that angels come in different colors. Since they are creatures of light, the color they appear is the part of the light spectrum they have chosen to express part of their nature. Pink means love, yellow means intellect or faith or joy, and purple means spiritual integrity, fortune, or majesty. There is no definitive list of colors and their symbolic meanings, however. New-Age angels who appear in white are reflecting the highest vibration since they are combining all of the colors at once.

Are Ghosts the Same as Angels?

People frequently report seeing angelic images who look like deceased loved ones.

Are these ghosts? Or angels?

They are both to New Age writers.

The angels might be likened to the "happy dead," whereas ghosts are perceived to be the "sad dead." Both serve to give messages.

In her book, Sophy Burnham titles her first chapter "Angels and Ghosts I Have Known." She states that when she was thirty, she looked up and saw a ghost standing in a doorway. She didn't see this with her physical eyes but with "some inner knowledge."[9] She also experienced three "visits" from her deceased mother. She says, "She was trying to tell me what it was like after death: We'd made a pact that she would try." Burnham sees her mother smiling with great love—"such love I thought my heart would break." She concludes, "On this material plane, I suddenly understood, we are not *supposed* to meet so totally: we are not strong enough to take such undiluted love."[10]

Burnham makes a clear delineation between ghosts and angels. She writes this about ghosts:

"Ghosts are attached by their longing and troubled memories to this physical plane; or else they are lost shadows, unable to reach the other side. Ghosts are found in every culture, and all people agree on how they look. You can see through them, or else they appear as a milky, misty substance with rippling edges. They have no feet. Since they retain their own personalities, they are as dear or as wicked as they were in life. Some disturb because they are themselves disturbed or troubled. They come in on the channels of mediums, or they stand behind chairs in ancient homes, or they drift weeping and disconsolate through rooms, drawing plangent music in their wake. Or they play jokes, as if to show us dull, blind humans that they still exist. Some spirits are truly evil, bordering on the demonic; they can possess you. They do great wrongs. But usually they are our loved ones returning in concern or to tell us everything's all right.

"When a spirit enters a room, you feel a chill, as if a door's been left ajar, and when it touches you or when its body passes through you, you feel an arctic cold. All these signs mark the characteristics of a ghost."[11]

In contrast, Burnham states that angels are characterized by warmth and light, have iridescent color or brightness, and flood a person with laughter and happiness, or great serenity. They carry messages.

New Age Writer Karen Goldman contends that there is no Angel of Death, but that when a person dies, an angel greets him to let him know he's actually still alive. Thus, we're all on the same plane. Ghosts and angels are just a higher form of "life."

New Ager Rosemary Gardner Loveday has a little different take. An English clairvoyant, medium, and psychic healer, she has said, "They (angels) gather around me when I do meditation or say my prayers. Thoughts come to me, and I write them down on paper."

She believes that angels assist in the healings that she conducts, and believes:

"Angels are human souls who have evolved and evolved, probably through lots of lifetimes, to get to the stage of being an angel. They work on very high vibrations. I think we come into this world to learn our lessons, such as, we've got to learn patience and learn not to be angry. We've got to develop spiritual qualities. Well, the agony of life is learning, but if you can grow spiritually, then you become closer to God—and nearer to the angels. I think angels are souls who have gone through the agonies of learning, and they have reached that high level of vibration in realms of light. Then they come back as angels, to bring that light and God's love to people."[12]

Belief #3: Angels come in various forms— all forms of *help* to humans is angelic in origin.

For many, angels are a way of explaining intuition, or extrasensory perception. The messages angels bear, according to some, are the "hunches" we feel about things that are about to happen to us or to others, nearby or far away.

Angels are considered by others to be feelings of love. They are equated with the impulses that drive us toward good deeds or loving actions. They are synonymous with compassion, generosity, and goodness.

Angels are thus "traits" of humanity that are positive, and which cause a person to evolve upward to a higher level of self-realization.

In sum, angels are not only those who help us and the methods they use, but ultimately, angels are us. In the New Age there's very little of a good nature that angels aren't.

From a Christian point of view, we can see an unholy trinity at work. New-Age angels serve the work of the Father—they are omnipotent, omniscient, and omnipresent with us. New-Age angels also serve the role of the Son—they reveal, help, and redeem man, raising man up from his present level to one higher. And, New-Age angels serve the role of the Holy Spirit—they continually prompt man toward his better nature.

As I said, this is an unholy, totally human trinity—one that is attempting to take on divinity for itself.

A Close Look at New Age Teachings

The best way I know to give you a thorough introduction to what the New Age teaches about angels is to let you read for yourself the words of one New Age writer, Karen Goldman. She has had two best sellers about angels: *The Angel Book—A Handbook for Aspiring Angels* and *Angel Voices*. Goldman believes the angels direct and guide her writings, but she also credits Sedona Institute in Phoenix, Arizona and the Self-Realization Fellowship for their support. She is clearly embedded in New Age thinking.

She begins *The Angel Book—A Handbook for Aspiring Angels* with these words:

> "Welcome to The Angel Book, a gift from angels everywhere to every heart. The Angel Book is the first handbook ever for the aspiring angels within us all, designed to help us understand and experience the essence of angels. It is a description of our journey back to our own "lightest selves," not some farflung celestial creatures with harps and feathers. It is a book about all of us, just as we are inside right now, a road map to the higher realms within us. A love letter from our angels, our Heavenly counterparts, it is, therefore, a handbook to Heaven . . . . The Angel Book captures the essence of angels; we learn what it means to fly, how to make miracles, and get our own wings . . . . The Angel Book will show us where to find our nearest angels so that we can ask anything we want to know, all by ourselves, anywhere, anytime, and for any reason." [13]

And she means it!

Goldman contends that angels have been kept "hidden in the shadows of religion" and that when we "get to the level where angels do exist, there's really no difference between any of us . . . if we look inside ourselves to understand the essence of just one 'angel,' we'll find that we can easily understand all angels." [14] The mark of an angel, according to her, is love.

She states:

> *When we accept ourselves as angels, we are gifted, guided, unified beings. Our natural mission is love. Our natural home is Heaven. God has given us this freedom. The reason we do not yet manifest it entirely is only our own silly selfishness, our pride, and our ignorance.* [15]

Selfishness, pride, and ignorance may, indeed, keep us from Heaven, but the rest of this statement is utter nonsense from a Bible point of view. Self-acceptance is not redemptive. Our mission as Christians is to love our neighbors as ourselves, but that is not our "natural" stated, according to God's Word. "Agape" or "divine love" for others is possible only when we open ourselves up to God's love, and become vessels for that love made available to others. Our natural home is not Heaven. It is earth. Our eternal home is a gift of God to those who love Him and seek to live according to His truth.

A Subtle Mix of Truth and Lie

Like so many of the New Age books on angels, Goldman's book is a mix of what is true according to the Bible, and what is false. She contends that angels:

- are everywhere . . . *which is true.*
- are always trying to reach a person through that person's own good thoughts, inspirations, and warm feelings . . . *which is NOT true. Angels aren't reaching out to people except as God commands them to do so.*
- are stronger than they look . . . *which may be true.*
- can be felt in every atom of creation . . . *which is NOT true. It is God who indwells every atom of creation by virtue of His creative power.*
- often work behind the scene and often go unnoticed . . . *which is true.*
- know "just what it feels like to be you" . . . *which is NOT true. Angels do not know the joy of personal salvation or the relationship we have as human beings with God Almighty. They are not indwelled with God Holy Spirit.*
- are nearer to people than they may realize . . . *which is true.*
- have a wingspan that is broad enough to lift the heart of the entire world . . . *which is NOT true. Angels are created, finite beings. They have no redemptive power whatsoever.*
- talk through a person's conscience . . . *which is NOT true.*
- never grow old . . . *which is true.*

- are happy at our success . . . *which may or may not be true.*
  *The Bible does not grant us insight into how the angels feel
  about us.* The Scriptures state only that: "there will be more
  joy in heaven over one sinner who repents than over ninety-
  nine just persons who need no repentance" (Luke 15:7).
  If angels rejoice over anything, it is over the fact that we turn
  to God, are forgiven by Him, and live godly lives.
- emerge from within us . . . *which is NOT true.*
- speak to everyone . . . *which is NOT true. The Holy Spirit
  is the One who woos each heart toward Jesus.*

Ten Major and Dangerous Lies

Ten of the most erroneous and dangerous of the lies in Goldman's books are these . . .

(1) *We should seek out angels with an open heart
through our "feelings."* There is no Bible basis for this whatsoever. We are to seek God and Him alone. The first of the two great
commandments given by Jesus is this: "You shall love the Lord
your God with all your heart, with all your soul, and with all your
mind" (Matthew 22:37).

(2) *Angels work miracles,* and sometimes the only way we
know an angel has been present is "by the miracles he leaves blos-
soming in his path after he is gone."[16] Only the Lord God works
miracles. He is the author of all natural and supernatural law, and
He alone is capable of superseding those laws.

(3) *All angels speak the truth.* Goldman leaves no room for
evil angels, or demons, who lie. The Bible teaches that fallen angels—which we call evil angels or demons—are lying spirits, full of
deceit, incapable of speaking truth.

In *Angel Voices*, Goldman only briefly explores the idea that
we can be evil angels, although she never directly identifies them
as such. She writes, "In the shadows of my darkest dreams I am a
hurricane with red-streaked splotches and gold elbows, in a bris-
tling black cape. My hair is spun from iron needles. My teeth grip
the night in one embrace. But when I awaken I am an angel."[17]

(4) *When a person is lost in life "an angel will get right
inside your heart with you and show you the way home."* [18]
Hardly. Angels throughout Scripture work externally to man. It is

the Holy Spirit who convicts the heart about the truth regarding Jesus Christ, and it is the Word of God, including the word of Jesus, that speaks the truth about God the Father.

(5) *If you "give an angel an inch . . . you gain a ticket to Heaven."*[19] Angels have no redemptive power. It is only the blood of Jesus that provides a person entrance to Heaven.

Goldman also states that:

"There are as many ways of becoming an angel as there are angels themselves. There is no proper way to do it. It is not important how you become one. Any way you get to Heaven is just fine. Whenever the next moment arrives when you feel you are ready to fly, look around you. There are always openings in the field of angels.

"Your trip to Heaven is a journey only you can navigate for yourself. If you will listen to the angel inside you, you will find directions coming to you as sweetly as music." [20]

Jesus taught, *I am the way, the truth, and the life. No one comes to the Father except through Me* (John 14:6).

Goldman closes *The Angel Book* with these words, **"Congratulations! . . . Your ascension has begun!"**

Hardly. No person is capable of reaching Heaven by his own will. The people at Babel once tried it.

In her second book, *Angel Voices*, Goldman makes these claims about the redemptive work of angels, and their approach toward judging humanity:

1. "Their verdict is always innocent, their sentence always love."[21]
2. "As we open to our angels, we become healed by our own surrender; changed by what we receive; happy and whole by what we remember."[22]
3. "Heaven never wishes to punish, but only to heal; never to accuse, but to vanquish all misery."[23]
4. "When the Soul doors are open to experience angels, reality becomes transparent. You can see the workings of creation."[24]

Again, this is not what the Bible tells us. Angels have no redemption or healing power in and of themselves. They give only God's verdicts and edicts, not their own. As for heaven, while it may be true that God has no desire to punish, a part of His nature as a Just and Righteous God is to reward those who diligently seek

Him and to keep from His presence all those who willfully disobey His commandments.

We do not need to experience angels in order to see God at work, to understand creation, or to experience ultimate reality. Ultimate reality lies in Christ Jesus and it is the Holy Spirit who opens our eyes to see the world as God sees it.

A False Concept of Grace

Also of special importance to note in Goldman's second book is her concept of grace. Once again, we find a mishmash of truth and falsehood. It's important as we read her statements to keep in mind the Bible definition of grace: "the work of God."

To Goldman . . .

- "Grace keeps Time moving, our bodies breathing, our souls humming. We are all living in a state of grace." That is true. Time, and all natural laws are God's work.

- "Grace is a treasure, a package of soul flowers received by intuition to be opened delicately and appreciated forever." That is *not* true. Grace is a *gift of God, not of works, lest anyone should boast. For we are His workmanship, created in Christ Jesus for good works, which God prepared before hand that we should walk in them* (Ephesians 2:8-10). It is impossible for us to bear any grace not given to us by God!

- "Grace is a sweet gift, and when we own it, it illuminates night with bright singing and morning with flight." True and *not* true. Grace *is* a sweet gift, but we do not own it in and of ourselves. We receive it as a gift from God, not a gift resident in our own beings. The difference is subtle, but vast.

- "Grace can be found by opening the door to our inner angel and harmonizing ourselves with that place." That is *not* true. We receive grace from God and we find it by opening ourselves up to Him and inviting the Holy Spirit to cleanse us, guide us, and reveal truth to us.

Here, Goldman makes a very subtle and deceptive clarification. She writes, "To manifest more grace in our lives, to receive gifts of Spirit, we have only to open our inner doors."[25] This sounds very close to what the apostle Paul wrote to the Ephesians with one important difference. Goldman never refers to the *Holy* Spirit. She refers only to human spirit, and she exalts it to a deified plane.

(6) *Angels reward your love with an expansion of your own being.*[26] Angels are not capable of reward. God is the *rewarder of those who diligently seek Him* (Hebrews 11:6).

(7) *"What is considered 'genius' by the world is simply the 'angel' within us acting without our interference.* This is how great men and women function. It is how great, brilliant, and masterful works are done and how man's 'greater purpose' can be realized."[27] This is tantamount to believing that we are all "possessed" by an angelic spirit! Such a statement leaves no room for the creativity of God, or individual endowment of traits and talents that are acted upon by a person's will. Even the Holy Spirit, who indwells man at man's invitation, does not "possess" man. Man always retains his own will unless he invites *evil* to possess him, according to God's Word.

(8) *Angels are omnipresent with us and share our emotions.* Goldman states that the angels sing, "Our care is your care. Our passion is your passion. Our heart is your heart. We are with you in your light and your darkness. We stand by you in your unhappiness and your joy."[28] That is not the cry of angels. Angels say that of the Father. They live and move and have their total being in Him, not us. Rather, that is the heart's cry of the Father toward us. He longs for us with care, passion, and compassion. He is the One who is with us always.

(9) *We become angels.* Goldman claims in *Angel Voices* that once we become angels "we have no fear. No dangers of earth can rise against us. We are creatures of magic and love, unstoppable and invincible—and nature knows it. Yet this is our birthright and our calling. We can exist beyond the trap of our mortality. We are meant to transcend our skin and feel the fires of Heaven glowing within us; to know the healing waters of joy and compassion that flow simultaneously through everything known and unknown, cleansing everything. To witness the miracles of creation and dissolution, exploding in every atom of space all around us . . . to produce miracles of sanity and hold jewels of freedom in our

hands. As angels we can known intimately that which was never born and will never die as the foundation of all things known."[29]

Regardless of what Goldman may claim, we are human beings locked into fleshly existence as long as we reside on this earth. We cannot become angels, nor should we desire to do so. The only true inner cleansing any of us can experience is forgiveness and release from our sins, which is God's alone to grant to us in His mercy. We are not destined to become miracle workers, only to have a relationship with the true Miracle Worker, Jesus Christ.

(10) *Angels serve only to uncover our innate goodness and divinity.* Goldman's books represent the basic New Age tenet that man is inherently good. She states in *The Angel Handbook*: "You don't have to try to be somebody new or better or different to become an angel. Just recognize that you already are somebody perfect and heavenly. Then, just be you."[30]

She expands this idea in her second book, *Angel Voices*, stating: "Within the mind of God is the heart of all things. Within the heart of a human being is the clear mind of God."[31]

Goldman uses the words "inner angel," "angel self," and "the angel within" to describe "that part of us which she says is like an angel."

She also makes statements such as these:

- "To become an angel you must discover your own inner light for yourself and let it shine."
- "The real distance to Heaven is only as far as it is to your real Self."
- "The nearer you live to your own angel heart, the nearer you live to Heaven."[32]

Man-Made Miracles

She writes, "When you let your inner angel out to play, unusual forces come to your aid. Little miracles begin to happen all around you. Things take place for your benefit that seem to defy logic. Perfection begins to make itself known to you through ordinary events. You begin to unveil the deeper meaning of your life, the hidden truths of this world. You finally arrive at a profound and exquisite vision of the universe." This is New Age thinking at its best—just peel away all the ugly layers of your life and you will find perfection and be capable of divine activity.

The Bible takes an opposite approach: man is born with a sinful nature and must be redeemed from it through faith in the living God. Jesus made it very clear in His teachings that only One is inherently good—our Heavenly Father. (See Matthew 19:17.) We do not become good by looking within ourselves, but by accepting His sacrificial death on the Cross. We are renewed in spirit when the Holy Spirit indwells us and convicts us of error, and when we choose God's ways over the desires of our sinful flesh. It is by that process that we acquire the mind of Christ.

Goldman states that an angel is any person who helps another person believe in miracles, raises your spirits, looks you in the eye with love, and "helps you grow."[33] Furthermore, everyone on earth is an angel "for at least a moment."[34]

Goldman has angels, friends, hope, the Holy Spirit, and human potential grossly misconstrued into a mishmash of platitudes that make it seem as if everybody and everything is wonderful if we only think it is.

Can Nirvana be far away?

Not in Goldman's thinking. She advocates:

"You can make fully discovering your angel the object in your life. Then, one day, you'll identify with this angelic self alone and you will always be in Heaven. It is as actual as you are. It is never separate from you. It is your heavenly soul—who you really are. It is you. There is nothing more than you could ever be . . . . To be truly human is to become Divine."[35]

A very similar lie was voiced in Eden.

And There's Still More Lie . . .

Goldman makes very direct statements about angels that gives angels the specific roles assigned to Jesus and the Holy Spirit in the Holy Bible. She says,

- "We can always call upon our angels when we have lost our light."[36] *No . . . we are to call upon the Lord.*
- "Use light to create magic with the Grand Magician. Through His Creation you will find the doors to Him. The doors can be seen everywhere to the discerning eye, felt everywhere to the discerning heart."[37] *No . . . the Lord God is not a magician. He is Creator. The door to God is not creation, but Jesus Christ, who openly called himself the Door* (John 10:9).

- "As human beings, we have one continuous invitation to open any door to join Him."[38] *No . . . there is only one door, not many. Jesus said, "I am the way, the truth, and the life. No one comes to the Father except through Me"* (John 14:6).
- "An angel's inspiration can restore integrity, righteousness, and humility to a self-obsessed world."[39] *No . . . that is not the work of angels, but of the Holy Spirit.*

Goldman contends that angels embody light and wisdom. Angels may appear to be bright and shining, but they are not synonymous with light. They may appear wise, because they speak God's Word, but they are not synonymous with wisdom.

A Goal of Oneness

The Hindu-Buddhist concept of "oneness"—which is basic to New Age thinking—is evident throughout Goldman's writings. She states, "To the angels, we are all one perfect child with many different faces."[40] She writes in *Angel Voices:*

- "There is a way of 'knowing' that like an angel defines gravity, defines the intellect, eludes the most scholarly and renowned. It is the experience of unity, by instantaneous knowing, that we are one with all creatures and all Divine Providence."
- "The greatest message of the angels is that we are not alone but that we are an integral part of One Divine Consciousness with infinite members."
- "Only in Oneness do we find true happiness. Its roots are in the unlimited soil of Being."
- "A pure soul sees itself simultaneously everywhere—in the shape of a tree, a river, a town, or a sunset. It does not need mirrors. It sees all parts of itself at once because there is nothing it is not."
- "If our training has been opposite to these Truths, we must train ourselves to find them, where they are. The answers are not on the shallow, mundane level of our questions. Mundane problems require mundane solutions, but the thrill of life's greatness, of our beauty, and Heaven's magic is not found in the world of separation and fear. It is a little higher up where all is One."
- "Receptivity is the window to open to the breezes of Oneness."

- "In Oneness, there are no 'others,' only different views of our greater angelselves."[41]

This is a denial of our individual creation and our uniqueness in Christ Jesus. The apostle Paul noted that there is only One Spirit, one baptism, one faith. But *many* gifts. We are unique beings, set in unique times and situations. We express ourselves creatively and are invited by God the Father to take an active part in His ongoing work on the earth. We are not of the same creative order as the trees, rivers, or sunsets. Of all God's creation, man alone received the "breath" of God.

Goldman's foremost goal, it appears, is to achieve, and to help others achieve, a communion with angels, and in that communion, to find union and a great sense of joy. She writes:

"When we commune as angels with all Life, we see everything in the light of our joy."

"In communion with angels, we experience the most Heavenly qualities, the holiest, noblest, selfless ambitions, complete with unending power to achieve them—true soul-sprung values and morals, acceptance and wisdom, toward all."

"All our troubles cease the minute we merge with the Source of all solutions."[42]

There is nothing in God's Word that implies that we ever become "one" with God. We retrain our distinct selves. It is not communion with angels that brings out the best in us, but the indwelling power of the Holy Spirit that regenerates our hearts and renews our minds so that we think, act, and speak as Jesus Christ would think, act, or speak in our circumstances and situations of life—but always with our own personalities, talents, and traits!

Constant Contact with the Angels

Goldman's advice is to "stay in contact with angels and your life will become dreamlike, ushering in all the good you ever dreamed possible, deeply nourishing all your truest loves, finding Peace and grace supremely, feeling cared for and guarded and guided through Eternity."[43]

She has angels sorely confused with the Holy Spirit of God, who never promises us a dreamlike existence, but rather, a supreme reality.

How do we get into contact with angels?

Goldman writes, "Come to the island of angelic thoughts within you. Breathe. Let yourself be surrounded by angels. Think of it as a journey into yourself, where you can dance with birds and find the volcano of Truth within you and see the clouds of love wrapped around the mountain of your spirit."[44]

Nice poetry, but not truth.

And what is not truth is lie . . . deadly, insidious deception.

Goldman claims that as a person journeys to become an angel, "there are no wrong ways or paths of no return—for all roads, even crooked and broken, eventually lead again to the Supreme One from whence they have also begun."[45]

This is one hundred and eighty degrees contrary to what Jesus taught. He stated very clearly, *Enter by the narrow gate; for wide is the gate and broad is the way that leads to destruction, and there are many who go in by it. Because narrow is the gate and difficult is the way which leads to life, and there are few who find it* (Matthew 7:13-14).

The Bible speaks of consequences that are not all "good" for everybody:

- *Do not be deceived, God is not mocked; for whatever a man sows, that he will also reap. For he who sows to his flesh will of the flesh reap corruption, but he who sows to the Spirit will of the Spirit reap everlasting life* (Galatians 6:7).
- *For the wages of sin is death, but the gift of God is eternal life in Christ Jesus our Lord* (Romans 6:23).

Pretty Words Don't Equal Truth

Goldman's books are filled with "pretty words." They soothe and entice and lull a reader into a false conclusion, "that's a nice little idea."

In fact, you may be tempted to say, "Oh, Phil, lighten up. She's just writing pretty poetry."

On the contrary . . . Goldman's ideas have a consistency to them from start to finish. They embody in "snippet" form the very tenets of New Age philosophy, with a coating of sugar to make them go down easier.

What she writes does not in any way exalt Jesus Christ as Lord. Her writings, throughout, are permeated with the concept of self-love and self-exaltation.

To her, man *is* god.

That is not pretty poetry . . . it's pure lie.

When we read words such as hers we must continually be in prayer, asking the Holy Spirit to help us discern lie from truth. We must pray as Solomon prayed, *Give to your servant an understanding heart to judge Your people, that I may discern between good and evil* (1 Kings 3:9).

9

Attempts at Conjuring Angels

A number of books on the market today propose to teach a person how to interact with angels. In essence, they teach how to "conjure" angels—how to make contact with them and then develop a relationship with them.

Why do this?

Many reasons are offered by New Age writers.

Angels supposedly can be used to help a person:

- overcome addictions
- achieve dreams
- define personal goals
- bring about both physical and emotional healing
- resolve troublesome relationships
- lose weight

Angels have been said to increase our capacity for trust, revive the innocence and wonder we experienced as children, and deepen our capacity for compassion and forgiveness.

Angels have been attributed to helping avert atomic meltdowns and bring families closer together.

Angels are said to "help us make life a true and meaningful experience."[1]

Various techniques are proposed. Some of them are quite lyrical. In her book *Angel Letters*, Sophy Burnham describes the process this way:

"We send letters to our angels. And letters come back to us, like leaves floating on the air. They land on the pond of our consciousness so softly sometimes we hardly feel them, and only by the ripples growing outward in ever-larger concentric circles do we recognize their presence, see the fallen leaf."[2]

One writer has even suggested that a person have a picnic in a park and invite the angels to come.

But for the most part, the writers present highly systematic approaches.

This is not to say that *they* perceive their approaches as systematic or manipulative. Quite the contrary. Part of the New Age deception is to claim that a person only puts himself into a limbo-like position in which angels and other supernatural events *might* happen to him. Alma Daniel writes, "You can't reach the angels willfully. You can only reach them through surrender. You can't command, 'Now I will speak with my angel! Now!' Rather, you have to open yourself as a tool, an instrument for them to come through you."[3]

Others, however, teach that once you know your angel's name, you can call upon your angel at will.

In either case, all New Age teachers instruct their followers to "open themselves up" to angels as a prerequisite for channeling their messages or energy.

This is best done, of course, if you are a basically good person. New-Age angel author Burnham chooses to believe that "angels come most commonly . . . to children, saints, and primitive people, to the innocents, who perhaps can perceive more clearly than we."[4]

A Panoramic Look at the Methodology Proposed

Again, I believe the most valid way to survey what New Age writers think and say about this matter of "interacting" with angels is to take a look at several of the foremost books presently on the market.

One of them, *Ask Your Angels*, offers a five-step method called the GRACE Process, which uses a divination process called the Angel Oracle.[5] The three authors—Daniel, Wyllie, and Ramer—claim, by the way, that an angel named Abigrael helped them create and write their book.

The GRACE Process they propose involves:

- *Grounding—focusing all one's mental, emotional, and physical energies into a calm and harmonious balance (achieved through meditation, breathing, and visualizing techniques)*
- *Releasing—*getting rid of negative self-beliefs, worries, and concerns until one gets to the place of forgiving both self and others
- *Aligning—*getting into a state of relaxed awareness and getting back into touch with "the part of you that never stopped believing in angels" (using advanced meditation techniques, chanting, and visualization, including the visualization of one's own wings growing from golden seed pods connected to the vertebra in the back)
- *Conversing—*asking questions and writing down answers (recognizing that angels use chills, goose bumps, tingling at the back of the neck, visions, tears, fragrance, and intense emotions)
- *Enjoying the Connection—*using the Angel Oracle for guidance.

The Angel Oracle is a three-part deck of cards. The first cards are assigned to the four archangels Uriel, Gabriel, Raphael, and Michael. When you pick one of these cards at random (after shuffling the cards and putting them face down), you supposedly connect with the problem-solving, creative, healing, or dreaming qualities of this angel.

The second set of cards has sixteen types of angels—from companion and connecting to technology and nature. Choosing one of these cards supposedly activates the angel associated with the card to help the person bridge the archangel function and the activity chosen from the third set of cards.

The third set of cards has twenty-four activities or situations. When a person picks one of these, he is told to pursue what the card says, knowing that his angel (from the second set of cards) is going to help him.

Thus, you might pick the archangel of healing, and then the angel of environment, and the activity of spend time with someone you love . . . and end up going on a vacation to a beautiful high-desert place with your spouse in order to get over an allergy.

I can't help but think that common sense might yield the same result.

Linked to the Zodiac

One writer, Tim Gunns, links angels to the sun-sign chart. Each of the four traditional archangels is linked to a season: Rafael–Spring, Uriel–Summer, Michael–Autumn, Gabriel–Winter. Each of the twelve signs of the zodiac are linked to a "key word" that is linked to an angel, that is in turn supposed to inspire a specific trait. For example, Aries is linked to the words "I am" to call upon the angel of "power and authority" to inspire "courage."

Use of Tarot with Angels

John Randolph Price starts his latest best seller, *The Angels Within Us*, with a verse from Psalms: *For he will give his angels charge of you to guard you in all your ways* (Psalm 91:11).

His book is anything but Christian, however.

An angel–who calls herself the Angel of Creative Wisdom, also known by some as Isis–supposedly appears to Price to tell him that there is a cord made of three tones. These tones are love, will, and understanding–and when they are blended, the sound of wisdom is heard.

Wisdom, the angel supposedly says, is taught by angels–twenty-two of them to be exact, which correspond to the twenty-two cards in the Tarot. Each of these angels has the name of a mythological god.

The angels Price identifies are the angels of . . .

- Unconditional Love and Freedom
- Illusion and Reality
- Creative Wisdom
- Abundance
- Power and Authority
- Spiritual Understanding
- Loving Relationships
- Victory and Triumph
- Order and Harmony
- Discernment
- Cycles and Solutions

- Spiritual Strength and Will
- Renunciation and Regeneration
- Death and Rebirth
- Patience and Acceptance
- Materiality and Temptation
- Courage and Perseverance
- Service and Synthesis
- Imagination and Liberation
- Truth and Enlightenment
- The Creative Word
- Success

Who *wouldn't* want to have more of any of these traits, or experiences?

The appeal of the New Age in angels is to the most basic of human desires for a "better quality of life."

In order to get into contact with each of these angels, Price offers a guided meditation. The one he gives for encountering the Angel of Death and Rebirth is one I found especially interesting—it is a mix of words that "sound good" but which pack an evil meaning:

"As I look within and contemplate the magnificent Presence I AM, I understand that the only death that I shall ever experience is the giving up of the old to receive the new. I am ready to do that now. I am willing to take the final step.

"I am no longer afraid to give up my humanhood and accept my Christhood because I know that as I move through the fog toward the Bridge of Light, You are my shield and protector. If I walk through fire, I will not be burned. If there are waters, they shall not overflow me. If enemies should encamp against me, they shall not find me, for I will be hidden in You.

"I now walk the path to the Bridge. There is darkness, but I am not afraid. My miscreations seem to be beckoning to me, but my eye is single. And now I see the Light piercing the night and the faint outline of the Bridge is visible. I walk steady toward the Light.

"As I step upon the Bridge, I see You, my divine Reality, and with each step we move closer to each other. We stop at the middle pint, and I see You in all your glory, a pure Light Body of God embodying the fullness of universal being.

"I now take the final step. Slowly we begin to merge . . . and I feel the Light and the Love and the Life. The divine infusion is taking place. I am being Christed. I am filled with the Presence.

"It has happened. The sense of separation is no more. The duality of I and You is now only I, the One. I AM that ONE.

"I rest now in the One I AM."[6]

The Bible tells us that Jesus is the Light. He is the Life. We are not to merge with Him, but to accept Him as the only begotten Son of God. We will never be totally one with Jesus and we will never be completely like Him. We are not begotten. We are made.

Remember that this is a guided meditation intended to invoke the Angel of Death and Rebirth. This angel is considered the key to a person's evolution from one spiritual level to another!

In reality, the person is opening himself up to true spiritual death—possession by an entity other than God Almighty.

Price goes on to tell how these angels work, what happens when a person projects their own ego into the process (rather than rely on the angel), and what can block the "energy flow."

Each angel is linked, of course, to a archetype (such as Tao, Krishna, Master of Heaven, Spirit for the "Angel of Unconditional Love and Freedom," a planetary energy (which includes planets, the sun, and zodiac constellations), and a Tarot symbol . . . as well as to a part of the physical body for purposes of healing. (The Angel of Success is useful especially to those who have problems with their skin, hair, skeletal structure, or who have poor skin tone, excessive wrinkles, unnatural hair loss, and easily breakable bones!)

One almost hates to ask, *What next?*

Angels Conjured to Help Us Create

One of the more prolific writers about angels from the New Age perspective is Terry Lynn Taylor. She has written *Messengers of Light: The Angels' Guide to Spiritual Growth, Guardians of Hope: The Angels' Guide to Personal Growth, Answers From the Angels: A Book of Angel Letters,* and most recently, *Creating with Angels: An Angel-Guided Journey into Creativity.*

She advocates that "when we fill our everyday lives with spiritual essence and ask the angels to join us, we create angel consciousness . . . Angel consciousness helps us keep heavenly qualities alive right here on earth."[7]

As the first part of this process, we are to seek personal freedom. This includes a willingness to drop rigid beliefs, to be flexible, to be a good friend to yourself, and to respond more to gut-level feelings and intuition.

The problem with most people's intuition, of course, is that it is not at all God-centered!

Taylor advocates that each person make a list of his or her current truths. On an equal plane, Taylor lists these as three of her truths: "God is love," "Life is strange and wonder-full," and "Our imagination is a place of truth and beauty." She quotes Fritz Perls:
> "I do my thing, and you do your thing.
> I am not in this world to live up to your expectations,
> And you are not in this world to live up to mine.
> You are you, and I am I,
> And if by chance, we find each other, it's beautiful.
> If not, it can't be helped."

The Scriptures warn against every person doing what is right in his own eyes. (See Deuteronomy 12:8.) Making one's own definition of truth can be dangerous business. Living totally unto oneself without responsibility for other people is the line of argument that Cain used as a justification for killing his brother Abel. (See Genesis 4:1–16.)

Next, Taylor advocates that when you sense something is wrong or amiss in life, that you ask your angels to help you flood light out through your solar plexus for protection, or to visualize the angels helping you put on a "light suit" of armor.[8]

A person then moves on to create the unexpected, privacy, enjoyment, celebration, dance, originality, vision, possibilities, education, relationships, and so forth. Included on the list of things to create is religion. Says Taylor, "Creating your own religion is a good way to free your spirit and 'know God on your own terms.'"[9]

Taylor presents a variety of techniques for creating various "realities," from making shrines to renting movies, from meditating to designing courses in angel studies. She invites people to "visualize

a door to the angelic realm, and as you fall asleep imagine it opening and allowing passage for you and the angels to play" as a means
of creating spiritual sleep.[10]

As a means of inviting Spirit into us (note that she doesn't say
Holy Spirit) she suggests that a person make something with a
mistake in it so that the Spirit can enter at that point. The mistake
might be a coffee stain, a misspelled word, a typographical error,
or a drop of paint where it doesn't belong.

Of course, to Taylor, each person is responsible for creating
his or her own play, harmony, happiness, wildness, fun, love,
kindness, generosity, and so forth.

But also on Taylor's list of things for a person to create are
three that I believe deserve special attention:

(1) *Self-Love.* Taylor states that each person is "a vessel of actual God light" and that we sometimes "forget we are made of
God." When we once again recognize that we are a "vase of God,"
then we supposedly regain love of ourselves.[11] Of course, if we all
did this, Taylor tells us that we wouldn't recognize our planet because all unkind, selfish, greedy, and negative acts would disappear. She suggests that we each ask our guardian angel to remind
us to love ourselves, and that we talk and walk in the park with
our guardian angel and think of nothing but ways to express love
to our own selves.

(2) *A Meaningful Relationship with Your Own Guardian Angel.* Taylor quotes a character from "Mister God, This is Anna,"
who says, "Most of an angel is in the inside and most of a person
is on the outside." Rather than be external to us, Taylor and many
other New Age writers see angels as operating inside the human
spirit. Angels are considered to be the muses that cause us to produce art and music. They are source of our whims and fantasies.
They are what give us a sense of humor or cause us to giggle. In
New Age thinking, we each are possessed, or are capable of being
possessed, by angels.

(3) *Faith.* Taylor cites a Buddhist belief that humans on the
earth are here to work out the issues of greed, doubt, hatred,
sloth, and agitation. She says, "Expressing our creativity will help
with all five issues. Having faith in angels can be your guiding

light. Angels give sight to faith. Instead of blind faith, you receive clear knowing that the highest good is always available to you."[12]

Sorry . . . but true self-love cannot be separate and distinct from a love of God and a love of others. They are linked by Jesus in the form of a command in Matthew 22:37-39.

Angels are external created beings. The only created spiritual beings characterized in the Bible as actually *possessing* a human body are demons.

Faith does not come from angels or involve angels in any way. Each person is given a measure of faith. That faith grows and becomes increasingly "useful" when we hear the Word of God preached in its fulness. (See Romans 10:17 and 12:3.)

Guided Meditations

Taylor provides very specific "guided meditations" in her book *Creating with the Angels*. She calls them journeys.

A person begins a journey by accepting love and requesting divine help.

Then the person takes relaxing deep breaths, and repeats a mantra or prayer.

She advises a person to define their "sacred space" with candle light, music, flowers, special stones, or to burn incense or hold a special crystal—all of which she suggests that a person do "lightly, not seriously."

And then, a person should ask his angel guide to come and guide him on a journey, which seems to embody certain hypnotic suggestions.

The angels do this by tapping into positive energy systems in the universe, and in the process, they supposedly align the person's soul with the personality.

The three journeys Taylor describes are intended to take a person to a place from which he or she will return with self-love and acceptance; knowledge of the person's angelic reflection; or blessings and privileges.

The second of these journeys presents the core of Taylor's belief about angels:

"In heaven, all light beings guard the sacred qualities of love, joy, happiness, mirth, peace, and divine humor. These qualities are kept alive by the exchange going on between humans and angels. Humans need help keeping sacred qualities alive on the earth, and this is why we have a guardian angel. Our guardian angel protects our spirituality by reminding us of who we really are. Our guardian is our angelic reflection . . . . When you declare yourself an angel-in-training, you will find that you naturally vibrate to a higher frequency, that you will be able to tune into the realm of heaven in your meditations and spiritual practices.

"Your guardian angel has known you since the beginning of your soul's first imprint. You will now merge in complete alignment with your guardian angel. You feel comfortable and at peace. With each breath, your heart opens, and love flows in from the divine source of all life. Warm, glowing peace surrounds you and washes through your mind, cleansing the window of your soul . . . you begin to feel your entire body tuning to light."[13]

Angels Help with Writing

There are times when I might wish for an angel to appear and do my research and writing for me. But that is only a whimsical wish. I am always keenly aware that my writing is hard work—although some of the ideas might be ones that I would consider to be "inspired," I trust that the inspiration comes solely from the Holy Spirit.

New Age writers, however, often see angels directly involved in their writing. In fact, some of the power that New Agers expect to be able to tap into is an ability to write. For some, this is considered to be "automatic writing," in which the writer need only hold the pen and let the spirits take over all processes related to content.

Rosemary Ellen Guiley says:

"When I began work on Angels of Mercy, the angels came out in force. It seemed I had a small army looking over my shoulder to weigh in with their various influences. When I set off to interview someone, my angelic band came with me and was joined by another band of angels attached to the person I was meeting. Indeed, David Cousins, a clairvoyant and healer whom I met at his home in Cardiff, Wales, commented that the room was packed with angels who wished to participate in our conversation."[14]

Guiley also claims that she has *felt the guiding presence of a "speaking angel." I have never seen him—though others have—but I sense his presence. He is a facilitator who helps me organize and deliver talks.*[15]

The Power of the Word

The power over the written and spoken word is something New Age writers not only feel they experience, but something they *desire*.

Biblical prophets, by contrast, did not *seek* to write or speak God's words. They did not produce the Scriptures through self-initiated techniques or as the result of meditation. The Bible tells us *prophecy never came by the will of man, but holy men of God spoke as they were moved by the Holy Spirit* (2 Peter 1:21).

There is a great deal of difference between receiving visions and dreams from God—knowing and openly acknowledging that these visions and dreams have come from an external entity—and in developing or projecting dreams that come from within one's self.

Jeremiah repeatedly said, "The word of the Lord came to me." Ezekiel says that a word "came to him" from God, and in God's timing. In fact, he says this nearly fifty times in the book that bears his name! Neither of these great prophets ever felt that an *angel* was speaking through his mouth!

Five New-Age Practices Used in Conjuring Angels

The goal of New Age practices, however, is to evoke an "altered state" in which a person might experience spiritual awakening. Peak emotional experiences such as excitement, tension, peace, quietude, and a deep sense of relaxation are all promoted within the New Age as "thinking skills" that flow out of this altered state. In point of fact, they are feelings or intuitions.

The five techniques most commonly used for achieving this altered state of consciousness are:

- meditation
- vocalization of mantras
- visualization
- naming
- and the manipulation of flowing energy

We'll take a look at each of these since all are advocated by the writers who seek to help people interact with angels. But first, we need to note that all of these practices are related to Eastern religions—specifically Hinduism, Jainism, and Buddhism. These religions have a much different concept of the universe than Christianity or Judaism (or even Islam).

Judaism and Christianity hold to a position that the universe is "tripartite"—heaven, earth, and hell, and that each part is populated accordingly with angels, humans, and demons. The Eastern religions do not believe in a tripartite universe—they recognize only the earth, with all pertaining to heaven and hell residing completely within an individual person.

In Judaism and Christianity, the means of communication between God and man is considered to be prayer.

In the Eastern religions, communication is totally with the self. Others might help the person learn how to communicate better with Self, sometimes called Higher Self. In the Americanized version of the Eastern religions, such "persons" are angels. In the East, the function of revelation is given to other beings, generally reincarnations of supposedly holy people or incarnations of various deities.

The foremost Eastern method of self-realization, or self-communication, is considered to be meditation.

Meditation Is the Key Technique

Meditation to the Eastern religions is not simply a means of "contemplating" something.

It is a systematic means of lowering the body's energy flow—metabolism, heart rate, breathing, and brain waves—to enter into an "altered" state of consciousness. In this altered state, spirit is regarded as being above the natural drives. Spirit reigns supreme in this state, according to Eastern religions. It is a highly desirable state. Most Eastern-religion devotees wish they could live there most of their lives.

You surely noted in reading the New Age methods for conjuring angels that meditation played a key role in getting people into a state where they might "receive" the help of angels.

What's Wrong with Meditation?

There's nothing wrong with meditation . . . as long as it is done the *Bible* way.

The Scriptures include the word meditation. It is regarded as a valued spiritual practice. What a great many people today don't realize, including many Bible-believing Christians, is that the concept of meditation in the Bible means something very different than the way meditation is practiced in yoga or in other Hindu-Buddhist spin-off religions.

Meditation in Hebrew literally means "to mutter." The concept of meditation was the repetition of God's laws—to mutter them to oneself over and over and over—until they became part of the person's very thought processes. Meditation was a means of memorizing God's Word—largely in a time when God's Word was passed down primarily through oral means. But it was also something more. Meditation of this type meant that throughout a person's day, his or her focus was continually on God's opinion and on God's plan for mankind. Nothing was done in life that wasn't in some way put up against the mirror of the truth of God's Word.

It's very difficult to engage in an ungodly practice while muttering God's true and righteous Word to yourself.

The Hebrew people were told to meditate for two main reasons: so that God's law could shine a light on their path—in other words, so they could live a life that was not only pleasing to God but also a life that made sense and was fulfilling to the person. And, so they could pass on God's law to their children. In Deuteronomy 6 we find the admonition to talk about God's Word continually with our children—from sunrise to sunset, and in all situations throughout a day.

In no way does the Bible concept of meditation include relaxation techniques, a focus on images or senses, visualization, the speaking of mantras, or the "calling up" of angels, spirit guides, or other spiritual experiences.

The purpose of meditation in the Bible is not so that a person might have a spiritual experience. It is so that a person might continually be called to remembrance of God's commandments. The purpose of meditation is to help a person obey God.

The word *meditation* has been completely twisted and distorted by false religions and the New Age movement. It has come to be considered a means of having a relationship with the divine. That relationship is rooted in experience, not obedience. It is based upon human power to "feel" first and think later, whereas the Bible calls us to hear and do. Feelings are peripheral in God's Word. They are a byproduct of our obedience and our relationship with God, not what leads us *to* God.

Meditation from a Hebrew understanding of God's Word is a highly desirable thing.

Meditation from a Hindu understanding is not.

The late Dr. Walter Martin, Bible scholar and founder of Christian Research Institute, had this to say about yoga and transcendental meditation:

> "Transcendental Meditation (attained through Yoga), is pantheistic in nature and one's goal is to lose one's personality in the oneness of God. This takes away from the unique and separate personality of God. Being in the living presence of God. The reality of Life. It is eternal truth. It is absolute in its eternal freedom.

> "In all its forms, Hinduism (including the practice of Yoga) denies the biblical Trinity, the Deity of Christ, the doctrines of atonement, sin, and salvation by grace through the sacrifice of Jesus Christ. It replaces resurrection with reincarnation and both grace and faith with human works. Peace *with* God is not achieved by looking inside oneself, but by looking up to Him of whom Moses and the prophets did write 'Jesus of Nazareth, the Son and Christ of God.'"[16]

Just to Relax?

There are those who say that they only engage in yoga-style meditation (stretching, breathing, focusing, using mantras, and so forth) in order to "relax."

The question must arise, "why resort to meditation for relaxation?" There are numerous other ways to relax one's body. True relaxation comes after we have worked hard at the tasks we see before us, are fully trusting God's purposes to be done in our lives, and are living in right relationship with God and our fellow man. The person who has put in a full day of physical labor (or perhaps mental labor with a heavy dose of physical exercise), is eating the right foods, places his full confidence in God, and is keeping God's commandments is, generally speaking, a person who has no difficult sleeping, or playing.

Rather than resort to meditation for relaxation, a person will find that he probably gains much more benefit from curling up in an easy chair with God's Word, and then praying for God's help in living out what God's Word tells him to do.

The person who actively seeks to create an Alpha state of brain waves, is a person who is ultimately seeking a man-made man-empowering experience. Whether or not that is the intended goal of a person, that is the *result* of these New Age meditation techniques. If you are wanting a God-empowering experience, go with God-empowering and God-ordained spiritual practices, such as prayer, the reading and contemplation of God's Word, the memorization and recitation of Scripture, and worship with other Bible-believing Christians.

The person who engages in Eastern meditation may be relaxed and "open," but the question arises, "open to what?" Very often, the person has opened himself up to evil spirits.

One person has been reported as saying:

"Recently I was meditating and experienced a sudden in redible expansion, or explosion of colors, particles of indigo and gold, into a space so vast I do not have the words to truly describe what this looked like or how I felt . . . except that I was being shown by angels that there is so much wisdom and infinite love within myself! A few weeks after that I started to notice, behind my left shoulder, a brilliant white light, a loving presence. I can see it almost any time, and sometimes I have mental dialogues going on, and I feel as though I am being helped and guided through my problems and uncertainties."[17]

This person went on to say how an image named Jesus had helped her make her daughter's bed in a miraculous way!

Eastern religion opens up the senses and the spirit of man—and leaves the spirit and senses wide open to an evil assault.

Most people wouldn't dream of disrobing and walking through their city streets naked as a jaybird.

And yet thousands of people a day disrobe "spiritually" and lay down in the presence of evil and invite evil spirits to speak to their naked souls.

In contrast to Eastern meditation, Christian meditation is an intensely intellectual activity. It ponders deeply God's Word, studies it, commits it to memory, and recalls it continually. Biblical meditation is a matter of filling up the mind with God's Word. It is *not* an emptying of the mind to make room for an inner spiritual experience.

In sum, Christian meditation and Eastern meditation are very nearly opposites.

The Use of a Mantra

A mantra is a word that is repeated as a chant while one is practicing yoga or some other technique in order to relax the body and enter into an altered state of consciousness.

The idea of a mantra originated in the Hindu religion. The Mother Goddess Kali is said to have used her mantra word *om* to create the world. This same word is the mantra *aum* used by the Church Universal and Triumphant (a New Age group).

A mantra is intended to invoke a spirit guide to come and make its presence known. It supposedly "magnetizes" the "presence." It is the form of "prayer" considered appropriate to Eastern meditation.

In sharp contrast, *The Lord's Prayer* given by Jesus in the Bible requires active participation, not a meditative and silent emptying of thought from the mind.

One of the ways that chants and incantations work is that they overload the mind with "noncoherent information." The mind goes "numb," as it were, as a protective mechanism to cope with the confusion. Basic mental faculties no longer work properly. The person has literally "scrambled their minds." The impulse is for the mind to attempt to come out of this state with strong images and impulses that are not true ideas, but rather, visual images, intuitions, and feelings.

The New Agers, of course, see many of these as symbols to which they then attach meaning. Thus, they receive "guidance" from their meditation. The relaxed state and resulting sensory scrambling is perceived as the Higher Self responding to the lower self. In other words, prayer to the self is answered.

The New Age philosophy includes a belief that angels listen to all prayers of mankind and that angels know the thoughts of men and women. The Bible approach is that God hears all prayers and knows all thoughts.

The New Age also holds to the opinion that if a person prays for the guidance of angels, and is sincere and receptive to receiving it, the angels will give him guidance. The Bible approach is that *God* hears and answers prayer.

Techniques of Visualization

As a part of meditation and in accompaniment to mantras, various techniques related to visualization are advocated by New Age Writers as a means of contacting and tapping into the supposed aid offered by angels.

One of these visualization techniques is the use of "third-eye attuning," which uses a mandala—a circular design from Eastern religions. The idea here is that a person is to stare at the mandala until he has it firmly visualized as being imprinted on his forehead just beneath the skin. This symbol is supposedly helpful, then, in aligning the person with his angel.

Actually, a mandala is any form of "magic circle." Carl Jung used mandalas to express the human psyche. They are used in various cultures. Terry Lynn Taylor suggests that a person design his own mandala and put himself at its center.

Right to Imagine?

Mental visualization techniques *for the purpose of spiritual experience* are contrary to God's Word. The Bible tells us plainly that we should be *casting down imaginations and every high thing that exalteth itself against the knowledge of God* (2 Corinthians 10:5 KJV).

Lust, envy, greed, and virtually all evil practices begin first in the imagination.

The Bible presents a *doing* concept of worship and obedience. We are not only to hear the Word of God, but to *do it*. We are to be obedient to God's commandments, and in the doing of God's commandments, we gain a full experiential knowledge about what God perceives as being right and wrong. We obey as an act of our will, as an exercise of free will to choose God's way over our own way.

We are also to accept God's plan of forgiveness of man—to believe that the Lord Jesus Christ is our atoning sacrifice and to receive into our own lives, by faith, what He did for us on the Cross. In so doing, we have a *relationship* with God. That relationship is not that we become God, or that we are united with God, but rather, that God imparts His Holy Spirit to us, to enable us to live out our obedience to His commandments with a want-to-desire rather than a have-to mind set.

Nothing is required of us other than that we love God and walk in His ways, to the glory of His name.

Neither our relationship with God, nor our obedience to His commandments, requires visualization or imagination. It is in the imagination that man generally devises ways to deny relationship, or to bypass God's commandments. Our visualization ability is often directed toward seeing what it is that we want, and what we want to do and be.

Christian Visualization?

Visualization is very popular in some Christian groups today, where it allegedly is used to help a person lose weight, quit smoking, or achieve a deeper spirituality or closer walk with Christ. Some are encouraged to "visualize" their healing, or their ownership of a new car, as a means of exercising their faith.

The New Age contention is that a person can use his or her imagination to create what they want in life, be it wealth, power, material goods, health, or spiritual guidance.

The primary danger of visualization comes when a person couples an altered state of consciousness with visualization. Be wary of anyone who attempts to get you to relax first, and then to visualize. And be especially wary if that person asks you to visualize anything that is not clearly promised to *all* people in God's Word. For example, if you are being asked to visualize a brand new Cadillac, ask yourself, "Does God's Word promise a brand new Cadillac to all followers of Jesus Christ?" No. Visualizing such a thing and calling it a "promise of God," or a "step of faith," is heresy. God's promises apply to *all* people in all cultures and all generations. They are always given to further His Kingdom, not to fulfill the wishes of men and women.

Furthermore, the Bible never asks a person to put their minds on hold prior to engaging in a spiritual experience. A. W. Tozer taught that people who imagine God wind up with an imaginary god. He warned, "true faith is not the intellectual ability to visualize unseen things to the satisfaction of our minds, it is rather the moral power to trust Christ." He also wrote, "The wise Christian will not let his assurance depend upon his powers of imagination."[18]

Remote Viewing

One of the aspects of "seeing" that is popular in the New Age is the idea of "remote viewing." People supposedly are capable of using telepathic power to describe objects or activities that are miles away.

In out-of-body experiences, people claim to see various objects—or to see things at an unusual angle which are not readily visible to the naked eye . . . everything from shoes on window ledges to the performance of various medical procedures. This type of viewing is nearly always linked closely to an Alpha state of brain waves.

The Bible does not ask us to enter an altered state, or to "see things," other than in the context of believing that God's will might be done. The "eyes of faith" spoken about in the Bible as well as numerous references to spiritual eyes—are all associated with believing that God is in control of the universe and that His will is unfolding according to His plan.

Naming One's Own Angel

Naming one's guardian angel is an important part of angel ritual in the New Age. Guiley contends, "We must discover names for our guardian angels if we wish them to manifest in their fullest magnitude. Name is an important ritual: it defines, and it invests life, power, and potential. Without names, we cannot call out to the higher planes; we cannot invoke or evoke the beings, forces, and energies into our own dimension."[19]

A similar belief has been penned by William Gray, author of *Inner Traditions of Magic*:

"The purpose behind the principle of naming anyone or anything at all, is to direct and hold the energy of Consciousness in some particular way at some special point or portion of Existence. It is essentially an act of cocreation, and therefore Magical. Humanity gives names to whatever exists, while Divinity gives Existence to whatever is Named. When a human being 'utters a name,' the object of that name has its primary existence only in their own mind or 'imagination.' When Divinity Utters a Name, Existence manifests wherever it is intended, even in material form, because everything including ourselves is 'in the imagination of God.' And that is far beyond the imagination of Man."[20]

Thus, discovering the name of one's guardian angel is a vital initiation, of sorts, into being able to operate with angelic power. A person must learn his or her guardian angel's name in order to "perform" in the name of that angel. Some would say to create with angel power. Others claim to write or speak under the power of an angel. Some claim to heal in the name of an angel.

Alma Daniel says, "I've made regular contact with LNO (the name of her angel). I do that just by closing my eyes and calling to her, and asking her a question. She will come in and I will write down the answer. Basically, it's *channeling*."[21]

The question naturally arises, "In which name are these people operating?"

They most certainly are not operating in the Name of Jesus Christ of Nazareth.

There is power in naming, but the ultimate power over all things resides in the Name which is above every name, and to which every other name must one day bow—the Name of Jesus. (See Isaiah 45:23 and Romans 14:11.)

Controlling the Energy Flow

The concept of God being associated with energy is a very big part of the Hindu religion. In *A Book of Angels*, Sophy Burnham records her conversation with a great Hindu teacher about angels. She writes: "He spoke instead of the Almighty God. . . . God cannot be seen without a form, God in boundless compassion takes on a body to appear to the worshiping devotee. This realization of God, said this teacher, comes in the form of energies, or *shaktis*. Often the shakti appears as a goddess."[22] They do not function as messengers, but rather, it seems, as "impulses." They very often in Hindu literature are associated with music, dance, and sexual behavior. They are creatures of pleasure.

The Use of Kundalini

Many of those who attempt to conjure angels use the Kundalini, a Hindu concept and technique. The word Kundalini means "coiled up" like a sleeping snake. It refers to a pool of energy that supposedly resides at the base of the spinal column, and which can be channeled upward to activate other energy sites along the spinal cord and in the brain called "chakras." The energy released and channeled is supposed to be both divine and a means of divination. It is said by New Age devotees to be the source of genius, psychic abilities, and ultimately, it is regarded as the path that leads to "enlightenment" and to tapping into the "cosmic consciousness."

Anatomically, such a flow of energy does not exist, and yet those who attempt to manipulate this source of power regularly claim it as a physical reality.

The energy is ultimately seen as being pulled upward from the earth, with the brain being the final repository. Rather than have the brain initiate ideas, it "receives" them from the tailbone. Something of a reverse mechanism, I suppose.

This may sound like an esoteric out-of-the-mainstream philosophy and practice to you, but those in the New Age are not only devoted to kundalini practices, but engage frequently in practices to tap into chakral energy sites. For many, it is a daily practice.

One of the most interesting aspects of kundalini practice is that those who experience what are called "full kundalini awakenings," often report experiences and images that are very much like those who report near-death experiences. (There are those who now believe that so-called near-death experiences are actually extremely relaxed biological states which have nothing to do with the actual death process.)

Madam Helena Blavatsky, who is the founder of the Theosophy religion, openly has stated that "Satan, the Serpent of Genesis

is the real creator and benefactor, the Father of Spiritual mankind
. . . the ever loving messenger." She regards Jehovah as the cruel
adversary of man.[23]

Through the centuries, of course, the serpent figure has always been associated with Satan. In Hinduism, Krishna bears the
title "Visuki, Lord of the snakes" and "Ananta, the holy serpent."
Buddha supposedly was saved from a terrible flood by sitting on
a snake. The gods Vishnu, Brahma, and Shiva—the trinity of Hinduism—are associated with serpents.

Serpentine power linked to the kundalini? It's not surprising.

Don't Fall for It!

If someone suggests to you that you, as a Christian, begin to
use relaxation techniques, Eastern-forms of meditation (such as
yoga), mantras, mandalas, visualization techniques, guided imagery, sexual activity, or rhythmic dance as a means of entering
into a more spiritual state . . . don't fall for it.

You may enter into a spiritual state, alright, but not necessarily
a *holy* spiritual state.

Trust God to give you the spiritual experiences He desires for
you to have. Stick to methods and practices related to His Holy
Word. You don't need to relax to feel God. In fact, there's no place
in God's Word where you are admonished to "feel" God in order
to know God!

As well intentioned or sincere as a person might be in bringing these practices into the Body of Christ, they are sincerely
wrong.

Run from evil. Don't consort with it. And by all means, don't
expose yourself to it willingly!

10

How Angels Fit
Into the New Age Agenda

THE Reverend Mark Buntane, well-known missionary to India, spoke at the church my father pastored some twenty-five years ago. I have very vivid memories of his presentation. He spoke about a coming of Hinduism to America, and how Hindu missionaries were being sent out from India to spread their belief in America. The primary technique they intended to use to gain popularity in America was yoga.

Mark went through various yoga positions in his presentation and told how each represented a prayer in Hinduism, an invocation to various gods to instill the person with their power. Mark was very bold in warning the people present that yoga was tantamount to an invitation for demons to indwell a person's thinking, especially when it was coupled with transcendental meditation techniques intended to "open up" the person to an inflow of energy.

Very few people that night took Mark Buntane seriously, at least as far as I could tell. There we were, in southern California, in one of the most successful churches in the area. The Jesus Movement was taking off all around us. Our church was sponsoring more than forty missionaries around the world, and had more than forty outreaches into our community. The prevailing opinion seemed to be that as Christians, we were untouchable by such a philosophy. Yoga was perceived to be something that only the sprout-eating, psychedelically bell-bottomed hippie leftovers were likely to pursue.

How wrong we were.

Today, Hinduism has been up-scaled, slicked down, and popularized by the media to be a very sophisticated religion replete with Hollywood stars and love-and-peace gentility. Had this Hinduism been presented to us in the guise of an old beat-up VW bus with peace signs scrawled on it, we would have been wary of it. Instead, we in America have been fed the convertible-black-BMW version of Hinduism.

We as a culture have bought into it hook, line, and sinker.

The messages are blatant in the cartoons our children watch and in many of the movies that have become big draws. The philosophy has filtered into all of the talk shows and many of the commercials we see on television. The catch phrases of the Hinduism-Buddhism philosophy have worked their way into the mainstream of our language.

Defining the New Age Movement

The New Age philosophy is a blend of Eastern religions (something of a western variant of Hinduism and Buddhism), occultism, and evolution theory. It claims that all religions are equally valid and all are merely different paths back to God. It's key tenet is that all human beings are divine—all are gods. We get in touch with our "god-ness" through altered states of consciousness. When we do, New Agers contend, we get in touch with our true Inner Self—who is always right and should always be obeyed—and we subsequently realize that we are all One with the rest of humanity, the planet, the solar system, and the entire universe.

The New Age movement is not limited to one particular cult or group. It seems to be alluring to those who are spiritually minded but unchurched, and to those who have had negative church experiences in the past (especially experiences heavily laden with superstition, nonbiblical practices, abuse, or fear).

Throughout the seventies and eighties, reincarnation and the "law of karma" (essentially the law of cause and effect according to an undefined cosmic balance sheet) were central to New Age philosophy. In the new outcropping of New Age books, however, reincarnation is not emphasized. In its place is a belief in "spiritual progression" during one's lifetime and beyond.

This new twist in the movement has opened the door for many Christians to be sucked in. Whereas Christians could once readily identify and reject New Age teaching because of the emphasis on reincarnation, the new emphasis on angels and the afterlife has a much closer alignment with what many Christians *think* they have grown up believing.

What they don't understand is that the New Age understanding of the afterlife and angels is far different than the one they learned in Sunday school.

Rooted in the Satanic Occult

The term "occultic" can be used to describe New Age practices and beliefs. Many associate the word occult only with Satan worship. The broader definition of the word includes all who attempt to unlock secrets; activities, events, and techniques that go beyond the five senses; and anything that deals with the supernatural, including the presence of angelic or demonic forces.

Occultic paraphernalia, which includes everything from crystals to zodiac medallions, is sold annually to millions of customers. The mailing list for occult materials in 1980 stood at nearly four million names and addresses in the United States. The explosion of interest, of course, has rapidly increased since then.

One estimate today is that as many as one quarter of all Americans are involved in at least some aspect of occultism on a regular basis. These practices include such things as:

- *divination* (including ESP, astrology, cartomancy or use of Tarot cards, palm reading, crystal ball gazing, numerology, "postviewing" events, or reading meaning into such things as tea leaves, smoke curls, bones, animal entrails, and so forth). The purpose is to find meaning or future direction.
- *magick* (which is different from stage magic). Magick makes regular use of invocations to demons, charms, symbolic rituals, fetishes, and drugs. The purpose is to call upon hidden powers for personal assistance.
- *spiritism* (primarily through mediums). The purpose is to gain contact with the dead. In the past, the spirits which were

summoned were supposedly from the unseen world called
Summerland. In the New Age, these spirits need not be "dead,"
but may be spirits inhabiting the Ethereal or Astral Plane.

- *mysticism* (which attempts to create an altered state of
consciousness through drugs, hyperventilation, yoga,
hypnosis, rhythmic dancing or music, biofeedback, and so
forth). The purpose is to have a supernatural experience.

Divination, mysticism, spiritism, and magick techniques and
purposes are all a part of "angel conjuring" as it is advocated by
today's New Age writers.

The Bible's Warning.

The Bible speaks very sharply against various occult practices.
I suggest that you look up the verses provided with each occultic
practice below and see what the Bible has to say for yourself.

Astrology

*Take heed, lest you lift your eyes to heaven, and when you
see the sun, the moon, and the stars, all the host of heaven, you feel
driven to worship them and serve them* (Deuteronomy 4:19).

Also: Genesis 1:16–17; Deuteronomy 17:2-5; 1 Kings 17:16,18;
2 Kings 23:5; Psalm 148:3; Isaiah 47:12–15; Jeremiah 31:35.

Witchcraft

*Give no regard to mediums and familiar spirits; do not seek
after them, to be defiled by them: I am the Lord, your God.* (Leviticus 19:31)

Also: Leviticus 20:6; Deuteronomy 18:10-12; 1 Samuel 15:23;
2 Kings 9:22, 17:17, 21:6; 2 Chronicles 33:6

Divination

Nor shall you practice divination or soothsaying. (Leviticus
19:26)

Also: Leviticus 20:6, 27; Deuteronomy 18:9-13, 20; 2 Chronicles 33:6; Isaiah 8:19-20; Jeremiah 14:13-16; Ezekiel 13:6-9, 23;
Acts 8:9-13, 13:6, 16:16; Galatians 1:8-9; Ephesians 6:10-18[1]

Only for Weirdos?

You may be tempted to say, "Only weirdos buy into all that."
If so, then two-thirds of our nation are weirdos.

A 1989 poll reported in *Parents* magazine, stated that nearly two-thirds of those polled believed in at least one type of "paranormal" phenomena:

- 34 percent believed some people can consistently predict the future
- 33 percent believed there are spirits or ghosts who make themselves known to people
- 25 percent believed certain people have mental or psychic powers to make objects move
- 22 percent believed some numbers are either lucky or unlucky
- 14 percent believed a person's spirit or soul could be reincarnated
- 14 percent believed in lucky charms or objects capable of bringing about good fortune
- 11 percent believe astrology can accurately predict the future
- 8 percent believed quartz and other crystals can increase a person's mental and physical abilities.[2]

A national opinion survey conducted in the mid 1980s by the University of Chicago concluded that almost *half* of American adults believe they have had contact with someone who died.[3]

As for those who have made statements regarding reincarnation (either their past lives or their expected future lives), you'll find the list of names includes such famous Americans as Henry Ford, Benjamin Franklin, General George Patton, and Walt Whitman. George Washington reported seeing an angel. Abraham Lincoln attended a number of seances after the death of his son, Willie. These are hardly people out of the mainstream of American life!

The great likelihood is that the high school graduate of fifteen years ago could not name one witch or satanist in his graduating class. I know that in my high school graduation class of one thousand seniors—graduates from a public high school in Southern California, which was far from being a back roads or Christian-school environment—we did not have one student who openly proclaimed himself or herself to be a witch or satanist. Today, virtually every high school student knows at least one person in their own school—small, rural, middle American schools—who claim to worship Satan or who deal in occultic practices.

The change in our culture in the last fifteen years has been dramatic!

New Age practices—and especially the current fever of interest in angels and the afterlife—are clearly within the "mainstream" of America today. The New Age is no longer on the fringe. Furthermore, it is growing in both acceptability and popularity among people who would be shocked to think they are dabbling in Hinduism or Buddhism.

The Road to the New Age

Those who claim to have frequent conversations and contact with their "personal angels" nearly always come to this point after years of personally exploring the metaphysical realm—encounters with spirit guides, Indian medicine men, Tibetan monks, tuning themselves into the energies of the Great Mother, studying ancient Egyptian gods, focusing on the energy meridians of the earth, and so forth. They claim angels speak to them with specific directions, use their own vocal chords to speak, or communicate telepathically by giving them "integrative insights" and "knowings."

Others claim to have become connected to their angels after death or near-death experiences.

Typical of these angel-conversant New Agers is Susan Ragsdale who is quoted in Taylor's book, *Creating with the Angels:*

"I discovered Siddha Yoga and devoted myself to a spiritual master, Gurumayi Chidvilasananda. I continue to meditate, read scriptures, and chant praises to the Lord in Sanskrit.Following this path has opened my heart to love, and I have been blessed with immense gratitude. Through God's grace,I have attained humility, and I simply want to serve and be an angel."[4]

The story of Roseann Cervelli blends Christianity with the New Age in a particularly insidious way. This woman is identified in *Angels of Mercy* as one who has been channeling angels for a number of years. She was raised a Catholic and then in her twenties, went through a period of questioning the church and became increasingly unsatisfied with it. By her own admission, she went through an agnostic searching and studied Edgar Cayce's material for a number of years. Then she began studying about healing and consciousness, and eventually what she called "Christ consciousness."

She had a priest lay hands on her and pray for here about 1980 and she felt an "opening" to mystical experiences. After that, she would enter into meditative states where she would feel one with the entire world. She is reported as saying, "I'd see a face, like the face of my daughter, and then her face became somebody else's face, which became somebody else's face, and so on, and before I knew it, I was enveloped in this oneness. These were my first experiences with the spiritual energies—very loving and embracing. I didn't understand at all what was happening. I thought I was going crazy. But I trusted the experience, because it *was* happening to me."

The experiences lasted for about a year, and by then, she had learned to enter meditative states on her own. At the end of 1981, she met a woman who channeled an entity named Matthew. He spoke to her about healing and soon she was into prompted writing. She said, "As I wrote, it transformed me. It was like there was a spirit in my head, and it would go into my heart and I would emotionally *feel* what I was writing, and I could feel it changing me as I wrote." When she called to tell her priest about this, he told her she had received a wonderful gift.

Before long another entity named Elliott was channeling messages to her, and then an entity named John. Then the three—Matthew, Elliott and John—informed Roseann that they were going to be replaced by another energy—angels—who would give instruction at a higher vibration. This level of energy lasted two to three years, and then an energy that called itself Angels of Light and Truthful Revelation took over.

How did her life change? Roseann claims that she now has greater self-esteem, is less judgmental, and she no longer feels separated or lonely, but a "part of everything—part of the trees, part of the mountains, part of the people. Along the way, she and her husband divorced, although she claims they don't really know why and that "it was just the way it was supposed to be."

She says, "If we separate ourselves from angels or from a voice of love, we're also separating ourselves from God. And we are not separate from God. We *are* God, sparks of God, so we are sparks of angels, we are sparks of each other. So we are one."[5]

The Personification of Godly Traits

In many ways, those who have bought into the New Age philosophies have "personified" various traits of human nature and turned them into angels. Love is an angel. So is hate. It is in this way that an entire host of angels can be seen to dwell within any one person.

In the past, people would have called these various traits part of human nature. The New Age, however, deifies mankind, and therefore, these traits are a part of mankind's "divine" nature. Because they are considered part of a divine nature, they surely must be given some sort of divine name. The next logical step is to call them angels.

The fact, however, is that love and hate are human emotions and behaviors. They reflect a choice of will regarding good and evil that man makes on a daily basis. An angel doesn't cause a man to choose good. That is man's prerogative and privilege *as a human being.*

Why is the New Age philosophy so opposed to man simply being man?

Because if man is limited to his humanity, he is not God. It is Satan's intention to convince man that men and women *are* God. The Bible records that as his purpose from the first few pages of Genesis.

Furthermore, if man is simply man, then he is flawed. He is capable of sin. If he sins, he is separate from God. Someone or something must bridge that gap. Man needs a Savior. That is the message of the Bible.

The New Age, however, claims that man is not flawed—he simply hasn't progressed yet to his full potential. Man doesn't sin, he only makes mistakes that help him grow. He eventually will arrive, perhaps after his death. Man needs no Savior in the New Age philosophy. He is capable of saving himself and of remedying all that is wrong, both on an individual basis by the individual, and on a world-wide all-of-humanity basis by the human collective.

Consider the conclusion drawn by Morris Margolies in *A Gathering of Angels:*

"The archetype of all Jewish angels, the Archangel Michael, is
guardian and lifesaver through all of the Rabbinic literature.
He rescues Abraham from the fires of Nimrod. He protects
Sarah from being defiled by Abimelech. He saves Lot from a
Sodom in flames. He rescues Jacob from the threatening
clutches of his brother, Esau. He prevents Laban from carrying
out his design to harm Jacob. He snatches Tamar from the
stake. He shields Shadrach, Meshach, and Abednego from
Nebuchadnezzar's searing furnace. He confutes Haman's
accusations against the Jews in the domains of Ahaseurus.
And, at the end of humanity's long trail of tribulations,
Michael will defeat Samael-Satan in mortal combat, thus
relegating the symbol of evil to oblivion."

Many Bible-believing Christians no doubt would agree in generally terms with Margolies to this point. Man can not help himself, and therefore, God sends angels to rescue certain people in
order for them to fulfill their God-ordained purpose on the earth.
But note Margolies' next line:

"Michael is the heavenly model of what man should be, what
man can be."[6]

We Reside in Angels?

There are other New Age teachers who believe that "cosmically speaking," angels don't reside within us, but rather, we reside within them. We don't have control over our lives, because
we exist in their greater whole. The angels are in charge of us and
direct our movements, not from an inner impulse, but because
they are all around us. Rather than prompt us toward our higher
selves, they corral us and move us toward the direction of the
Higher Self.

Still other New Age writers state that all angels come from
"other realms" or "other star systems."

In both variations of thought, the mind and spirit of man are
divinely inspired, compelled, and motivated by the angels.

The point the New Age makes repeatedly is this: God is *not*
separate from man. He is inside us and we are god. In that, God is
not holy. We are. Man's supposed divinity is the basic lie that the
New Age writers propagate.

Inconsistencies in the Movement

A major inconsistency in the New Age philosophy, in my opinion, regards the New Age opinion of "perfection." From the New Age point of view, any evil that might exist does so in order to provide a contrast for a person—with the notion being that the person will choose good and run away from evil. Moving toward good and away from the bad is called "spiritual progression." Some label this as becoming angels.

The New Age contends that everything in the afterlife is good. There is no hell. Everybody ends up "perfect" in the afterlife.

But . . . what of those who don't "embrace the light" and "reject the darkness."

Old Hinduism and Old Buddhism had a concept of reincarnation to deal with that possibility. The folks who hadn't embraced the light simply came back in another form and got another chance to try again.

New-Age variants of Hinduism and Buddhism, however, reject this notion of reincarnation. Instead, they have adopted the idea of "spiritual progression," with the ladder only going one way . . . up.

But still, they leave unanswered the question: "What happens to those who willfully go *down* the ladder, or to those who don't choose to go up the ladder, or to those who don't even know a ladder exists?"

Furthermore, if everything ends up as goodness and light in the afterlife, and ends up that way for everybody, why bother with the struggle to progress spiritually now? The conclusion must be drawn that spiritual progression has the most benefit in the here and now—that it brings some type of earthly reward. What is the reward that is being sought?

Aha. In that we can see several clear underlying motives.

What Does the New Age Offer?

What does a person get out of pursuing the New Age methods of "becoming a god," "becoming an angel," or "becoming fully enlightened?"

Plenty. At least, as promised by New Age writers. The three big benefits are:

- **Peace**—the New Age promises inner bliss, love among all people, and abiding peace. Philippians 4:7 tells us that the peace of God "surpasses all understanding." It is not something that we can arrive at in our own minds. It is a gift of God. And furthermore, it is a gift of God that "guards your hearts and minds through Christ Jesus." Peace does not flow from our minds. It is God's gift to us to protect our minds!
- **Purse**—those who are involved in New Age teaching and various "support services" make billions of dollars a year. The purpose of many of the seminars offered related to angels, spirit guides, and the flow of inner energy are intended to help a person "maximize their potential," which is a New Age way of saying, "be successful." The goal of many of these methods is a desire to unleash genius, artistry, or healing power. The motive of greed is very cleverly masked in a *stated* desire to inspire, bring about the betterment of mankind, to find wholeness, and so forth. Nevertheless, a great deal of money changes hands and the root desire for many is to improve their *tangible* quality of life.

This comes as a surprise to those who envision the New Age as being the religion of the flower children of the 1960s.

The world of the occult is *not* impoverished. Let me give you just two examples.

About ten years ago, I was privileged to take a sixty-day missions trip that included two weeks of ministry in Sri Lanka, the former island of Ceylon. While there, we traveled to the lush interior of the island where the main rubber plantations are located. In the midst of this very rural and agricultural area stood a very large Temple. Inside the structure, we found an area about six feet wide and eighteen feet long. This interior structure was covered inside and out with gold. Since we were not Buddhists we were not allowed to enter this area, but we were able to peak inside from the entry way. Inside the gold room, large jewels had been encrusted into its ceiling. The wealth represented by that structure was incalculable.

It's purpose? The Temple was a shrine to a supposed tooth of Buddha.

Closer to home . . . .

The deaths of a Southern Methodist University business professor and his wife, the daughter of a North Dallas physician, shocked Dallas a few years ago. This couple had been on a search for New Age enlightenment and they ultimately bought into the lie that they were the original Adam and Eve who had since lived 800,000 life times. Their names were changed to Jupiter and Venus, and shortly before their deaths, they had been led by their Dallas spiritual guru in suicide practice sessions (so they might kill each other simultaneously). Before their deaths, they had given more than $110,000 to their spiritual guide. Eight other followers of this guru have all died in suicide or in sudden accidents, and all had made their guru their beneficiary of their wealth.

She had been a woman who supposedly "looked like someone's grandma." She offered a doctrine of forgiveness of sin and a reinforcement of pleasure—that they would find bliss in every sexual encounter and comfort with wealth.[7]

- **Power**—both fame and influence are goals of New Agers, although they individually might say just the opposite. New Age books, including the crop of angel books, nearly always point to famous people in the past who used certain techniques to do the work that made them famous. Some books go so far as to label these famous people as angels, or as the recipients of incredible angel influence.

Nearly all New Agers are very open about expressing a desire for inner power. That's the entire reason for channeling energy, the very motive toward becoming more enlightened.

Collective Power

Another purpose stated in many of the books is that of collective power. Actually, the words power and empower appear frequently in these works.

What are we to do with this power?

One author might advocate that we "heal the planet," while another, that we "raise the vibration of love on planet earth." There is no consensus. The net impression, however, is that we are to make ourselves and our world *better*.

That simply is not possible if sin is never confronted, which it isn't in the New Age philosophy. Rather, sin is dismissed by New

Age teachers as being no longer relevant . . . or as an aspect of goodness . . . or as a concept we have now outgrown in our evolution
as human beings. In other cases, sin is considered a "mistake," and
since we learn from our mistakes, we should embrace our sins and
consider them beneficial for our growth and progression.

All of this stems, of course, from a root New Age belief that
man is a self-contained god. God does not exist apart from man or
external to man. There is no reason to think of God as "Holy"—
which means separate and distinct from sin—because God is perceived to reside within it and to fully embrace the concept of sin.

The New Age, in sum, offers peace, purse, and power to men
and women *on earth*. It claims that heaven *can* be experienced
here, and should be.

The New Age philosophy is not a slight twist and bend away
from the truth. It is a totally controverted world view of the truth.
From the perspective of the Bible, the New Age calls black *white*,
and white *black*.

Opening Up the Self to Channel Power to the Self

To a New Age person . . .

Abraham was having a mid-day trance induced from staring
into the bright noontime heat.

Jacob was having a battle with his own inner guilt.

Hagar was guided by an inner angel to overcome her fear of
Sarah and return to Abraham's provision of safety.

All spiritual experience is contained within.

As described in the previous chapter, prayer in the New Age
is largely a matter of a person opening himself up to power, and
channeling power into himself.

Prayer is largely perceived as talking to oneself, except of
course, that the Self would be capitalized. It is considered a matter
of speaking and believing for one primary purpose: healing. This
healing is thought to be both physical and spiritual. The spiritual
healing, however, is a "healing" that takes a person from one spiritual plane to another.

New Age writers regularly contend that angels heal. Karen
Goldman states in *The Angel Book* that "the angel in you can heal
you in many ways. Angels can help to heal illness, poverty, anger,

despair. There is an abundance of pure healing energy, joy, creativity and unwavering inner strength available for you at all times."[8]

If you think the lines are getting blurry between Christian terminology and New Age terminology . . . they are!

A book that exemplifies this is *Healing Words* by Larry Dossey, M.D. In his book, Dossey uses a variety of names for Almighty God—such as Supreme Being, Absolute, Goddess, God, Allah, Krishna, Brahman, the Tao, the Universal Mind, Alpha and Omega, the One. Some of these, of course, are Christian in their origin. Others decidedly are not.

After an upbringing in a one-room country church in Texas—where he claims that ministerial students regularly spewed forth sermons marked by hellfire, damnation, and eternal punishment—Dossey claims to have discovered the philosophies of the East, particularly Buddhism and Taoism, while in medical school. He now considers himself an "eclectic."

He eventually felt compelled to include prayer in his medical practice. He did not pray with patients or directly for specific outcomes, but rather, his prayer was, "May the best possible outcome prevail."

He writes—

"As part of the ritual I devised, I would shake several rattles and gourds, paraphernalia used worldwide by shamans and healers to 'invoke the powers.' These curious objects had been given to me by patients and friends over the years. When I used them, I felt a connection with healers of all cultures and ages. Although I had never imagined that I—a white-coated, scientifically trained modern doctor—would be behaving like this, my prayer ritual was deeply satisfying."[9]

As a fellow Texan, let me assure you that if Dossey attempted this approach with me, I would not find it at all satisfying! To be fair, however, Dossey claims that he did not foist his prayers on anyone and that he prayed for his patients when they were not present.

A New View of Prayer

Dossey dismisses the old biblically based views of prayer as ones:

"developed when a view of the world was in place that is now antiquated and incomplete. In this century our fundamental ideas about how the universe works have changed. We have redefined our ideas about the nature of space, time, energy, and causation. These bear little resemblance to the views that dominated human thought for millennia in the West, and that shaped our concepts of prayer. In addition, our basic ideas of the structure and function of the human psyche have been radically transformed and continue to evolve. If our world view has changed, perhaps we should also reevaluate our views of the nature of prayer."[10]

He advocates a "modern" model of prayer and cites it as having these characteristics:

- prayer can affect past events even though they seem already to have taken place, as well as the present and future
- one does not pray to an entity outside one's Self because the "Divine within" concept is at work
- there is no external God to whom one must appeal, but rather, to the internal god in the person
- prayer originates in the conscious or the unconscious; unconscious and even "dream prayer" is possible.[11]

Dossey, of course, contends that the Self is immortal and eternal, and cannot die. Therefore, any sickness is but a transitory experience toward a better life. There is no reason to pray against sickness and disease, but rather, that the person will quickly move toward the good that is going to come as a result.

He notes that one of the most common New Age exercises for promoting health is to visualize "pure white light" washing over one's body. It is the *state* of prayerfulness that heals.

Speaking Healing Words to the Self

Dossey quotes two young people with AIDS in his book. They take different approaches, but both are within the New Age philosophy and this approach of speaking healing words to one's Self.

One young person says, "Put on your gloves and fight 'em (viruses), go ten rounds. You have to beat it . . . . You have to challenge AIDS . . . . I do combat against my virus. Sometimes I go into my body and I fight my cells and I defeat them . . . . I didn't get to the leader yet in my dreams, but I know he'll have . . . every kind of weapon you could think of, machine guns, bazooka, power-pack, everything . . . . When I kill him, that will cure it in real life."

The other writes, "I deal with this disease by looking at it as one of the best teachers I've ever had. I treat it with respect. I try to love it. I talk to it. I'll say, 'You're safe with me. Do not worry. I do not hate you.' I am not sure if befriending this virus within me has any healing impact, I know that it helps me to carry on. If my attitude is good and I am happy and generous, I feel I can live with this virus within me for a very long time."

The Biblical Approach

The Bible presents a much different approach to healing and to healing prayer. Jesus did not ask people to visualize floods of bright white light. He didn't tell people to "get inside their own heads" and do battle with disease. Neither did He tell people to befriend their ailments. Jesus cast out disease. He saw disease and all forms of destruction, depravation, and death as Satan's work. He said, *I have come that they may have life, and that they may have it more abundantly* (John 10:10). He gave His Name to His disciples to use in praying for the sick, and in so doing, His disciples saw the blind see, the lame walk, and demons cast out. (See the book of Acts.)

Jesus, Angels, and Healing

In John 5:2–9 we have an account of a man who was healed as he lay by the pool of Bethesda. The story begins:

Now there is in Jerusalem by the Sheep Gate a pool, which is called in Hebrews, Bethesda, having five porches. In these lay a great multitude of sick people, blind, lame, paralyzed, waiting for the moving of the water. For an angel went down at a certain time into the pool and stirred up the water; then whoever stepped in first, after the stirring of the water, was made well of whatever disease he had. (vss. 2-6).

A legend had taken hold among the people that an angel periodically stirred up the waters in the pool of Bethesda, and that the first person into the waters was healed.

Jesus appears on the scene and speaks to a man who has been lying by the pool for thirty-eight years. He asks him, *"Do you want to be made well?"* (vs. 6)

The sick man answered Him, *"Sir, I have no man to put me into the pool when the water is stirred up; but while I am coming, another steps down before me"* (vs. 7).

This man is waiting for an angel!

Jesus does not address the matter of angels or stirred-up waters. He says to the man, *"Rise, take up your bed and walk." And immediately the man was made well, took up his bed, and walked* (vss. 8-9).

Jesus clearly demonstrates that it is *He* who heals, not waters and not angels.

At the same time, we should note that Jesus did not denounce the pool of Bethesda or tell the sick man that the waters there had no curative powers. It may very well be that the waters were capable of providing relief for some who were ill, and that God did periodically send an angel to stir up the waters as a means of healing a particular person. This passage does not say that the angel healed, only that an angel stirred the waters.

The point is—God heals. Angels don't. An angel might direct a person to a place of healing or to a man or woman of God who might pray for their healing, but angels do not heal directly.

Channeling Various Spirits

In conjuring angels, New Agers openly admit that they are "channeling" angel power to themselves.

You may be asking yourself, "But why would anybody want to listen to what a channeler has to say?"

Primarily because the person is channeling "spirit guides" who have wonderful, loving things to say. The message always begins with words that make the listener feel good . . . at least initially.

New Agers claim not only to have channeled the spirit of Jesus, but of Michael the Archangel, Moses, Jeremiah, Peter, Paul, and other long-dead prophets and saints, as well as an assemblage of Babylonian kings and queens, and Egyptian pharaohs and priestesses.

One of the terms that is common in the New Age is the phrase "Christ energy." This is the energy that a person supposedly gets when he channels a major Christ-like figure into his subconscious. (Actually, this isn't far from the ancient pagan practice of eating an enemy's heart in order to ingest the courage and power of that enemy. In this case, a person is channeling the energy of an entity in order to ingest spiritually its power.)

Jesus is considered to have *used* Christ energy during His ministry on earth, but New Agers do not believe He was the source of that energy. "Christ light" is a term they use to denote one of the seven fundamental spiritual energies they believe permeates the universe.

The New Age is Organized . . . With Specific Goals

Even though the New Age cannot be pinned down to one particular set of beliefs, dogmas, or religions, the goal of the overall movement has been well-stated by a number of people. The goal is world domination.

This has been stated in a thirteen-point plan often called the Master Plan or simply The Plan by New Age leaders. The principal aim is to establish one political, social, and religious system for the entire world.

This plan was first elaborated by Meishu Sama, a New Age pioneer from Japan who came to the New Age via atheism and then Shintoism. He wrote about The Plan in 1931 and claimed it was a "revelation" disclosed to him about a time when "negative vibrations" would be removed from the earth in an earthshaking purification process.

The New Age religion will be a revival of the religion of ancient Babylon in which mystery cults, sorcery, occultism, and immorality flourished.

Babylon Revisited

What was the spiritual climate of ancient Babylon? These are all religious practices, rituals, and doctrinal beliefs mutually embraced by the Babylon of yesterday:

man-as-god doctrine	karma
occult visualizations	palmistry
sexual licentiousness	fire worship
psychic mind powers	self-love
reincarnation	numerology
evolution doctrine	necromancy
goddess worship	levitation

astral travel	astrology
drug abuse	divination
alcohol abuse	shamanism
occult meditation	decrees
nature-earth worship	hypnotism
altered states of	Mystery Teachings
consciousness	initiation
magic words (mantras)	occult symbolism

Every one of these practices and beliefs has had a major resurgence in the last twenty years.

Ushering in the New Age

According to Sama, the Plan will be ushered in when the New Age Messiah, the Antichrist with the number 666, comes to unify the world and oversee the new order. Spirit guides help man inaugurate the New Age and pave the way for the Antichrist, who will be called the Great World Teacher. (Note: New Agers openly refer to Antichrist and the numbers 666.)

The three rallying cries for the New Age World Religion will be "world peace," "love," and "unity." The teachings of this religion are to be taught around the world. New Age leaders will teach that Jesus is neither God nor the Christ. All religions are to become integral parts of the New Age World Religion, but most Christian principles will be discredited and abandoned. Children, especially, will be taught the New Age dogma. Science and the New Age World Religion will become one. And Christians who resist The Plan will be exterminated so the world can be "purified."

Does this sound like science fiction?

New Age writer Vera Alder has said,

"There is actually a Plan and a Purpose behind all creation . . . . World Unity is the goal towards which evolution is moving. The World Plan includes: A World Organization . . . A World Economy . . . A World Religion."[12]

Another New Age writer, John Randolph Price, has said,

"The Gathering is taking place. (New Age believers) in all religions are uniting again—this time in a New commission to reveal the Light of the World . . . and begin the Aquarian Age of Spirituality on Planet Earth . . . . The revolution has begun . . . the pace is quickening. Throughout the world, men and women are joining in the uprising (and rising up) and are coming forward to be counted as part of a new race that will someday rule the universe"[13]

Alice Bailey outlined in 1946 the conditioning that she believed was going to be necessary for the New Age to initiate a "New World Order." She told her New Age disciples to emphasize the following:

- The evolution of humanity with particular attention to its goal of perfection.
- Relation of the individual soul to all souls.
- The belief in the spiritual Hierarchy will then be deduced as a result of a belief in the previous two goals . . . it will be taught that the "Kingdom has always been present" to a relatively few people.
- After these teachings have taken effect, it will be emphasized that there are those among us who have already reached a goal of "soul control."

Bailey also instructed her followers to teach mind control and meditation techniques to the masses. Color and music therapy, as well as holistic health, were to be emphasized. Symbols such as the rainbow, Pegasus, the unicorn, the all-seeing eye, and triple-sixes were to be increasingly displayed. The movement was to keep a low profile until 1975, taught Bailey, at which time there would be a no-holds-barred drive.[14]

The Drive Toward Oneness . . . Excludes Christianity

The prevailing word for the New Age, once it has been established, is "oneness." One world government. One world economy. And one world religion.

New Age writer Lola Davis wrote in *Toward a World Religion for the New Age*, "A World Religion for the New Age . . . is needed to meet the needs of thinking people . . . and to unify mankind."[15]

A New Age World Religion has support from some very influential people in our times, according to Texe Marrs, who identifies these supporters in his book, *Dark Secrets of the New Age*: singer John Denver, former astronaut Edgar Mitchell, former Notre Dame head Theodore Hesburgh, the late science fiction writer Isaac Asimov, physicist Fritjof Capra, and author John Naisbitt.

Again, these are figures well-known in the mainstream of America; they are not fringe personalities.[16]

John Randolph Price, head of two major New Age groups—the Quartus Foundation for Spiritual Research and the Planetary Commission for Global Healing—boasts that "more than half-a-billion (New Age) believers are on the planet at this time working in various religious groups. New thought concepts are spreading more rapidly than any other spiritual teaching."[17]

For all its emphasis on love and peace, the New Age cannot accommodate true Christianity. Christians are considered the arch enemies of New Age philosophy. Love and peace are extended to all *but* Bible-believing, Jesus-worshiping Christians.

Why?

New Agers will not say, of course, that they despise Christians because of Jesus Christ and His shed blood. Rather, they will tell you that Christianity is "separatist," "elitist," and thus, cosmically undemocratic.

The New Age teaches that all religious paths have some "light" to them . . . except Christianity. Jesus is labeled as being "anti-unity."

Jesus warned His disciples that they would one day be called devils, with the inference being that those of the devil will be called good. (See Matthew 10:24–25.)

The kingpin argument, of course, is that eventually Christians will be perceived as being the only stumbling block to the ushering in of the New Age. That is why they must be eliminated. They are all that is keeping the New Age from being a reality. The demise of Christians will actually be perceived as being an act of love on behalf of those who desire oneness with all on the planet.

What's a Christian to Do and Say?

The Christian response must not be to quake or waver in the onslaught of New Age thinking, but rather to:

- discern clearly what is happening,
- to obey God's commandments and to refrain from evil and all appearance of it,
- speak boldly the Gospel of Jesus Christ, and
- trust God with the outcome.

More than preach against the New Age, we must be bold to preach the good news that Jesus Christ came to save man from himself, and to restore man to His true and genuine Heavenly Father.

We do well to remember something C. S. Lewis wrote in *Mere Christianity*:

> "Look for yourself, and you will find in the long run only hatred, loneliness, despair, rage, ruin, and decay. But look for Christ and you will find Him, and with Him everything else thrown in."[18]

11

The Great Emphasis on "Experience"

SCIENCE, to my knowledge, has not proven the existence of angels, nor have angels' voices been recorded, or their images captured on film. While some people claim to have seen or felt angels, others around them have been oblivious to anything unusual.

What some of us know about angels we know because someone has *told* us of an experience—an experience they cannot explain other than to say they have been touched by the supernatural.

Today, people seem to be having those experiences with greater frequency and intensity. And, they more openly talk about them.

In an article titled *Psychics at Work*, Jane Mersky Leder wrote: "According to writer and sociologist Andrew Greeley and colleagues at the University of Chicago, a growing number of Americans are reporting paranormal or mystical experiences. National surveys by the Gallup Organization support Greeley's findings. More 'ordinary' Americans are having psychic experiences or are less reluctant to talk about experiences they've been having all along . . . . Some feel the failure of organized religion to meet the spiritual needs of many is partially responsible."[1]

Today in our nation there are more than 1,500 national and regional religious groups, and nearly half of them are "non-

conventional." Mostoftheselurepeopletothempromising religious experience, warm personal relationships, and a strong sense of
purpose.

How Can Personal Experience Be Denied?

It is very difficult to counteract another person's personal experience. That is one of the reasons I believe so much is being said
about angels and spiritual experiences today. The devil has de-
cided to start using a tactic Christians have been advocating for a
long time.

For decades we have said in our churches, "Just present your
personal witness of Christ Jesus. Tell what you know about Him
and how He has forgiven you. You don't need to be a Bible scholar
or know everything there is to know about theology. Simply tell
your story."

Christians have done this . . . and now when others come saying, "This is what happened to me," many Christians gullibly swal-
low what they say as being true, or are left wondering how they
can argue against someone else's "personal experience."

More Than a Personal Witness

The importance of relaying our personal experience is a
sound approach to witnessing, but it is not *all* that we are to do.
As Christians, we are to *begin* with a presentation of our personal
witness and relationship with Christ Jesus. But we are to grow
continually in that relationship so that we do become thoroughly
familiar with the Bible and we do have a sound theology, which
means simply a study of God.

As we come to know more of God's Word and have a deeper
relationship with God, we are also to share that. We are to tell *all*
that we know. That is truly what it means to be a witness. Begin
with your personal experience, but don't end there!

And just as importantly, when others tell you of their personal
experiences, don't take those statements as a conclusion or as a
definitive statement of truth. *Begin* with their statements about
the truth and check them out. Put what they say to the test. Seek
verification.

Consider the relationship you have with your spouse or a beloved member of your family. You met that person on a particular

day and time. Perhaps it was at the time of the person's birth, or of your own birth. The loving relationship you have with the person stems from that moment. It is the foundational basis for what you know about the person. Nobody can invalidate that first encounter, or the bond that developed, or the fact of your great love for the person. But . . . in all likelihood as your relationship with the person developed, you came to *desire* to know more and more about that person.

In my relationship with Cynthia, following our initial meeting after a church service, I wanted to find out everything I could about her! I wanted to talk with her and find out what she thought, how she felt about certain things, and what she believed. I wanted to spend time with her, experience the way she experienced life, and see the world partly through her eyes.

The same holds true for a genuine relationship with Jesus Christ. Once we have met the Lord and acknowledge Him as our Savior . . . we seek to know more and more about Him in order to become more and more like Him. We grow in a knowledge of His Word. We give increasing thought to how He lived His life and to what God says to be true.

Experience isn't enough. We must become disciples, which means followers and students. The apostles—those who lived in the closest relationship to Jesus on this earth—called Jesus "Rabboni," which means master teacher. They loved Jesus and had countless experiences with Him, but they also wanted to be His disciples, His students, His followers. They sought to pattern their entire life after His example.

When we have a spiritual experience, therefore, we must not only live and breathe that experience, or base our entire relationship with the Lord upon it. We are to verify our experience against God's Word. We are to go to the Bible and ask ourselves, "How does my experience line up with all of the Scripture?" If there is anything in our experience that doesn't match up with the full Truth of God's Word, then we need to reevaluate our experience.

It is only when we do this that we can evaluate correctly our own experiences, as well as those of others.

Are we to evaluate the experience of others?

Yes.

Jesus taught, *Beware of false prophets, who come to you in sheep's clothing, but inwardly they are ravenous wolves. You will know them by their fruits* (Matthew7:15-16).

Not All Spiritual Experience is of God

Not every spiritual experience is of God.

Too often we tend to conclude, "I had a spiritual experience. God has favored me." We may feel warm and wonderful after such an experience—whether it is a dream, a vision, a revelation or insight, an ecstatic outpouring of emotions, a gift of the Holy Spirit, a sweet time of communion with the Lord. In our "feeling good," we may automatically conclude that every spiritual experience we ever have is holy.

Satan and his demons are also spirit beings. They are capable of influencing human thought and behavior. They are masters of deception, including deception in the realm of spiritual experience. *Some* spiritual experiences are *unholy* spiritual experiences.

We must always keep in mind that spiritual experiences come in two varieties—ones from the Holy Spirit of God, and ones from the "unholy spirit."

The yardstick against which we measure these experiences is not the intensity of our feeling or the subject matter of the experiences—such as heaven or an angelic visitation—but God's Word. God's Word alone is the criterion against which all spiritual experience is to be measured.

Culture and Spiritual Experience are Intertwined

We must also keep in mind that it is impossible for us, in our finite minds, to segregate fully what is holy and divine from what is rooted in our own backgrounds and cultural experience. In other words, we cannot take a spiritual experience and isolate it from everything else and say, "That was a purely divine moment." We filter all experience through the background of our own culture. We perceive, understand, and remember experiences uniquely and individually, and in part, on the basis of our own backgrounds and cultures.

If you were born and raised in the United States of America, there is a great likelihood that you have memories related to the Fourth of July. If you see something that is red, white, and blue in coloring, you probably think of our flag, our nation, or of something patriotic. If you see fireworks bursting in the sky, you probably think about the Fourth of July, even if the fireworks are being seen at Disneyland on the second of April! In sum, you have a cultural propensity toward certain colors and experiences that a person from another nation would not have. To a person from another nation with a green and yellow flag, the colors red, white, and blue are just that—red, white, and blue colors. Fireworks may be interesting and beautiful, but they have no embedded meaning. And when the fourth of July comes up on the calendar, that day is likely to be "just another day" to the person who is not a citizen of the United States of America.

When we have spiritual experiences, our first impulse is to relate them to something else that we know or have experienced in our own past. Our culture helps us interpret or make sense of the spiritual experience.

This is neither a good nor bad thing. It is simply the way we human beings function. It is part of the way we have been created. If we have had bad past experiences in certain areas, we tend to interpret similar present-day experiences in their light. The same for good experiences.

Part of the redemptive power of Jesus Christ is that He gives new meaning to our pasts. We can ask the Holy Spirit to heal us of past wounds so that they do not cause a misinterpretation of His work in our lives. The gifts of the Holy Spirit, to a great extent and to the extent we allow them to operate in our lives, can give us a new framework for evaluating God's love and mercy extended toward us. Even so, we are in a constant struggle all our lives to separate what is "of the flesh" and what is "of the Lord."

This is yet another reason for relying on God's Word as the criterion against which we evaluate spiritual experience. When we seek to evaluate or interpret that experience according to our own wisdom, we fall short. We inevitably see, understand, or remember what has happened to us in terms of our cultural background and past experiences.

Our Desires Impact Spiritual Experience

We must also consider the fact that our personal desires impact our interpretation of personal experience. Again, this is part of the way we human beings are made.

We want things to turn out in our favor.

We want things to be orderly and good.

We want things to be according to our wishes and desires.

This is true on earth for virtually every situation you can describe. We are self-absorbed and self-centered creatures, and to be anything else is to be at least partly redeemed and refashioned by the Holy Spirit. Apart from Him, as kind and gentle and generous as we may claim to be, we are creatures bent on "looking out for number one"—ourselves!

The fact of the matter is that no one wants to face divine judgment. We'd rather believe that God loves everyone and would destroy no one. We'd rather think that everyone—indeed, every living creature—goes to a "better place" when he or she dies. We do not like for things to be out of our own control or beyond the realm of our own understanding. We are finite beings and we struggle greatly with the idea that God is infinite.

How many times have you heard a person say, "I felt so helpless in that situation. There was nothing I could do." They might be describing an accident or the serious illness of another person, or even an experience of being with another person who was suffering or dying. The fact is, we all would *like* to be able to do something, make a decision, fix it, and make it right according to our own thinking. Trusting God is one of the hardest things any of us will ever do.

This tendency we all have does not limit itself to what can be scientifically proved. If anything, it is more pronounced when we come to matters that are beyond our ability to prove them. In the realm of "mystery," we want even more to exert our control and to have our own dreams come true.

In our humanity, we all desire:

- **no right and wrong answers or criterion.** If such exists, we just might be wrong!
- **no judgment based on our behavior.** After all, if there is a judgment, we might find ourselves on the wrong end of it, having failed to do certain things required of us.
- **no limitations.** If there is limitation, it might bind us or thwart us in a way we personally don't choose to be limited. No limitations includes no variation in rewards. We'd just as soon everybody be rewarded equally.

In sum, we want things to work out in our favor. This is especially true when it comes to the afterlife. We want Heaven to operate according to OUR will and be a place of comfort and ease according to our own definitions.

That is not the case. Heaven has been created for us, but it is not created by us. Heaven operates solely according to God's design and judgment. God's way prevails in Heaven.

Spiritual Experiences Boost the Ego of Man

Spiritual experiences tend to boost the ego of man. They exalt man. They say to the average man, "I must be alright, or even better than alright, for this to have happened to me."

Will Baron has said, "Even if a person believes in Satan's existence, the visit from an angelic being tends to so inflate one's ego that he is reluctant to consider the possibility that the mysterious visitor is other than a divine being sent from God."[2]

Some who claim to have had angelic encounters or near-death experiences clearly state that they are telling their stories to bring "comfort" or "consolation" to others, while overlooking the state of their souls. Those who tell their stories of spiritual experiences face a challenge: who will receive the glory? In telling their stories, will they ultimately bring as much or more attention to themselves and the experience they reportedly have had as they do to God? There is grave danger in usurping God's glory and in telling about spiritual experiences without openly acknowledging God the Father as the Source of all good gifts.

As believers, our spiritual experiences are to lead us to these goals:

- **presentation of the Gospel to those who haven't heard.** The proclaiming of the Gospel initially is used by the Holy Spirit to bring about conviction in the unrepentant heart, not comfort or consolation.
- **edification to the Body of Christ.** In order to be truly edifying, any experience we have in the Lord must be one that we openly admit, acknowledge, and believe to be available to all people. Nothing about a spiritual experience is intended to set us apart as charmed, uniquely gifted, or semi-divine. The spiritual experiences God gives to us—whether visions, dreams, gifts of the Holy Spirit, healings—are intended not only for our benefit, but for the encouragement of others. God is no respecter of persons—what He does for one, He desires to do for all.
- **destruction of the devil and his minions.** Our intercession is intended to scatter the enemy and cause him to flee.

Spiritual experiences are not intended for self-glorification. A genuine biblical experience with an angel doesn't bring glory to man, and only rarely brings comfort. The glory always goes to man. For man's part, he usually gets hard work and an opportunity to trust God even more.

Above all . . .

We as Christians need to make certain that our spiritual experiences are within the context of the Body of Christ. When you take a look at the places where spiritual experiences abound today—whether miracle manifestations or angelic encounters—very often you will find that they are not happening where the people of God are mature in their faith and are busy doing the work of the saints. Rather, they are in places of great darkness, or where the miracle or angelic experiences penetrate the darkness and are a sign to *unbelievers*. If you or someone else has a spiritual experience that is profound, ask yourself, "Why?" Is this a sign to unbelievers? Is it an experience that is compelling people to accept Christ Jesus as their Savior? Is it a means of propelling you or a body of people closer to the Lord Jesus?

A Gallup poll about religion in America asked this question: Have you ever had a religious experience—that is, a particularly powerful religious insight or awakening? Sixty-three percent of those polled said "no."

This would seem to indicate that two out of three Americans—although they claim to attend church and read the Bible—may *not* have had a personal conversion experience to the Lord Jesus Christ.

Another topic subjected to polling was the importance Americans place upon having a deeper relationship with God. More than half (56 percent) said it was very important. Another quarter (26 percent) said it was fairly important.

Taking these two polls together, one might conclude that while Americans believe that having a deeper relationship with God is important, they don't believe they've had an experience that they could define as life-changing or "deepening" their relationship with the Almighty. Such persons seem ripe for the plucking. They *want* more of God, or more in the way of spiritual life. But what they are doing now isn't satisfying them.

What will happen to these people when someone comes along offering them a spiritual experience? What will happen to Christians when someone comes along offering them a experience that seems more loving and more "spiritual" than the one offered to them through their church?

On the one hand, we need to be calling people to accept the sacrifice that Jesus made on the Cross, to receive the forgiveness of sins, and to be empowered by the Holy Spirit to repent of their sin and lead righteous lives. On the other hand, we need to say to people: turning to Christ is not necessarily an *emotional* spiritual experience. You accept Jesus as Savior as an act of the will. A blaze of emotion or a "spiritual high" may not be a part of that decision in one's life.

We as Christians need to make certain that our spiritual experiences are not something we are waiting impatiently to have, or that we expect God to give us. For every person who claims to have seen an angel once in their life, there are tens of thousands who have not. (Apparently, "seeing angels" isn't something that God considers to be an important spiritual experience for the vast majority of His people.)

There are other things that God *does* require or expect of His people—to stay filled with His Holy Spirit, to read and apply the Word of God to daily life, and to be in constant prayer. There are other things that God desires for *us* to desire: the good gift of agape love, as well as all the gifts of the Holy Spirit. God desires for us to *want* to bear the fruit of the Spirit in our lives. (See Galatians 5:22–23.)

"Seeing angels" is neither a badge of spiritual discernment nor a reward for good spiritual conduct. It is not something we are to desire.

12

The Subtlety of Deceit

THE lies set forth about angels by the New Age writers may seem blatant as presented here. You may find yourself saying, "Well, I'd certainly never fall for any of that."

In actuality, the lies in the material presented by authors such as these are stated with great subtlety. What has been quoted in previous chapters is a concentrated dose of what is much more "watered down" in today's New Age books about angels. When taken as a whole, many of these books seem to come across as "nice little collections of quotes," as "cute ideas," or as "definitive historical surveys."

One must read very carefully and with a knowledge of both the New Age and the Bible in order to pick up the phrases that are central to the New Age movement and which are directly opposed to a biblical view.

The language often crosses over—but be aware that what you as a Christian mean when you use a traditionally Christian word may not be at all what what the New Age writer has in mind.

If you are questioning the purchase of a book about angels, read the biographical sketch of the author. It will give you a clue as to the person's philosophical orientation.

Then look for these "lies" about angels:

- Angels are people who are living at a higher state of consciousness and goodness than normal folk.

- We will all be angels some day, once we have fully evolved, or perhaps in the afterlife. In the meantime, we need to strive to become angels.

- We not only can get in touch with the angels, but we should, since angelic encounter is always to our benefit.

Look also for New Age techniques of meditation, communication (healing words, positive thoughts, use of mantras), and visualization that are advocated as a means of gaining contact with angels, or with one's "angelic Self."

Look for mention of the "tools" of the occult—the use of Tarot cards or other systems that can help a person "know" what angels are saying.

Look for talk of a higher state of spirituality or a new awakening on the earth.

You'll find a lot of emphasis on love, oneness, acceptance, gentleness, goodness, and niceness in these books.

Question a heavy emphasis on experience being the basis for truth. Recognize the spirit at work if the Name of Jesus is dismissed as unimportant or "just another name." At that point, you are dealing with openly defiant evil.

If someone asks you to enter an altered state of consciousness to contact your personal angel . . . don't.

If someone asks you to pay your hard-earned money for a seminar designed to give you an angel experience . . . don't.

If someone asks you to incorporate mystical techniques in order to unlock spiritual secrets—even in the name of the Church or with an intent of furthering your relationship with Jesus Christ . . . don't.

The devil rarely shows up to say, "I'm here to capture your soul." His techniques are usually far more subtle, more along the line, "I'm here to give you something wonderful that you can't live without and which you surely must want."

Do not listen to him.

No Substitutes

The New Age readily substitutes angels for God and His Son, Jesus Christ. Always keep in mind the two main reasons why.

First, angels as they are presented by the New Age are non-judgmental. They help everyone without regard and without prejudice. Angels are not depicted as being reserved to aid the saints of God; they are presented as being available to everyone. If you "buy" this, there is no reason to face sin. And the result is that you never feel a need to turn from their sin to embrace Jesus Christ. The redemption of man is "cut off at the pass", as it were, before he feels convicted of sin. The end result, of course, is that he may die in his sin, never having accepted the atonement of Jesus Christ.

Second, angels as they are presented by New Age teachers are nonthreatening, wise, and loving. They are presented as offering help, whether we request it or not, and even if we ignore them. Again, they are a substitute for what is a very painful truth: we are sinners until we come to Jesus Christ and ask God's forgiveness through Him.

If the devil can convince people that they don't *need* a Savior, he has won.

The angels of the New Age have little resemblance to the description of angels in the Bible. They are like a caricature of the real thing.

No Confusion

If you find yourself "in doubt" about what someone is saying with regard to angels, run to your Bible and stay there. The Scriptures tell us, *God is not the author of confusion but of peace* (1Corinthians14:33). The author of confusion, so integral to deceit, is Satan. He would like nothing more than to plant seeds of doubt in your mind about the working of angels. He would take great delight in confusing you as to their origin and their work on the earth.

I once saw a T-shirt with these these words contradicting the New Age philosophy:

"There is a God. You're not Him."

If someone attempts to confuse you as to whether you just might be your own god, run from them!

Fallen Angels—

Two Takes on Ancient Foes

13

Angels, Demons, and Demons in Disguise

AT the outset of this chapter, we may do well to remember the words in a song Elvis Presley made famous:

You walk like an angel,
You talk like an angel,
But my, oh my
You're like the Devil in disguise!
Oh yes you are!

Deception about the fallen angels is just as rampant in today's New Age literature as deception about God's elect angels.

Fallen angels are called evil angels in some Christian literature. Various Bible translations refer to them as unclean spirits, devils, demons, and Satan's minions. The most popular term for them is demons, which is the term we will use most of the time in this chapter.

Once again, let's turn first to what the Bible says about demons.

The Truth About The Devil and His Demons

C. S. Lewis wrote:

"There are two equal and opposite errors into which our race can fall about the devils. One is to disbelieve in their existence. The other is to believe, and to feel an unhealthy interest in them. They themselves are equally pleased by both errors and hail a materialist or a magician with the same delight."[1]

The Bible states clearly that both Satan and the demons are real. They are classified as the enemy of all righteous people. (See Acts 13:10.)

Demons, as characterized by the Scriptures, have these characteristics:

Demons are spirit beings.

They do not have bodies of their own. They are described as rulers, powers, and spiritual forces in Ephesians 6.

Just as the elect angels, demons are spirit beings that are able to talk, think, feel, and act. They are referred to as "unclean spirits" (Matthew 10:1 and Luke 11:24), a description that not only describes their nature, but also describes their relationship to man. What they possess they foul.

Demons were originally in fellowship with God but "did not keep their proper domain."

Jude 6 speaks of the fate of the rebellious angels:

"And the angels who did not keep their proper domain, but left their own abode, He has reserved in everlasting chains under darkness for the judgment of the great day."

1 Timothy 3:6 tells us that the fault leading to the devil's condemnation was pride.

Demons are knowledgeable about God and tremble before him.

Demons know Jesus Christ is God. One such demon-possessed man claims this in Mark 1:23–24.

The Bible tells us clearly that the devils know who Jesus is, and that He is the Son of God. James 2:19 tells us "even the demons believe—and tremble!" Matthew 8:28–29 tells of two men from the country of the Gergesenes who cry out to Jesus, "What have we to do with You, Jesus, You Son of God? Have You come here to torment us before the time?" These demons not only proclaim that Jesus is the Son of God, but they know that a tormenting hell has been created for them.

No matter how kind or loving an evil spirit may present itself to be, it will do its utmost to avoid or deny that Jesus Christ is the only Son of God, or that Jesus Christ is God's Son come in the flesh.

Demons are organized and under authority.
Beelzebub is called the ruler of the demons in Matthew 12:24.
Demons oppose God's people and attempt to destroy Christ's Kingdom. (Ephesians 6:12 and 1 Peter 5:8)
They are allowed to roam the earth and torment unbelievers. (See Matthew 12 for Jesus' teaching about a spirit that finds seven other spirits more wicked than itself and returns to indwell its victim.)
The number-one job of demons is to oppose the saints of God. Their foremost technique toward that end is temptation—to get people to turn their backs on God's will, as expressed in God's commandments, and to pursue their own will and fleshly desires. The pattern of their temptation activity is set out in 1 Timothy 4:1-2:

- **Demons seduce us to pay attention to something that is contrary to God's will.**
- **Demons set forth a false "doctrine" or teaching about that thing or person**—in other words, they call what is wrong, right, and what is right, wrong.
- **Demons "speak lies of hypocrisy"**—which means that they defame or unjustly bring condemnation upon those who are choosing right or who are in living in accordance with God's commandments.
- **Demons sear the conscience of their victim so** that a person can no longer tell right from wrong.

This pattern is evident throughout the Old Testament, where we read repeatedly how evil messengers from Satan turned the people's hearts from God to idolatry. The pattern is evident in our world today as we see millions being wooed away from their Christian upbringings to pursue false religions.

We have an example of this type of seduction and "false doctrine in I Chronicles 21. The chapter begins, *Now Satan stood up against Israel, and moved David to number Israel.* That sentence, in a nutshell, describes the work of Satan—he makes a stand against a person or people, and then moves upon a person to do something that is contrary to God's orders. God had never authorized a census. In fact, God expected his people *not* to number themselves, but rather, to place their trust squarely in the Lord so that no matter how many or few they might be, they would be trusting God for victory. Joab said to David, "May the Lord make His people a hundred times more than they are. But, my lord the king, are they not all my lord's servants? Why then does my lord require this thing? Why should he be a cause of guilt in Israel?"

David proceeded with the census nevertheless and God was displeased. He struck at Israel and David repented. Through Gad, the Lord offered David one of three punishments: three years of famine, three months of enemy war and takeover, or three days of the "sword of the Lord" with the "angel of the Lord destroying throughout all the territory of Israel." David chose the latter punishment, putting himself squarely into the hand of the Lord with a proclamation, "His mercies are very great." (See 1 Chronicles 21:3–13.)

Then David lifted his eyes and saw the angel of the Lord standing between earth and heaven, having in his hand a drawn sword stretched out over Jerusalem. So David and the elders, clothed in sackcloth, fell on their faces (vs. 16). The angel commanded David to go the threshing floor of Ornan the Jebusite and build an altar there. David made a burnt offering on the altar he built and *the Lord commanded the angel, and he returned his sword to its sheath* (vs. 27).

The altar that David made was on Mount Moriah, the same mountain on which Abraham offered Isaac as a sacrifice to the Lord. It is the mountain on which the Temple of God was later built. An act of disobedience opened David's life to destruction. An act of worship stayed the hand of the angel and brought deliverance to David and Israel.

Demons readily accept worship.

One of the best ways to tell if someone is acting according to the Lord is to see if they will accept worship. If they do, they are not of God. True men and women of God, and the angels of heaven, do not allow themselves to be worshiped. The devil, on the other hand, delights in the worship of men. So do his demons and those who do his work.

The devil has been described as being capable of transforming himself *into an angel of light* (2 Corinthians 11:14). This disguise is intended to dazzle, and to evoke the awe and worship of mankind.

It is a false aura and glow, however. The worship given to the devil is equally false, and ultimately is destructive to the soul.

Demons can occupy a human body.

In fact, numerous demons can indwell a human being. The demons in one man in the Bible referred to themselves as Legion. (See Mark 5:8-9.)

We have an example of this type of possession in Acts 16:16-19:

Now it happened, as we went to prayer, that a certain slave girl possessed with a spirit of divination met us, who brought her masters much profit by fortune-telling. This girl followed Paul and us, and cried out, saying, "These men are the servants of the Most high God, who proclaim to us the way of salvation." And this she did for many days.

But Paul, greatly annoyed, turned and said to the spirit, "I command you in the name of Jesus Christ to come out of her." And he came out that very hour. But when her masters saw that their hope of profit was gone, they seized Paul and Silas and dragged them into the marketplace to the authorities.

The Bible described this girl as being "possessed" with a demon who controls her actions completely, including the words she speaks. Note that the demon speaks words that are truthful—Paul and his associates have come to proclaim the way of salvation—but that the motive is one intended to bring derision and to hinder the very work of salvation. Also notice that when the evil angel is commanded to come out of the girl at the name of Jesus Christ, it does, and the girl is so transformed that her masters recognize immediately that she has been cleansed of this evil angel and is no longer going to be an agent of divination for them to use.

The elect angels of heaven do not indwell people, only demons. The elect angels, in obedience to God—who created the free will of man and honors man's choices—do not take away man's free will. Demons, on the other hand, are in disobedience to God. They delight in taking away man's free will because in so doing, they take away man's ability to choose to follow God.

As an attribute of possession, demons can cause mental and physical disorders. (See Matthew 9 and Mark 5:2-5.) Demons have a particular power to affect the human body—to cause it to become blind, dumb, deaf, have seizures; to speak, screech, or scream with unnatural voices; and to twist and contort in unnatural ways.

Keep in mind that demons know how man is made. They understand both the physical desires and mental capacities of mankind. They know how to manipulate man.

Demons also can possess or control animals. The demons Jesus cast out of one man went to indwell swine (Mark 5:13).

Demons can transform themselves into highly appealing entities—even as "angels"—or appear as apparitions of people.

The apostle Paul tells us in 2 Corinthians 11:14 that Satan "transforms himself into an angel of light" in order to deceive people into thinking that he is something other than what he is. He is the master of deceit. Jesus said of him, *when he speaks a lie, he speaks from his own resources, for he is a liar and the father of it* (John 8:44).

Demons are also called "familiar spirits."

Have you ever met a person and said to yourself, "My, that person is familiar?" Or have you seen someone and said, "Why, they look just like my friend!"

Demons have the capacity to make themselves appear to be familiar—to take on the likeness of entities or people whom a person has known or knows.

Demons will be judged and committed to the pits of darkness.

It may be that a portion of the evil angels have already been apprehended and cast into hell. Various theologians read this meaning into 2 Peter 2:4, where it states, *God did not spare the angels who sinned, but cast them down to hell and delivered them into chains of darkness, to be reserved for judgment.* Jude 6 may also allude to a partial judgment of the rebellious angels—*the angels who did not keep their proper domain, but left their own abode, He has reserved in everlasting chains under darkness for the judgment of the great day.*

Either way, the Bible tells us that a final judgment is a certain reality one day.

Lucifer will be shut away from a thousand years, a time we call the "millenium:"

I saw an angel coming down from heaven, having the key to the bottomless pit and a great chain in his hand. He laid hold of the dragon, that serpent of old, who is the Devil and Satan, and bound him for a thousand years; and he cast him into the bottomless pit, and shut him up, and set a seal on him, so that he should deceive the nations no more till the thousand years were finished (Revelation 20:1-3).

After this time, Lucifer will be *released for a little while* and will go *from his prison and will go out to deceive the nations which are in the four corners of the earth* (Revelation 20:3,7-8).

Finally, *the devil, who deceived them, was cast into the lake of fire and brimstone where the beast and the false prophet are. And they will be tormented day and night forever and ever* (Revelation 20:10).[2]

Angels Have More Power than Satan

Unfallen angels are more powerful than fallen ones. That is a great truth of the Bible we don't tend to hear often enough, in my opinion. Frequently, I encounter Christians who seem to think that God and the devil are on equal footing, that they represent an equal clash between good and evil. Not so! God and Satan are not equals. One is the almighty King of the Universe, absolute in power, omniscient and omnipresent. The other is a creature of God who rebelled and has been cast from God's presence.

The ultimate demise of Satan is at the hand of *unfallen* angels. Revelation 12:7-9 describes this battle for us:

War broke out in heaven: Michael and his angels fought with the dragon; and the dragon and his angels fought, but they did not prevail, nor was a place found for them in heaven any longer. So the great dragon was cast out, that serpent of old, called the Devil and Satan, who deceives the whole world; he was cast to the earth, and his angels were cast out with him.

Later in Revelation we find this description of the casting of Satan into a bottomless pit:

Then I saw an angel coming down from heaven, having the key to the bottomless pit and a great chain in his hand. He laid hold of the dragon, that serpent of old, who is the Devil and Satan, and bound him for a thousand years; and he cast him into the bottomless pit, and shut him up, and set a seal on him, so that he should deceive the nations no more till the thousand years were finished (Revelation 20:1-3).

In neither account do we find Jesus, the Father, or the Holy Spirit engaged in the battle. We find elect angels—unfallen, loyal, created beings of God—able to defeat the devil and all his demons at the command of the Lord.

In his book on angels, Billy Graham notes:

"We must not get so busy counting demons that we forget the holy angels. Certainly we are up against a gigantic war machine. But we are encompassed by a heavenly host so powerful that we need not fear the warfare—the battle is the Lord's. We can boldly face Satan and his legions with all the confidence of the old captain who, when told that his outfit was completely surrounded, shouted, 'Good, don't let any of them escape.' If your valley is full of foes, raise your sights to the hills and see the holy angels of God arrayed for battle on your behalf."[3]

As far as know, the elect angels are more numerous than demons. But, we do not know the exact proportion of angels to demons. Our main clue lies in Revelation 12:3-4 when John writes:

And another sign appeared in heaven: behold, a great, fiery red dragon having seven heads and ten horns, and seven diadems on his head. His tail drew a third of the stars of heaven and threw them to the earth.

Many theologians consider this to be a description of Lucifer's fall to the earth, along with a third of the angelic host. If so, that still leaves two thirds of God's angels as loyal subjects. Since God created angels, He could, of course, create as many angels as needed. The devil, as a created being, as no means of creating more demons.

One thing we do know with certainty is that the Bible has more to say about angels than about devils or demons.

We Must Discern Their Presence

The evil angels have their agenda: to take as many people to hell with them as they can. Toward this end, they are highly active.

Demons are not passive creatures, just as the elect angels are not passive.

We must continually be alert to the fact that demons are at work in the world. This does not mean that we need to be looking for a demon behind every door or under every bush. It does mean that we need to be savvy about them. We are to be "wise as serpents," which means that we are to be just as wise as the demons! But we are also to be innocent as doves. We are to know about them intellectually and at a distance, never experientially.

The apostle Paul foresaw a day when *some will depart from the faith, giving heed to deceiving spirits and doctrines of demons* (1 Timothy 4:1). This should give us double warning that we need to be on our toes in today's world when it comes to spiritual discernment. Always be aware that:

- Not all spirits are good ones.
- Not all spiritual experiences are Holy Spirit-ual experiences.

We are admonished, *Beloved, do not believe every spirit, but test the spirits, whether they are of God* (1 John 4:1).

Fighting Spiritual Battles Against Demons

Our warfare as human beings today is ultimately spiritual in nature. Ephesians 6:12 tells us:

> *We do not wrestle against flesh and blood, but against principalities, against powers, against the rulers of the darkness of this age, against spiritual hosts of wickedness in the heavenly places. Therefore take up the whole armor of God, that you may be able to withstand in the evil day, and having done all, to stand.*

Our primary goal as believers in the Lord Jesus Christ is not to conjure spirits or have spiritual experiences with angels, but rather, to proclaim the Gospel of Jesus Christ and to stand against wickedness. We are to do both steadfastly, with full resolve and without wavering.

What is the "armor" that we wear?

Our Battle Garb

Our suit of spiritual armor is not "paranormal." It does not involve the presence of a spiritual guide or angel ally. Our armor is:

- **truth**–the full truth about God's Word, will, and purposes, and about His Son, Jesus Christ
- **righteousness**–knowing we are in right standing with God
- **the preparation of the Gospel of peace**–having done our inner homework in prayer and study of God's Word
- **faith in God**–believing God is Victor over all and the Source of all goodness
- **salvation**–the full assurance that our sins have been forgiven (through belief in Jesus Christ as our sacrifice)
- **the Word of God**–the Scriptures themselves, spoken aloud to the enemy and to edify ourselves

This armor is not devised by some means of conjuring, Zen-like meditation, or secret chants. It is the result of a life lived in emulation of Christ Jesus. He is our armor. We are putting on His likeness. And we do that daily through study of God's Word, prayer, and acts of service to others.

Our armor, of course, is the antithesis of what the New Age is based upon, which is: lie and illusion, no standing necessary with God, a gospel of false peace, faith in Self, redemption through a higher state of self-realization, and mantras.

Note that when we are fully dressed for battle, we are told by the Apostle Paul to do two things: stand and *pray always with all prayer and supplication in the Spirit* (Ephesians 6:18). Our battle is not an offensive one. It is a defensive one. In 1 Peter 5:8-9 we read that our enemy, the devil, *walks about like a roaring lion, seeking whom he may devour. Resist him, steadfast in the faith.*

We Win! The good news is that when we fight spiritual battles according to the plan prescribed in God's Word, we win! Colossians 2:13-15 gives us the assurance of victory:

And you, being dead in your trespasses and the uncircumcision of your flesh, He has made alive together with Him, having forgiven you all trespasses, having wiped out the handwriting of requirements that was against us, which was contrary to us. And He has taken it out of the way, having nailed it to the cross. Having disarmed principalities and powers, He made a public spectacle of them, triumphing over them in it.

James 4:6-7 encourages us, *Submit to God. Resist the devil and he will flee from you.* Prayer is the foremost way we submit to God, stating openly, *not my will, by Yours, O God. Not my choices in life, but yours.*

Again, our posture toward the enemy angels of Satan is to be one of resistance and defense.

The Offense

What about the offense? Isn't a good offense the best defense, as many a coach has said?

The offense, in my opinion, happens as the Lord God directs His angels to intervene and take action on our behalf. Our offensive team in the heavenlies is one we cannot see, but we can be assured, they are winning!

Why do I believe this is so?

In the first place, we must recognize that mankind has been created to hold a position described by the Scriptures as "a little lower than the angels." (See Hebrews 2:7-9 and Psalm 8:4-6.) This does not mean that man is without honor. The writer to the Hebrews noted,

> *You have made him a little lower than the angels; You have crowned him with glory and honor, and set him over the works of Your hands. You have put all things in subjection under his feet.*

Man has his own role and function to fill in God's design. No angel can fill that place. No angel has independent free will. No angel can know the fullness of emotion or spiritual response that a person can know.

At the same time, no one person has more power, skill, or intelligence than an angel. Angels were created to give continual praise to God and to carry out God's orders. In order to carry out His orders, God endowed angels with power that far exceeds that of human beings. Not only are angels powerful, but they are highly intelligent. Stop to consider for a moment that the angels have been with God throughout eternity. They know God, God's methods, and God's desires far better than any of us. They have seen the sweep of humanity and know human nature better than we human beings know it. None of us is capable of holding our own in either a physical or an intellectual match with an angel.

All of which means that none of us can truly take on the enemy angels, or demons, with any hope of winning *in our own strength and power.* We can resist, but we cannot attack in a way that is definitively victorious.

When we resist the devil, we are in a position for God to send His holy angels to help us. The loyal host of heaven is capable of engaging in offensive maneuvers against fallen, disloyal angels. No fallen angel is a match for an angel authorized to take action and given power by God to defeat it.

This is a far cry from what many New Age authors advocate. From their perspective, man is smart enough to "direct" his own angels to do his bidding.

Using the Word. In her book, *Angels All Around*, Marilyn Hickey gives this advice:

"God has provided his angels to minister to the household of faith while the devil and his angels try to harass, tempt, and cause Christians to stumble in their faith. The key to angelic *ministry* or angelic *menace* for the Christian in this war is knowing the Word of God."

She goes on to give ten bits of strategic advice from God's Word:

1. Put on the whole armor of God. (Ephesians 6:11)
2. Know Satan's devices. (2 Corinthians 2:11)
3. Give the devil no place. (Ephesians 4:27)
4. Resist the devil. (James 4:7)
5. Be sober and vigilant. (1 Peter 5:8)
6. Overcome the devil by the blood of the lamb. (Revelation 12:11)
7. Overcome the devil by the Word. (1 John 2:14)
8. Cast out devils in the name of Jesus. (Mark 16:17)
9. Overcome the devil by the power of the Holy Spirit. (Romans 8:14-15)
10. Overcome the devil by faith. (1 John 5:4)

I recommend that you look up the verses next to the statements above and commit them to memory. Meditate on them, in the true Hebrew sense of the word. Learn them and let them sink deep within your heart and mind. And then, use them against the enemy any time that you sense the presence of evil. Voice these verses. Incorporate them into your prayers.

There is great spiritual power in the Word of God to defeat demons.

Take Action in The Name of Jesus

New Age writers would have us believe that all angels are benevolent and "on our side."

The Bible gives a very different picture. In fact, the foremost angel, the rebellious Lucifer himself, is continually berating and accusing Christians before the throne of God. In Revelation 12:10 we find this description:

Now salvation, and strength, and the kingdom of our God, and the power of His Christ have come, for the accuser of our brethren, who accused them before our God day and night, has been cast down.

Just as Satan had access to God to accuse Job, so he has access to accuse us. Lucifer is definitely *not* on the side of believing Christians!

The only thing that appears to knock Satan out of his accusing role in the throne room of God are actions taken in the Name of Jesus on this earth.

When the seventy disciples sent out by Jesus return to Him, saying, *Lord even the demons are subject to us in Your name,* Jesus responded with this statement:

I saw Satan fall like lightning from heaven. Behold, I give you the authority to trample on serpents and scorpions, and over all the power of the enemy, and nothing shall by any means hurt you. Nevertheless do not rejoice in this, that the spirits are subject to you, but rather rejoice because your names are written in heaven.

It is vitally important that you see the distinction between having authority over the devil or a demon in your own name, which is not possible, and having authority over the devil in the Name of Jesus. The spirits are *not* subject to our directives when we speak in our own name. They are subject only to us when we speak in the Name of the Lord Jesus Christ. It is to His name that every knee must bow.

The seven sons of a man named Sceva learned this the hard way. (See Acts 19:13–16.)

Deliverance for Those Ensnared

The Bible also holds out hope for those ensnared by demon power. Jesus and His apostles all had "deliverance" ministries. At times, the spoken Name of Jesus was all that it took for the apostles to cast out demons. (See Acts 16:18.) At other times, fasting and prayer was required. (See Matthew 17:21.)

Those who have been pursuing evil power, or who have been consorting with devils and their false teachings, are admonished in the Scriptures to turn away from evil and ask God's forgiveness. (See Nehemiah 1:9.)

New Age Lies About Demons

The New Age writers seem to be divided into two camps when it comes to demons.

On the one hand . . . there are those who believe that we not only have a guardian angel assigned to us, but also a "bad angel." The bad angel plays the role of making things *so bad* for us that we run toward goodness.

On the other hand . . . there are others who believe that there are no demons. All spirit guides work for our good.

One writer has said this about hell, heaven, and angels:

> "We make our own hells here on earth, in our minds and in the prisons of our hearts, and it is to escape these hells and our howling demons that the angels come—to tell us we have freedom."

The net effect, however, is the same for both of these approaches. Whether we see no bad angels, or we regard demons as working toward good, we are taught by the New Age writers to welcome and embrace these spirit beings.

Elena, one of the Superbeings that John Randolph Price claims to have channeled, says that Elena told him this about demons:

> "I prefer to think of them as angels of light—whether from earth or other worlds. They search, select and guide those men and women who may be suitable subjects . . . . A Master may then instruct, or plant the seed of a new concept . . . and the word is spread, taking hold and growing in the mind of to

others, until there is a wave of collective thinking sufficiently powerful to change events and shape the future."[4]

To be fair, I need also to state that there are a few New Age teachers who claim that dark angels exist and that they are *not* the flip side of our internal bright angels. Rather, as Guiley writes:

"The purpose of the dark angels is at the least to neutralize us as center of light and love and, if necessary, to destroy us— spiritually, psychically, even physically. They are engaged in spiritual warfare with the forces of light for control of our souls. The more we can be encouraged to petty acts of meanness and falsehood, to major acts of destruction and violence— the more we empty our souls of light and fill them instead with darkness—the stronger the dark angels become, and the further away we fall from God. The choice is ours, because both the forces of light and the forces of darkness present themselves to us. We choose which ones we want to follow. And when we choose darkness, the angels of light cannot rescue us unless we realize the folly of our choice and turn to them for help. When we ask, even with the smallest cry of despair, the smallest prayer, the help is given in the greatest abundance and love."[5]

Generally speaking, those who follow this line of thought are looking to angels for their "salvation" from the dark side of evil. They believe that salvation is a matter of a personal decision to pursue good. Thus, "salvation" is a matter of works, not faith or the grace of God.

The thinking behind this statement is also that those who are rapidly expanding their consciousness are subject to the greatest amount of evil attack, but that eventually the advancing soul is lifted above the level where dark angels have influence.

The biblical approach is that we are never above an attack of the enemy. Jesus Himself was tempted in the wilderness at the outset of his ministry, but also again just prior to His crucifixion in the Garden of Gethsemane. The Bible viewpoint would probably be that once a person has become so deluded by evil and has embraced so much of a lie, there is little fight necessary on behalf of the devil!

What About Possession?

New Agers never use the word *possession*. They have attempted to "sanitize" the concept of demon possession by calling it guidance or direction. Still, by whatever name possession might be called, New Agers readily teach that one should open up the soul to "help" from spirit guides and angels.

Possession by evil spirits has been sought after by people ever since the Greeks. In Sri Lanka, devil-dancing is a means of inviting possession in hopes the demons will help cure disease. In part of Asia and Africa, shamans invite demons to possess them so they can release their healing powers.

People described as "sensitives" or mediums often invite possession in order to pass a message from the dead to the living.

In Bali, Sanghyang Dedari trance dancing is done when two virgin girls mirror dance images after being possessed by spirits.

The New Age teachers do admit that the spirit "masters" often tell New Agers to do things they don't want to do. One New Age leader has said:

> "The old self, the ego, the personality, rebels. It resists the will of God. You then have to trust that God knows best what should be done. The little will of the personality has to bend to the greater will of God if you are to progress on the path of consciousness development."[6]

Christianity would say the same thing—with a **major** difference in meaning. We are to conform to the will of God by obeying the commandments of God as portrayed in the Holy Bible. The net result is not consciousness development, but holiness.

The Adoration of Lucifer

The New Age adores Lucifer. They refer to him as the "God of Light and God of Good." One of the most admired New Age teachers, David Spangler, has said that Lucifer is "in a sense the angel of man's inner evolution." He teaches that Lucifer is an agent of God's love:

> "Christ is the same force as Lucifer . . . . Lucifer prepares man for the experience of Christhood . . . . Lucifer works within each of us to bring us to wholeness as we move into the New Age."[7]

Lucifer is hailed as the "bringer of light" and the "morning star" in New Age literature. He is the one who will initiate the New Age, and who invites men and women now to prepare for it. Some writers blatantly claim that if a person has Lucifer in his soul, he has God within.

The origin of the idea that Satan is equated with light began in Babylonia and Persia from 1400 to 400 B.C. During that era, the religious cult of Mithraism thrived. It taught that in the last days the devil and God would be reconciled. Mithraism taught reincarnation and the progression of the soul through various stages or levels. The god Mithras was later worshiped as Sol Invictus, the Roman Sun God. Mithraism was a strong rival to Christianity in the second and third centuries A.D. . . . . And here it is again!

New Ager Benjamin Creme stated to a radio audience in 28 states and 11 nations that Lucifer came from the planet Venus some eighteen and a half million years ago. He went on to say that Lucifer made the supreme sacrifice for our planet and was both the prodigal son and the sacrificial lamb. It is Lucifer, according to Creme, who is responsible for our planetary evolution, including spiritual evolution.

Spangler has also written this about Lucifer:

"Lucifer works within each of us to bring us to wholeness, and as we move into a new age, which is the age of man's wholeness, each of us in some way is brought to that point which I term the *Luciferic initiation,* the particular doorway through which the individual must pass if he is to come fully into the presence of his light and his wholeness.

"Lucifer comes to give us the final gift of wholeness. If we accept it, then he is free and we are free."[8]

Just One Aspect of God

Rather than being the embodiment of evil, Lucifer to New Age writers is but one aspect of God, "dedicated to our growth by helping us strengthen our spiritual muscles." He allegedly teaches us about the necessary dark side of life and is:

"the shadow that reveals the light by contrast. In many ways we can't see the true light until we first experience the darkness . . . . Christ and Lucifer, while not exactly complementary to each other, are at least on the same side, integral parts of the same whole."9

Writers such as these advocate that we can now "free the so-called fallen angels from the negativity we have externalized onto them for all these long millennia" in order to free ourselves from the negative illusion of evil.10

The concept of the devil being just one aspect of God—God's "dark side" as it were—is also not new. In the ancient world, the gods were perceived to embody both dark and light. In nearly all of the pantheons in the ancient world, both good and bad gods live side by side, frequently doing battle with each other.

Within the monotheistic Hebrew religion, however, any "shadow" of God was perceived to be a manifestation of His Word—either His voice or touch. The shadow was an expression of God, a creation of God.

Satan in the Old Testament is primarily an accuser of the righteous. In the New Testament he is clearly the enemy, the accuser that attempts to bring man into the realm of Satan's own destructive power. Satan is portrayed as having the ability to test, tempt, and punish mankind.

Who Is at the Door?

Jesus is recorded in Revelation as saying,

> *Behold, I stand at the door and knock. If anyone hears My voice and opens the door, I will come in to him and dine with him, and he with Me* (Revelation 3:20).

Jesus, however, is not the only one standing at the door of your heart.

Have you ever had a "secret knock" that you used, perhaps, in your family or in a club of young friends? The rhythm of the rap let you know that it was a friend, not a foe, at the door.

More than ever, we need to know the sound of the Lord Jesus when He knocks on the door of our hearts.

His message is one of love from God, forgiveness offered by God, and obedience required by God.

The knock of the devil is one of love for self, forgiveness by self, and obedience only to one's self.

The difference is very subtle, and in that very deceitful. It only takes a crack in the door for the devil to come waltzing into a person's life.

One of the most astounding stories of New Age power is told by Will Baron in his book *Deceived by the New Age*. Will was brought up by devout Christian parents and regularly attended church until he was twenty-four years old. Then he became involved for five years in a metaphysical organization called the Lighted Way. He became a devotee of a noted Hindu-Buddhist guru named Djwhal Khul. And then . . . he was told that he should give up his metaphysical books and become a follower of Jesus Christ. He was told to regard himself as a New Age Christian, to accept Jesus Christ as his spiritual "master," and to listen to the "Holy Spirit" through his voice of conscience—just as he had done with Djwhal Khul in the past. He was also told to attend Christian churches and to interest his new friends there in meditation and various New Age ideas discussed, in his words, "in biblical-sounding terms."[11]

Two years later, Baron had a dramatic and genuine conversion to authentic Christianity. He says he discovered "that the Jesus Christ I was following was not the real Jesus, Son of God Almighty. I was devastated to learn that as a New Age Christian, I had been following false prophets and false teachings."[12]

As many who claim to have seen angels, or to have had near-death experiences in the afterlife, Baron saw a figure appear to him in intense golden-white light. The mysterious shining figure looked like Jesus Christ.

This experience happened after he had been in the Lighted Way organization for about a year, and on the particular morning in discussion, after he had been meditating for only about four or five minutes. Baron felt a brilliant light fill his being. He lost all sense of weight and discomfort and had no sense of apprehension.

In Baron's terms, the figure looked "kingly." He had a knowing, he says, that the figure was not actually Jesus, but Djwhal Khul. He asked the dignified handsome figure about his struggle in his spiritual life and the figure said, "Yes. Well, that is how it is."

He then asked about a specific problem he was having and the figure in light commented, "Don't worry about it."

Hardly words of comfort, in my opinion!

Khul claims that he is a human being born more than 350 years ago in Tibet, and that he has been reincarnated through a succession of people to the place where he is now a member of an elite group of human beings called "ascended masters." He has attained immortality and will never need to be reincarnated again. Kuhl claims that Master Jesus is alive on the planet, directing the destiny of Christianity by telepathically transmitting ideas into the subconscious minds of the leaders of the Christian church. He emphasizes that Master Jesus is a man who evolved himself over successive incarnations and initiations until he became an immortal "Son of God."

Khul is a master forger of the truth.

Baron says, however, that until he was soundly converted to authentic Christianity, he never had any doubts regarding the identity of the spirit that ruled his life. He writes:

> "The truth is, I never suspected I was a slave to demons
> masquerading as agents of light. My confidence in the New
> Age path and the spirit guides had been built up over many
> years . . . . I became a devoted 'believer' in the New Age, its spirit
> guides, and its philosophies. I then became an easy candidate
> for total 'possession.' Almost nothing could shake my faith in
> what I believed and cause me to doubt the authenticity of my
> spirit guide. Even my dedicated Bible reading could not pierce
> through the web of deception because I was twisting the
> meaning of many texts in an attempt to harmonize them with
> my existing metaphysical beliefs."[13]

What first led Baron away from his Christian roots? He joined a London-based international organization called Health for the New Age. He wasn't looking for spirit guides or occult practices, only information about an alternative healing technique that he thought could help him with a health condition he had.

The devil doesn't need much rope to trip you.

Perhaps the greatest truth of all that we can state about the demons and the devil himself can be summed up in two words: **Crafty Evil.**

Angels And The Afterlife

14

Embraced by the Light, or Embraced by Darkness?

ONE of the most popular books to hit the *New York Times* best-seller list in 1994 was *Embraced by the Light,* written by Betty J. Eadie. In this book, Eadie describes a near-death experience. Her depictions of the afterlife have sent readers flocking to book stores to "read all about it." According to *Charisma* magazine's June 1994 issue, Christian bookstore owners were bombarded with requests for Betty Eadie's book. Linda Vixie, associated editor of *Bookstore Journal* is reported to have told *National & International Religion Report* that some customers "get furious" at Christian retailers who say they won't stock the book.

Many seem to think *Embraced by the Light* is a Christian book.

It most definitely is not.

The deception in Eadie's book begins with the dedication:
"To The Light, my Lord and Savior Jesus Christ, to whom I owe all that I have. He is the 'Staff' that I lean on; without him I would fall."

It is on the basis of that claim, made as the first statement of her book, that many Christians apparently have been drawn into believing that her experience is a truthful representation of death and Heaven that is in agreement with the Bible.

While I do not question the truthfulness of her personal confession about Christ, I do question a number of aspects of Betty

Eadie's work. I am not saying that she is purposefully deceitful—or that she is attempting to hurt or mislead people. Her intent may very well be to help and comfort, as she has stated on many occasions. Still, several key points in her book are in direct contradiction to the Holy Bible. Therefore, I conclude that while she may not have an intent to deceive, she has been deceived on several points.

Who Is Betty Eadie?

In her book, Betty Eadie identifies herself as half Native American Indian by race. As a very young child (but old enough to be aware of what was happening to her), she and her siblings were abandoned by her parents and placed in a very strict Catholic boarding school. There, she was separated from her brothers. She remembers the school as having "gigantic brick walls and dark, cold rooms."[1]

She recalls that at the age of four, she had severe whooping cough and double pneumonia, and in the hospital, a doctor said, "It's too late. We've lost her" and pulled the covers up over her head. At that time, she saw a man with a beautiful white beard who cradled her until a nurse called out, "She's breathing again."[2]

She felt strong judgment from the Catholic Sisters that "the Indians . . . were heathens and sinners."[3] She later lived in a town where signs read, "No Indians or Dogs Allowed."[4] Much of what she came to know about God was rooted in fear. She also recalls an experience that she had in which she saw a light outside her window at night, and thinking that it was Jesus' Second Coming, she screamed. Eadie writes, "I had been taught that he would come as a thief in the night and would take the righteous with him and burn the wicked." It took her father several hours to calm her, and to convince her that she had only seen a search light advertising a carnival.[5]

As she grew older, she longed for a family and out of that longing, married at age fifteen and divorced at twenty-one after having given birth to four children, one of whom died. She later married and had three more children. Her last pregnancy was a difficult one and her physician had at one point even suggested an abortion, which she refused to have. She felt blessed, but "knew that something was missing." She writes, "My relationship with God seemed distant and filled with fear."[6]

Eadie states that she went to several churches, none of which satisfied her inner longing.

What Eadie does not tell her readers is that she has been a Mormon for years.

What Does She Say Happened to Her?

Eadie states that in the aftermath of a partial hysterectomy, she died and was taken to heaven in November of 1973. Her book relates what she saw.

Among the experiences she supposedly has in heaven, is an encounter with "two of my close friends before I came to earth."[7] They lead her on a tour of her new surroundings, in which she sees people working on manual looms creating garments for the new arrivals, a beautiful garden, and a reception room filled with pastel-garbed spiritual beings.

Eventually Eadie is encouraged to return to earth to complete her mission in life.

Eadie's book ends with the relaying of a vision she had of a little girl, the likeness of whom was exactly the same as that of a child she and her husband later adopted and with whom she claims to feel a very special spiritual kinship.

Her book was published some twenty years after she had the experience she describes. In the intervening years, she went through—by her own admission in the book—a deep depression and a bout with agoraphobia (to the point where she was too afraid to leave her own house and walk to her mailbox).

Key Discrepancies with the Word of God

What conclusions does Eadie reach about her experience that I question against the light of God's Word?

False Claim #1: We pre-existed our life on earth.

The "monks" who escort Eadie to heaven and who speak to her tell her that they have been with her for "eternities." She writes:

> "The fact of a pre-earth life crystallized in my mind, and I saw that death was actually a 'rebirth' into a greater life of understanding and knowledge that stretched forward and

backward through time. And I knew that these were my
choicest friends in that greater life and that they had chosen
to be with me."[8]

This concept of "foreknowledge" and prior existence is repeated several times in the book.

Eadie describes her death experience as beginning with a
deep rumbling, rushing sound. She feels drawn up into an almost
palpable great, whirling, black mass—feet first, with her head
slightly raised. She feels very calm and comes to sense other people and animals traveling with her in the blackness, although they
are at a distance and she has no personal connection to them.
Some of them linger in the "wonderful blackness."[9]

Next, she sees a pinpoint of light in the distance and she travels toward it at great speed until she is finally engulfed by the
brilliance of the figure of a man. She writes, "I felt his light blending into mine, literally, and I felt my light being drawn to his." She
feels great love and a sense of being home. And yet, she writes:

"I knew that he was aware of all my sins and faults, but that
they didn't matter right now . . . . I knew that I had known
him from the beginning, from long before my earth life,
because my spirit *remembered* him."[10]

She identifies this light-bathed person as Jesus and in her conversation with Him, she concludes that Jesus' mission was to
come into the world to teach love. She writes:

"This knowledge was more like remembering. Things were
coming back to me from long before my life on earth, things
that had been purposely blocked from me by a 'veil' of
forgetfulness at my birth."[11]

Much of what she states she understands about Heaven is
couched in terms of "remembering." She remembers, for example, the creation of the earth. She writes:

"All people as spirits in the pre-mortal world took part in the
creation of the earth. We were thrilled to be part of it. We
were with God, and we knew that he created us, that we were
his very own children. He was pleased with our development
and was filled with absolute love for each one of us. Also,
Jesus Christ was there . . . . Each spirit who was to come to
earth assisted in planning the conditions on earth, including

the laws of mortality which would govern us. These included the laws of physics as we know them, the limitations of our bodies, and spiritual powers that we would be able to access. We assisted God in the development of plants and animal life that would be here. Everything was created of spirit matter before it was created physically—solar systems, suns, moons, stars, planets, life upon the planets, mountains, rivers, seas . . . . It was important that I understand that we all assisted in creating our conditions here."[12]

Eadie claims that our bodies have an encoded memory of our eternal past. She says:

"I also learned that we do not have repeated lives on this earth; when we seem to 'remember' a past life, we are actually recalling memories contained in the cells (about an ancestor's life)."

There is no Scriptural base for such a statement. The Bible states that while we may suffer the effects of the "sins of the fathers, to the fourth generation," we can be redeemed from those propensities. In no place are we told that we can recall specific information about our ancestors. (See Exodus 20:5.)

The Bible does not teach that mankind existed prior to God's Creation, or that man assisted in the Creation.

The Bible does state that God knew about the existence of men and women "even before the foundation of the world." Mankind was God's plan prior to His initiating Creation. But, we were not party to that plan in its inception.

False Claim #2: We have chosen our own destinies, including our purpose on the earth.

A good portion of Eadie's book is devoted to a description of our purpose on this earth. She writes:

"I saw that in the pre-mortal world we knew about and even chose our missions in life. I understand that our stations in life are based upon the objectives of those missions. Through divine knowledge we knew what many of our tests and experiences would be, and we prepared accordingly. We bonded with others—family members and friends—to help us complete our missions."

She continues:

"We were given agency to act for ourselves here. Our own actions determine the course of our lives, and we can alter or redirect our lives at any time. I understood that his was crucial; God made the promise that he wouldn't intervene in our lives *unless we asked him.* And then through his omniscient knowledge he would help us attain our righteous desires. We were grateful for this ability to express our free will and to exercise its power. This would allow each of us to obtain great joy or to choose that which will bring us sadness. The choice would be ours through our decisions."[13]

Not only can we choose to come to earth, but according to Eadie, we can choose at which stage during pregnancy we want to enter our mother's womb.

Furthermore, we "are given the choice to remain on this earth until our bodies are buried or to move on, as I did, to the level to which our spirit had grown." She writes:

"Most spirits choose to remain on earth for a short time and comfort their loved ones; families are subject to much more grief than the departed one. Sometimes the spirits will remain longer if the loved ones are in despair. They remain to help the loved ones' spirits heal."[14]

The Bible certainly speaks of man's free will and his ability to function as free moral agents to choose right from wrong. What is wrong about Eadie's statement, however, is that our actions are not the sole determinant of the course of our lives. The Scriptures state that we are subject to influence by others and to circumstances that are not subject to our will: *He makes His sun rise on the evil and on the good, and sends rain on the just and on the unjust* (Matthew 5:45). There is much in life that brings us sadness or joy that is *not* of our choosing.

The Bible does not teach that a person becomes a comforting spirit to the living after he or she dies.

False Claim #3: Man's basic nature is goodness and light.

In facing a "council of men" in the afterlife, Eadie is allowed to review her life—in a series of hologram-like images that progress at a very rapid speed. She sees the ripple effect of both her bad deeds and good ones. As she sees how she had offended others, she sees the Savior stepping toward her and saying, "You're being too harsh on yourself." She concludes:

> "I realized that no real mistakes had been made in my life. Each experience was a tool for me to grow by."[15]

Eadie states:

> "Spiritually, we are various degrees of light—which is knowledge— and because of our divine, spiritual nature we are filled with the desire to do good."[16]

The Bible teaches that man does sin, and sin has deadly consequences. (See Romans 3:23.)

False Claim #4: Everything turns out alright for all people.

After her death experience, Eadie states that she stops by her home on her way to Heaven and invisible to her family, she sees that her children each "had their own free will to live their life as they chose. I knew that this free will should not be denied them . . . . There was no need for sorrow or fear. In the end each of my children would be all right."[17]

An Outcome-Based Eternity for All?

What about those who die as sinners, or atheists? Eadie writes:

> "Because of lack of knowledge or belief, some spirits are virtual prisoners of this earth. Some who die as atheists, or those who have bonded to the world through greed, bodily appetites, or other earthly commitments find it difficult to move on, and they become earth-bound. They often lack the faith and power to reach for, or in some cases even to recognize, the energy and light that pulls us toward God. These spirits stay on the earth until they learn to accept the greater power around them and to let go of the world. When I was in the black mass before moving toward the light, I felt the presence of such lingering spirits. They reside there as long as they want to in its love and warmth, accepting its healing influence, but eventually they learn to move on to accept the greater warmth and security of God."[18]

There is no reason, if one buys into this belief of Eadie's, for a person ever to make a commitment on earth to Christ Jesus. There is no judgment based on life's choices and behavior.

We hear a great deal these days about "outcome based educa-tion." The critics of that educational philosophy point to the fact that in outcome-based instruction, students never face failure. They continue to be praised, and promoted from grade to grade, until they stumble upon the right answers.

In many ways, the thinking presented by Eadie is tantamount to *outcome-based eternity*. A person will get there eventually . . . given enough time and an eventual, even reluctant acceptance of God's power.

False Claim #5: Jesus' primary mission on earth was to teach love.

Eadie claims that she "remembers" that Jesus came into the world to teach love. Eadie claims that she is shown in the after life that love is supreme, and we are truly nothing without love. We are here on earth primarily "to help each other, care for each other, to understand, forgive, and serve one another."[19]

The Bible says that man's highest purpose is to love God and have fellowship with Him. We are called to "obey" God in loving others; it is a commandment to fulfill our relationship with God. Jesus came to earth to be the sacrificial Lamb slain so that God might redeem man from his fallen state.

False Claim #6: All religions are equally good.

Eadie states:

"All religions upon the earth are necessary because there are people who need what they teach. People in one religion may not have a complete understanding of the Lord's gospel and never will have while in that religion. But that religion is used as a stepping stone to further knowledge. Each church fulfills spiritual needs that perhaps others cannot fill. No one church can fulfill everybody's needs at every level. As an individual raises his level of understanding about God and his own eternal progress, he might feel discontented with the teachings of his present church and seek a different philosophy or religion to fill that void. When this occurs he has reached another level of understanding and will long for further truth and knowledge, and for another opportunity to grow. And at every step of the way, these new opportunities to learn will be given."

She concludes:

"Having received this knowledge, I knew that we have no right to criticize any church or religion in any way. They are all precious and important in His sight. Very special people with important missions have been placed in all countries, in all religions, in every station of life, that they might touch others. There is a fullness of the gospel, but most people will not attain it here. In order to grasp this truth, we need to listen to the Spirit and let go of our egos."[20]

In this, Eadie strays from her Mormon theology since Mormonism contends that all other forms of religion are false.

The Bible contends that there is only One true and living God—not many gods. The Bible teaches that man is on dangerous ground when he attempts to create or follow other gods. Jesus said that He is *the* Way, *the* Truth, and *the* Life.

False Claim #7: A spirit of intelligence fills every particle of creation.

Eadie states:

"All things were created by spiritual power. Each element, each particle of creation, has intelligence in it, which intelligence is filled with spirit and life, and thus has the capacity for experiencing joy. Each element is independent to act on its own, to respond to the laws and forces around it; when God speaks to these elements, they respond, and they have joy in obeying his word."[21]

In seeing a beautiful garden, Eadie says, "Each drop from the waterfall had its own intelligence and purpose," and in examining a rose, she says, "I felt the rose's presence around me, as if I were actually inside and part of the flower." She concludes, "My joy was absolutely full again! I felt God in the plant, in me, his love pouring into us. We were all one!"[22]

This is pure pantheism—God in every cell of nature. The cells in a tree trunk do not have a mind of their own to choose to follow God's laws. Rather, they are created by God to follow His laws . . . period!

This link of thinking is at the root of Buddhism and its ying and yang philosophy of energy. Eadie is right on target with Buddhist thinking when she writes:

"Positive energy is basically just what we would think it is: light, goodness, kindness, love, patience, charity, hope, and so on. And negative energy is just what we would think it is: darkness, hatred, fear (Satan's greatest tool), unkindness, intolerance, selfishness, despair, discouragement, and so on."[23]

Eadie claims that:

"Simply by thinking positive thoughts and speaking positive words we attract positive energy. I saw that this is the case. I saw different energies surround different people. I saw how a person's words actually affect the energy field around him."[24]

The Bible fact is, however, that the manipulation of energy is not the end-all and be-all of our existence. We are not created to exercise energy, but to have fellowship with God and to do His bidding in our lives. We are created for His glory, not for the channeling of "vibes."

Further, Eadie describes laws as spiritual, physical, and universal and claims:

"When we recognize these laws and learn how to use their positive and negative forces, we will have access to power beyond comprehension. When we break one of these laws, going against that which is the natural order, we have sinned."[25]

It is not a sin to defy the law of gravity (and to fly in an airplane). A sin is something that breaches our relationship with God and causes us to move further away from His presence rather than closer to Him. A sin is ultimately choosing our own way over His way. The root of all sin is pride—thinking and acting as if we *can* control our own destiny, set our own agenda, decide our own fate.

Eadie describes human perfection this way:

"To become as perfect as mortal being can become, we need to bring the mind, body, and spirit into total harmony. To become perfect in the spirit, we must add to that harmony Christlike love and righteousness."[26]

According to God's Word, we do not do the work of perfecting ourselves. We simply are not capable of it! In fact, logic defies it. How can an imperfect creation make itself perfect? It can't! It takes the perfect and divine Holy Spirit indwelling us for us to be made whole.

While it is true that we are to *seek* to become perfect as He is perfect (Matthew 5:48)—which means to become whole even as

He is whole—our seeking leads us to a recognition that we must rely totally and completely on the Holy Spirit to do what we ultimately cannot do. We cannot achieve harmony of mind, body, and spirit on our own—no matter how much we exercise, how much education we attain, and how much we strive to love and be good. Our perfection is His work . . . and the Scriptures teach us that He is not only the Author, but the Finisher of that work. (See Hebrews 12:2.)

The Scriptures teach us:

> *Now may the God of peace who brought up our Lord Jesus from the dead, that great Shepherd of the sheep, through the blood of the everlasting covenant, make you complete in every good work to do His will, working in you what is well pleasing in His sight, through Jesus Christ, to whom be glory forever and ever* (Hebrews 13:21).

It is the shed blood of Jesus that brings us to a point of completion. He is the One who works in us . . . not so that we can control positive and negative energy, but so that we can do what HE desires for us to do.

False Claim #9: Imagination is the key to reality.

Eadie claims that we come to earth with our powers of imagination already well developed and then, using that power of imagination, we create our own lives, "to exercise our gifts and experience both failure and success. We are to use our free will to expand and magnify our lives."[27]

The Bible says we are to magnify the Lord and put our faith in Him—obeying Him, worshiping Him, and trusting Him to unfold HIS purpose in our lives.

False Claim #10: Every person is "engineered" for eternal life.

Eadie claims that she "was shown that the cells of our bodies were engineered to provide life indefinitely. They were programmed in the beginning to regenerate themselves, to replace old cells that had become ineffective or damaged so that life would not end." She acknowledges that the decisions made in the Garden of Eden "created conditions that make eternal life in mortality impossible." Still, she concludes that "there is still the power within us, using faith and positive energy, to alter our cells so that we can be healed—if it is right." Although she states that "we must remember that God's will is always involved in healing," she also claims:

"Positive self-talk begins the healing process. Once we have identified the illness or problem, we need to start verbalizing its remedy. We need to remove thoughts of the illness from our minds and begin concentrating on its cure. Then we need to verbalize this cure, letting our words add to the power of our thoughts. This creates an excitement in the intelligences around us, and they then go into motion, working to heal us. I understood that this verbalization can best be done in prayer. If it is right that we be healed, God will then assist us in the healing process."[28]

This line of thinking leads to at least two major conclusions that are not supported in God's Word.

(1) We might conclude that it is God's will that some be healed and others not be healed. The Scriptures depict, however, a loving God whose desire it is that all be healed. It is not God who keeps people from being healed, but the enemy of our souls—the devil, and the sin that he promotes and prompts.

(2) We might conclude from Eadie's statements that it is up to us to "think good thoughts" and "say the magic words" in order to put the healing process into motion. Healing flows from the Holy Spirit without any coaching from us. The Bible has numerous examples of people being healed by Jesus who didn't say or do anything on their behalf.

To think that we are responsible for our own healing can also lead us to a false thinking that, when we are healed, we have done the work! That definitely is not the Bible point of view. Man does not heal. God does.

Eadie also makes this amazing statement:

"I saw that most of us had selected the illnesses we would suffer, and for some, the illness that would end our lives . . . . We were very willing, even anxious, as spirits to accept all of our ailments, illnesses, and accidents here to help better ourselves spiritually."[29]

This attributes some type of redemptive power to sickness—that we are made better or more spiritual through illness. That conclusion cannot be supported by Scripture. Rather, the New

Testament presents a clear message that the shed blood of Christ Jesus is what redeems us from sin and that "by His stripes we are healed." (See Isaiah 53:5.)

I personally have known dozens of people who allowed illness—either their own or that experienced by a loved one—to cause them to become bitter against God, much to their spiritual detriment.

I also reject categorically her claim that we choose the ailments, illnesses, and accidents that we experience in life. Sickness and injury often come quite apart from our behavior. Many people are maimed and even die because they simply are in the wrong place at the wrong time. Others inherit genetic propensities toward certain illnesses. We live in a fallen world.

If there's benefit in suffering in and of itself, then there would be no reason in Jesus Christ's suffering in order to heal us!

Much of what she says is related to the "power of positive thinking." She openly states:

"Because I knew that all creation begins with thoughts, I also knew that the creation of sin, and of guilt, and of despair, and of hope, and of love all start within us. All healing comes from within. All misery comes from within. We can create our own spiral of despair, or we can create a trampoline of happiness and attainment. Our thoughts have tremendous power."[30]

This line of thinking quickly comes to a conclusion that "if you feel guilty, change your mind." That, in turn, causes people to justify their sin, to claim that sin doesn't matter, or to completely dismiss the idea of sin from their minds.

The Bible fact is that all have sinned and come short of God's glory. We are sinners, and in sin we are born. (See Romans 3:23, 1 John 1:7.) Our thoughts may be powerful in the making of choices to move toward God or away from him, but they do not change the facts of sin, guilt, and despair. Only God can totally cleanse us from sin. Once He has, we then, and only then, are *free* to forgive ourselves.

Other Non-Bible Contradictions

Apart from biblical accuracy, there are several points in Eadie's book that don't connect logically for me. Some of these contradictions are blatant.

Answered or Not?

In one section on prayer she states that all prayers are eventually answered and in the very next sentence states that many (but not all) of the insincere prayers of repetition are not heard.

What Progression?

Eadie claims that we choose to come to earth in order to "progress" spiritually, and that we do so with joy, and yet many people apparently choose dead-end lives, or choose only to live for a few hours, while others apparently don't achieve their purposes and live in a state of after-death limbo for awhile. Precisely what it is that a person gains by coming to earth is never clear to me? Apparently it is to advance from one spiritual level or stage to the next, but the criterion for that is never spelled out. Pre-earth spirits mingle freely with post-earth spirits in Eadie's heaven. No differentiation is made among them. So . . . why earth?

In one chapter she describes seeing a drunken bum who had bonded in the "before life" with a spirit who became a prominent attorney. Precisely what is to be gained by these spirit beings choosing to become a drunk or an attorney is never clearly spelled out, other than that "the drunk had sacrificed his time on earth for the benefit of" the attorney in reminding the attorney of his need for others and in motivating him toward a good deed.[31]

Eadie's Take on Angels

How does Betty Eadie regard angels? From my reading, I conclude that she considers angels to be "some of the righteous spirit children of our Father in Heaven (who) did not choose to come here to this earth. They have selected to stay as spirits with God and act as guardian angels for people here" or to become "Warring Angels" who do battle for us against Satan and his angels. The warring angels she describes as being "giant men, very muscularly built, with a wonderful countenance about them . . . dressed like warriors, in head dress and armor" . . . who "moved more swiftly than other angels" and who seem to have more confidence than other angels.[32]

In no place in the Scriptures do we have the notion that angels chose their role in creation. Neither do we have a depiction of offensive angels as being armor-clad or in some way more powerful than defensive angels.

The angels are motivated by prayer. Eadie sees:

"many lights shooting up from the earth like beacons. Some were very broad and charged into heaven like broad laser beams. Others resembled the illumination of small pen lights, and some were mere sparks. I was surprised as I was told that these beams of power were the prayers of people on earth. I saw angels rushing to answer the prayers. They were organized to give as much help as possible . . . . They always responded to the brighter, larger prayers first."[33]

What About the Demons?

Eadie does acknowledge the existence of spiritual beings other than angels.

Shortly after Eadie returns to earth, which is at her own volition after she is given more insight into her mission on earth, she claims that she began to recall her experiences in the afterlife and then she writes:

"I was about to close my eyes and drift off to sleep when I caught a movement by the door. I tried to raise up on an elbow to get a better look, and I saw a creature poke its head in. I cringed backward in fear. Then another one appeared. They were creatures of the most hideous and grotesque appearance imaginable. Five of them entered the doorway, and I was all but paralyzed with fear. They appeared to be half-human half-animal—short, muscular beings with long claws or fingernails and savage, though human, faces. They came toward me, snarling, growling, and hissing. They were full of hate, and I knew that they intended to kill me. I tried to scream but was either too weak or too paralyzed with fear to move. I was helpless as they came to within five or six feet of the bed.

"Suddenly a huge dome of light, almost like glass, fell over me, and the creatures lunged forward, seeming to recognize its threat to them. The dome protected me as they frantically flailed at it and tried to climb on it to get a better vantage point.

But the dome was too high to climb on, and they became more frustrated. They shrieked and cursed and hissed and began spitting. I was horrified as I felt trapped in my bed. The creatures were persistent, and I didn't know if the dome could hold up. I didn't even know what it was.

"When I thought I could bear it no more and my fear seemed about to overwhelm me, my three adoring angels, the monks, entered the room again, and the creatures fled. The angels said not to fear, that I was protected. They told me that the devil was angry at my decision to return to earth and that he had sent these powerful demons to destroy me. They explained that the dome would remain around me for the rest of my life. They said that the demons might try to get at me again and that I might see or hear them in the future, but the dome would protect me. 'Also know,' they said, 'that we are always near you to help and encourage you.' Moments later, to my sadness, the monks were gone."[34]

Strong Background Influences

Given Betty Eadie's background and the surgery she had just undergone, I do not find it in the least unusual that she:

- would see "men" at her death who were robed with light brown robes in a way that made her think of them as monks,[35] or that she would see pastel-garbed people who are friends[36]
- has a great sense of being "home" and loved in the afterlife[37]
- asks God why there are so many churches on the earth[38]
- concludes that her fear of God kept her from loving God[39]
- sees Eve as wanting "to become a mother desperately enough that she was willing to risk death to obtain it."[40]

Some of Eadie's concepts seem very Catholic. The warm embracing darkness some experience at death—through which they move slowly as they progress toward a state of being in which they are acceptable for entry into the next stage of their spiritual development—sounds a great deal like purgatory. Mormonism, however, also advocates a purgatorial progression. Hell is not a possibility for human beings, except perhaps for apostate Mormons.

Most of what Eadie states, however, is a direct reflection of her Mormonism.

The Mormon Influence

Although this is not a book about cults, I believe it is important that you know several things about Mormonism since they help explain part of Eadie's experience:

Mormonism not only claims to be authentic Christianity, but it alleges that it is the only true Christian religion. As a result of its self-claims, million of people, including Christians, think that Mormonism is a Christian denomination. It is not.

Mormonism differs from Christianity on nearly every major point of doctrine and foundation of authority.

The Book of Mormon and its so-called translator, Joseph Smith, are the central elements in the Church of Jesus Christ of Latter-day Saints—as opposed to the Bible and God the Father, Son, and Holy Spirit. Joseph Smith was an occultist who believed the entirety of Christendom was in deep ignorance and who claimed that because he had the Holy Ghost, he was "learned, and knew more than all the world put together."[41]

Mormonism contends that:

- the Bible is unreliable and incomplete
- God is finite, morally imperfect, always evolving, sexual, and polytheistic
- Jesus is a created god who was not virgin-born and who earned his salvation
- salvation is by works and is possible after death
- death is "purgatorial" involving three celestial kingdoms which are almost universalistic.

Specifically, Mormonism teaches regarding the afterlife that there is a "general salvation" that is given to all men. All people are resurrected from the dead and are given immortality. General salvation is given without a person seeking it. Individual salvation is something different. This, according to Mormon teaching, is something that a person acquires by faith and good works. The degree to which a person has achieved personal righteousness determines which of three "kingdoms of glory" he or she inherits at death. Most of humanity won't get beyond the lowest level.

Lukewarm Mormons go to the second level and worthy Mormons to the highest.

Mormons reject the biblical teaching of justification by grace through faith alone. (See Ephesians 2:8–9 and Philippians 3:9). They adhere to a position of "I have power to save myself." Sins are only forgiven by our own law-keeping. Mormons categorically reject the atoning death of Jesus on the Cross. From their perspective, Jesus was just another mortal who earned his righteousness and his subsequent place in heaven. What he did, we can all do.

Mormons believe that Jesus was the first and foremost of subsequent billions of spirit children, conceived through sexual intercourse between male and female "earth gods." His brother was Satan. Jesus came to earth to work out His own salvation just as all people must do, and he gained power in heaven after his resurrection. He is not seen as unique. Every exalted man will attain the same godhood that Christ now experiences, assuming, of course, that he has been a good Mormon.

Mormons believe that good spirits routinely visit the earth to give counsel and comfort, serve as guardian angels, prepare people for death, summon mortals into the spirit world, and escort the dying through the veil of death. Eadie speaks several times of a "veil."

Mormonism holds that man has a pre-existent, eternal spirit with the potential to earn godhood. Further, Mormonism holds that all pre-existent spirits helped God create the universe. Bruce McConkie, the leading Mormon theologian, has written: "We are the offspring of God. He is our eternal father; we have also an eternal mother . . . We were born as the spirit children of celestial parents long before the foundations of this world were laid."[42]

Mormonism places a high interest in and respect for spiritistic revelations and contacts. Ankerberg and Weldon note in their book *Cult Watch* that "from its inception Mormonism accepted spiritistic revelations from the so-called dead and other spirits." This led to a priority being placed upon the dead for spiritual assistance. The end result has been that contacting the dead has become a "theological necessity" within the Mormon Church. All of the major leaders in the Mormon religion through the decades have been people who claimed to be in contact with the spirit world of the afterlife.[42]

All Mormon contact with the dead is considered to be a godly practice. In part this is because death is seen as a step upward.

We should note, too, that the type of experience Eadie describes would put her in very good company, and earn for her a very good reputation, within Mormon circles.

A Co-Mingling of Truth and Fantasy

One of the key principles about deception is that the best deception is the one that is closest to the truth.

Betty Eadie's book is a prime example of truth and falsehood interwoven so tightly and cleverly that one who is attuned to the Truth will only see truth. The aspects of her writing that ring true with God's Word tend to overshadow those passages that are blatantly in contradiction with God's Word. The net result is that many Christians conclude that the entire message is true. It is only the mature and discerning believer in Christ Jesus who will wrestle with such a description long enough to ferret out truth from falsehood.

Let me give you an example. In talking about the importance of love, Eadie writes:

"We are here to have love for every person born on earth. Their earthly form might be black, yellow, brown, handsome, ugly, thin, fat, wealthy, poor, intelligent, or ignorant, but we are not to judge by these appearances. Each spirit has the capacity to be filled with love and eternal energy. At the beginning, each possessed some degree of light and truth that can be more fully developed. We cannot measure these things. Only God knows the heart of man, and only God can judge perfectly. He knows our spirits; we see only temporary strengths and weaknesses. Because of our own limitations, we can seldom look into the heart of man.

"I knew that anything we do to show love is worthwhile: a smile, a word of encouragement, a small act of sacrifice. We grow by these actions. Not all people are lovable, but when we find someone difficult for us to love, it is often because they remind us of something within ourselves that we don't like. I learned that we must love our enemies—let go of anger, hate, envy, bitterness, and the refusal to forgive. These things destroy the spirit. We will have to account for how we treat others."[43]

On the surface, this sounds like good Christ-centered teaching. I've underlined below, however, those passages that are NOT what Christ taught, and in parenthesis next to the underlined passage, the reason why not.

We are *here* to have love for every person born on earth. (Showing love for others is not our primary purpose on the earth. We are, however, to show love.) Their earthly form might be black, yellow, brown, handsome, ugly, thin, fat, wealthy, poor, intelligent, or ignorant, but we are not to judge by these appearances. Each spirit has the capacity to be filled with *love and eternal energy.* (Each human spirit has the capacity to be filled with God's Holy Spirit. Apart from His indwelling presence, we cannot have divine "agape" love, or have eternal life.) *At the beginning, each possessed some degree of light and truth that can be more fully developed.* (We are born in spiritual darkness and sin, but with a measure of faith to ACCEPT God's invitation to redemption.) We cannot measure these things. Only God knows the heart of man, and only God can judge perfectly. He knows our spirits; we see only temporary strengths and weaknesses. Because of our own limitations, we *can seldom look into the heart of man.* (God's Word says that we cannot know the heart of man.)

I knew that anything we do to show love is worthwhile: a smile, a word of encouragement, a small act of sacrifice. *We grow by these actions.* (Eadie seems to mean that we grow toward a divine nature in this way. God's Word says that we grow in our inner being as a result of God's grace, that is, His working in us. He makes us more like Jesus, and in that, we are enabled to love. Our love does not enable us to become more like Jesus. The process is exactly opposite to which Eadie seems to allude.) Not all people are lovable, but when we find someone difficult for us to love, it is often because they remind us of something within ourselves that we don't like. I learned that we must love our enemies— let go of anger, hate, envy, bitterness, and the refusal to forgive. *These things destroy the spirit. We will have to account for how we treat others."* (Most of all, we will have to account for how we

have responded to Christ Jesus. That is the ultimate accounting we
will do. Sin destroys the spirit, and sin involves more than a failure
to love our enemies. It is rooted in a failure to respond to God's love.)

Hot on the heels of this statement about love, Eadie writes
these words:

> "Upon receiving the plan of creation, we sang in rejoicing
> and were filled with God's love. We were filled with joy as we
> saw the growth we would have here on earth and the joyous
> bonds we would create with each other.

> "Then we watched as the earth was created. We watched as
> our spirit brothers and sisters entered physical bodies for
> their turns upon the earth, each experiencing the pains and
> joys that would help them progress. I distinctly remember
> watching the American pioneers crossing the continent and
> rejoicing as they endured their difficult tasks and completed
> their missions. I knew that only those who needed that
> experience were placed there. I saw the angels rejoicing for
> those who endured their trails and succeeded and grieving
> for those who failed. I saw that some failed because of their
> own weaknesses, and some failed because of the weaknesses
> of others. I sensed that many of us who were not there would
> not have been up to the tasks, that we would have made lousy
> pioneers, and we would have been the cause of more
> suffering for others. Likewise, some of the pioneers and
> people from other eras could not have endured the trials
> of today. We are where we need to be.

> "As all of these things came to me, I understood the perfection
> of the plan. I saw that we all volunteered for our positions
> and stations in the world, and that each of us is receiving
> more help than we know. I saw the unconditional love of
> God, beyond any earthly love, radiating from him to all his
> children. I saw the angels standing near us, waiting to assist
> us, rejoicing in our accomplishments and joys. But above all, I
> saw Christ, the Creator and Savior of the earth, my friend, and
> the closest friend any of us can have. I seemed to melt with
> joy as I was held in his arms and comforted—home at last."[44]

Yes, Betty, the unconditional love of God does radiate to all
people.

But no, Betty, we did not choose our positions and stations in the world. Our destinies and purpose are of God's design.

No, Betty, the angels do not rejoice in our accomplishments, but in our salvation.

No, Betty, Christ is not the Savior of the "earth," but of men and women who accept Him as their Savior.

No, Betty, most of us are not "where we need to be." Where we need to be is in right relationship with Christ Jesus, not in accomplishing a particular "difficult task."

What *Really* Happened to Betty Eadie?

How do I explain what happened to Betty Eadie?

I can't explain it fully. I'm not sure medical science or theology has all the answers in this area.

What I think as one human being to another is that she had a very powerful and realistic-seeming hallucination, dream, vision, or some other type of mental processing in the wake of anesthesia and in a time of great pain and recovery from a difficult surgery. A physician later confirmed to her that she had hemorrhaged during the surgery and again after it. I conclude that she went into shock as a result of that hemorrhage since that is often what happens. When the doctor and nurses found her in that state, the physician told her they had given her an injection, medication, and I.V.'s and she had returned to life. In so doing, the medical team apparently had some idea that she was alive, rather than dead. There was no mention of cardiac intervention. In sum, both Eadie's body and mind had been through a highly traumatic experience and I believe her resulting experience stems from the trauma.

As in most of our dreams, the images in her story seem to run together—and they cover the gamut from the sublime to the grotesque and frightening. Many of the elements can be tied to her own past, and her preconceptions, fears, and beliefs. She had both a hideous nightmare and a glorious vision.

In the end, it is her experience.

Her story in no way means that all people would have such an experience, or that people undergoing even similar experiences would draw the same conclusions she has drawn.

Where I fault Eadie is that she didn't follow up her experience with a sincere look at God's Word, which is the Holy Bible, *not* the Book of Mormon. She assumed, and seems to be content that we will also assume, that everything she thinks she experienced lines up with God's divine plan, purpose, and message to mankind. She believes that what she experienced is "truth." She says of her own experience that it was "sacred."[45]

No person has a corner on the "truth." We acquire bits of truth in our life *precept upon precept, line upon line . . . here a little, and there a little* according to Isaiah 28:10. Whenever we think we have acquired a precept, line, or "bit" of the truth, we are to check it out against the whole of Scripture. We are to talk about it with Bible-believing and Holy Spirit led brothers and sisters in Christ Jesus.

As I have stated earlier in this chapter, our spiritual experiences must be measured against the light of the Holy Bible.

If Betty Eadie had done that, she would have found that some of what she experienced is corroborated in Scripture, and that other parts are far afield. Rather, she has taken her entire experience to *be* truth, and she presents it as such.

The Scriptures tell us that Jesus alone embodied the Truth of God in His person (John 8:46). If we are to know the Truth, we must look to Jesus and live in His example and by His power. In Betty Eadie's vision of an afterlife, Jesus is only one part of the Truth. In reality, He is the complete Truth. Everything of value and importance begins and ends in Him.

Why the Desire to Believe Her?

I am not nearly so concerned with what Betty Eadie experienced as I am by the fact that so many people seem to *want* to believe her story.

What is it about her tale that people are so eager to believe?

I personally am not at all interested in a heaven with old looms and manual labor! I have no desire to float along feet first in blackness, or to experience the interior workings of a flower. I do not want to help corral spiritual beings and launch them toward life on earth.

I believe that what compels people to buy into Eadie's story is their own desire for a *no-fault* afterlife, and to exalt their own importance as human beings.

Eadie presents a picture in which man doesn't die, and in which he has total choice between good and evil. In her vision, we are tantamount to gods. We helped with creation. We choose to come to earth. We choose to go back at our death (within parameters). We have a built-in life-expectancy of eternity. All of life turns out fine in the end. We live in the light forever and very possibly, whisk ourselves off to other planets and galaxies for further spiritual progression.

The lie undergirding this thinking isn't far from what a certain serpent told a woman named Eve in a garden named Eden: *You will not surely die . . . your eyes will be opened, and you will be like God* (Genesis 3:4).

15

Death and Near-Death Experiences: When Are We Really Out of the Body?

BETTY Eadie, of course, is not the only person who claims to have visited a beautiful place in the afterlife and returned to earth to tell the story. A number of these experiences have been reported, most within the last thirty years.

These experiences have come to be called "near-death experiences" (often abbreviated NDE). They have been studied by medical researchers, written about by the New Age, and talked about extensively in today's media.

What do we really know about them?

To begin, we know that the term didn't even exist until 1975 when it was first coined by Dr. Raymond Moody, author of a book titled *Life After Life.* Moody described a mystical experience that happens to *some* people who *almost die* and called it a near-death experience.

We also know that a large number of people seem to have had this experience.

A Gallop poll conducted in 1982 reported that an estimated eight million people had near-death experiences at some point in their life. The number today has been estimated as high as eleven million.

What Happens in a Near-Death Experience?

In a "typical good clinical death experience," a certain sequence of events is generally followed, which is summarized below. You should note prior to reading this list, however, that not all people who report near-death experiences report all of these stages. The person:

1. Senses he is dying and begins to feel blissful.
2. Leaves his body, is surprised to see the body remaining behind, and has a heightened sense of euphoria.
3. Is unable to communicate with the living but may recall details of the room, various procedures being done to their bodies, or what people say.
4. Enters an area of darkness, commonly described as a tunnel.
5. Moves at a speed that increases and then encounters a light. Then moves even closer to the light.
6. Often encounters a "being of light," known or unknown. The person may have a sense of blending with this light Sometimes the being encountered is someone from the person's past, or it may be a religious entity (perhaps even Jesus). The being of light always seems very familiar and loving.
7. Enters a new world, usually a garden. The person often reports hearing music, singing, or beautiful sound.
8. May experience a panoramic life review. Thought seems to replace a need for speech.
9. May have an encounter with relatives or friends who have died previously.
10. Enters a world that is exquisite beyond words, filled with beauty and sights that cannot be described.
11. May encounter a barrier, such as a fence, wall, or river. Attempting to pass this barrier, he is often told to return to life or that it is time to go back to the body.
12. Returns to the body, often with an understanding that this was "not their time."

People who have this experience are often reported as having no fear of death. They sometimes but not always have a heightened interest in spiritual matters, but in some cases, they are less dogmatically religious than they were before the experience.

The overwhelming conclusion reported by many is that death itself seems to be painless, with no sense of choking or smothering

Some recall the experience as euphoric, others as a state of "non-feeling."

Early and Late Stages of Death

As we move into a discussion of the death process, it is important for you to know that physicians now make a difference between the early and late stages of death.

- *Clinical death* occurs when both heartbeat and breathing have stopped but life can be restored by CPR or resuscitation, things man can do. Clinical death is an early, and often reversible, stage of death.

- *Biological death*—or final death—occurs fully when the brain and body cells have died and rigor mortis sets in.

Once the clinical death process begins—perhaps with cardiac arrest or lung suffocation—life must be restored within a matter of minutes in most cases. Otherwise, the sensitive brain cells begin to die. Brain cells actually begin to die after four to eight minutes without blood flow. The death of brain cells is followed by gradual death of the body cells. This results in rigor mortis, the stiffness of biological death. At that point, death is irreversible by medical means. A reverse would truly require a resurrection, not a resuscitation. Man cannot resurrect—either himself, or someone else—in his own power.

As recently as thirty years ago, very few people were resuscitated after heartbeat and breathing had stopped. In the last few decades, however, great strides have been made in the use of injected medicines, electric shock, and CPR techniques, so that a good many people on the earth today have been resuscitated from "early death" experiences. Many of these were the victims of heart attacks or accidents (such as drowning or electrical accidents).

It is vitally important as you read about near-death experiences that you recognize that there is a difference between:

- resuscitation—which can happen prior to biological death, and
- resurrection—which overcomes biological death.

Resurrection is extremely rare. The Bible only mentions people returning to life on a few occasions. In the instances of Jesus raising the young man at Nain, and in the instance of Jairus' daughter, the procedure *may* have been one of resuscitation. In the case of Lazarus, who had been dead and in the tomb for four days, the case is one of resurrection. Jesus' own rising from the dead is also clearly an act of resurrection. (See Luke 7:11–15; Mark 5, 22, 39; John 11:14; Matthew 27:50.)

In the Old Testament, Elijah and Elisha both were involved in raising people from the dead. We do not know if these were resuscitations or resurrections. They may have been either.

The Bible does not distinguish between clinical death and final biological death. In part, that is because a clinical death process could rarely be reserved in ancient times. Once a person started to die . . . they died. It is only in recent times that man has been able to resuscitate using medical means.

The great likelihood is that most of those who have had near-death experiences have not actually died, biologically speaking, but they may have experienced "clinical death" and been resuscitated from it.

One thing we need to keep in mind is that a "near-death" experience may be very different from an "after-death" experience. Only the dead actually experience life beyond death. That realm is one that will always require faith.

It is interesting to note that *none* of the people who were raised from the dead in the Bible are recorded as having described their experiences in the afterlife. Lazarus isn't quoted about what he saw or did. Jesus didn't talk about His own in-the-grave experience. We do not know what the young man in Nain, Jairus' daughter, or any of the other "raised" experienced.

Apparently, God is content with it to be that way. We are to live in the here and now, with both feet planted firmly on this earth. The future is apparently best left in the future.

We Don't Die As We Did in the Past

Centuries ago, predeath visions were considered a part of the dying process. A French historian, Philippe Aries, has documented that before 1000 A.D. people had entirely different death experiences than people have today. When the person felt his time was near, he usually reviewed his life, asked forgiveness of those he might have wronged, wept in sorrow at leaving loved ones, and often had visions of God or of seeing those who had died previously. Dying people often had a strong sense that they had reached "their time to die." This was considered normal dying behavior.

Today, the process of dying is often quite different. People are rarely at home surrounded by their loved ones. Rather, they are often in hospitals hooked up to all kinds of machines and under the influence of strong medication. The medical community does its utmost to resuscitate and to prolong life.

Two sociologists, Barney Glaser and Anselm Strauss, have identified certain unwritten rules that physicians, nurses, family members and dying patients seem to follow: no mention of topics about appearance, the future, or medications. No tears are allowed in the presence of the patient. When things go awry, everyone pretends that nothing is amiss. Everyone tries to keep interaction normal, pretending that everything is alright. All interactions are kept brief.

It's as if the death process itself is being denied. And yet, death is a part of life. It faces all of us in one form or another.

I am not being critical of modern medical practices. Surely a number of people are alive today and living fruitful, fulfilling lives because of the resuscitation efforts of the medical community. We may well be robbing others, however, of a peaceful and more "natural" death experience.

The near-death experiences may not at all be in God's plan. They may be a result of man's intervention.

We Are Curious Nonetheless!

In spite of the fact that God's Word ignores the intricacies of the death process, or perhaps because God's Word is silent on the subject . . . .

In spite of the fact that no person who has truly been biologically dead has returned to life to talk about it, or perhaps because of that fact . . . .

We are a people very curious about the death process! It is because we are so curious that books such as those by Betty Eadie rise to become best-sellers.

The latest book along these lines to hit the best-seller list is Dannion Brinkley's *Saved by the Light*.

Brinkley claims to have had not one but two near-death experiences, the first as the result of a lightning strike in 1975, and the second after going into cardiac arrest while suffering from pneumonia.

Most of the book deals with Brinkley's first near-death experience, which occurred after he was struck by lightning while talking on a telephone during a thunderstorm. His heart stopped, but he was revived twenty-eight minutes later in a morgue.

As with other reports, he claims to have seen his body and then entered into another state where he felt engulfed by peace and tranquility. He then moved through a swirling tunnel, and encountered a silver form appearing like a silhouette through mist. The Being of Light engulfed him and he had a life review experience. The Being of Light, however, was regarded by Brinkley as a "friendly counsel, letting me feel for myself the pain and the pleasure I had caused others. Instead of feeling shame and anguish, I was bathed in the love that embraced me through the light, and had to give nothing in return."[1]

He then hears and feels energy fields, which he floats through to a garden setting and then he writes:

"Like wingless birds, we swept into a city of cathedrals. These cathedrals were made entirely of a crystalline substance that glowed with a light that shone powerfully from within. We stood before one. I felt small and insignificant next to this architectural masterpiece. Clearly this had been built by angels to show the grandeur of God, I thought. It had spires as high and pointed as those of the great cathedrals of France, and walls as massive and powerful as those of the Mormon Tabernacle in Salt Lake City. The walls were made of large glass bricks that glowed from within. These structures were not related to a specific religion of any kind. They were a monument to the glory of God."[2]

Again, Overtones of Mormonism

Although he doesn't ever say so directly, I assume that Brinkley is a Mormon. Later in the book he writes about the Mormon beliefs regarding near-death experiences and says:

"Their findings match everything that happened to me. They believe that upon the death of the physical body, the spirit retains the five senses of sight, feeling, taste, hearing, and smell. They feel that death leaves us free of illness and disability and that the spirit body can move with great speed, see in many different directions at the same time, and communicate in ways other than speech . . . . Many of the Mormon elders have had near-death experiences or gathered detailed accounts of them from fellow churchgoers."[3]

The future is revealed to Brinkley in a series of twelve boxes which open to show him fully dimensional pictures. One set of boxes dealt with visions of a demoralized America, another set with strife and hatred in the Middle East, and other boxes with nuclear destruction, a powerful Russian leader advocating environmental clean-up, a battle between China and Russia, economic earthquakes and a desert storm, and genetic engineering.

He is also shown seven rooms: a therapy room, a massage clinic, a sensory-deprivation chamber, a biofeedback room, a room for psychic abilities, a room for music therapy, and a reflection chamber. The purpose of these rooms supposedly was to bring a person into a deep state of relaxation so he might be guided into a spiritual realm. Brinkley is told by the Beings that he is to create centers that have these rooms, so that "people could come to reduce stress in their lives."[4]

The Beings tell Brinkley he must return to fulfill this mission and he returns to his body.

Once back from his electrocution and near-death experience, Brinkley had trouble putting reality together. He writes, "reality came in pieces like those of a jigsaw puzzle."[5] He continued to have visions in which he saw himself returning to the Crystal City and attending classes taught by the Beings of Light.

He later sought counsel from, was interviewed by, and worked with Raymond Moody, who is the author of *Life After Life*.

As a result of these experiences, Brinkley found that he could foretell the future and read the minds of strangers. He also tells of experiences in which he goes into trances and sees events in the past—and even enters past events as a "player" in the scenes. He found he was able to predict songs on the radio and foretell the scores of football games. He describes more of his experiences as being like being a cassette of a home movie popped into his head.

In 1989, Brinkley had a second near-death experience. The lightning strike had left his heart with only about fifty percent of normal pumping ability. A bout with viral pneumonia caused aortic valve damage and during the course of heart surgery to repair the valve, Brinkley again encounters a Being of Light, has a "life review"—which he reports as a much better experience than the first one—and this time, spends more time in the garden, where he sees beautiful flowers and "radiant earthlings."[6] He hears a chant that sounds like ALLAHOM to him and he feels himself blending completely with the heavenly realm. Then he takes a deep breath and is back in his body.

Brinkley is now working to establish the centers he saw during the first experience. The first one is in South Carolina, with its focus to help the terminally ill face death. He says:

"Thirteen Beings of Light told me to build these centers. They put it on me. They didn't ask if I wanted to build them, they just told me that this is what I had to do. When I pass, I will be with them forever. Knowing that, I am determined to pull it off."[7]

Brinkley has appeared on Russian television where he claims to have spoken about "spiritual capitalism—that all people should be free to worship the way they choose. There are many paths to righteousness . . . and that is good news for all of us, since no one seems to be on the same path, as far as I can tell."[8]

No Agreement on the Death Process

In many ways, Brinkley's book is in agreement with Eadie's. In other ways, it differs sharply. Both are heavily laced with the same Mormon underpinnings as far as I can tell. The discrepancies between his book and what the Bible teaches are along the same lines as those in the Eadie book.

What Brinkley's experiences do point out is that the death process isn't always the same. His first and second dying processes are actually quite different.

They differ also with those reported by other people.

Variations in Death Experiences

Dr. Kenneth Ring, in a book titled *Life at Death* published in 1980, noted that people who are "sickness prone" tend to experience deeper levels of near-death experiences. Those who attempt suicide rarely report the various stages reported by those who have had lingering illness or an accident. Women tend to have more near-death experiences when they are ill, but men tend to have them more as a result of accidental injury. Those who have their whole lives "flash before them" tend to be accident victims more than illness victims. And somewhat ironically, Dr. Ring found that people who had heard of near-death experiences tended to report fewer of them than people who previously were ignorant about them.[9]

Death experiences for those in accidents seem to be different than those who die from slowly progressing diseases, where there is more time for a life review. Accident victims speak more of feelings of falling and then a complete indifference or detachment.

Flash Forwards

A number of people who are dying of disease seem to have "flash-forward" looks into the future. Most seem to conclude, "God help me."

Deathbed vision of the future life vary with the degree of consciousness that the person has at the time. Some see themselves in younger, healthier form. Some see places or dwellings. Some see loved ones. Most see light. A few have visions of Jesus.

There are also recorded cases of those who have frightening flash-forward looks into hell. Their faces are often said to express great torture, shock, and horror. Others are reported to have talked of nearby demons, ready to drag their souls into hell.

Not All Recall

Reports vary regarding the percentage of these people who recall an experience of heaven or hell. Some say as low as twenty percent, others as high as sixty percent. The fact is that not all people resuscitated from clinical death recall any afterlife or "out of body" experience.

Different "Lights."

The exact nature of the light that near-death subjects see has been difficult for them to describe. Some say it is a light that wraps around the person in warmth. Others hear the voice of God in the light. Some see very bright lights, and others a soft glow. Most do not find the light at all discomforting or unnerving.

Certainly, not everyone sees bright, white light when having a near-death experience or an occultic experience. The self-styled "Great Beast" of the occult world, Aleister Crowley, visited the Great Pyramid in Egypt on his honeymoon in 1903 and spent a night in the King's Chamber. Ensconced there with his bride, he lit a candle and began to read an incantation. Suddenly, according to Crowley, a pale *lilac* light bathed the room, allowing him to continue the incantation without the candle.

One medium of the 1930s, Eileen Garrett, has described her trances this way:

> "the space behind the forehead clears and becomes suffused with soft light in which changing colors plan an important part, and I actually enter a dimension which is color."[10]

The fact that people see a great "light" as a part of near-death experiences does not mean that all are encountering Jesus, who referred to himself as the "light of the world" (John 8:12) and whom John saw as casting a light brighter than the sun in Revelation 22:5. The Bible tells us that Satan is capable of transforming himself into an "angel of light" (2 Corinthians 11:14).

According to musician Carlos Santana, "Supreme Power holds a chandelier, and in the light are Jesus, Krishna, and Buddha, but the crystals are the angels."[11]

The conclusion must be drawn that those who see figures or beings of light may *not* be encountering something of God. They may just as likely be encountering something from Satan.

It is also interesting to note that those who have glorious visions of an afterlife nearly always associate the light they see with forgiveness and love. This light, therefore, must not have anything to do with karma or reincarnation since karma never forgives and mercilessly requires that a person pay for misdeeds in previous lives. There is no final judgment day in Hinduism, and thus, there is nothing to forgive. One can't help but ask, why is there a "forgiveness" aspect to the light if there is no sin and no judgment, and thus no need for forgiveness according to New Age teachings?

What About An Out-of-the-Body Explanation?

While some near-death experiences seem to include out-of-body (OBE) experiences, virtually all out-of-body experiences that do not include death symptoms are drug-related. The drugs generally associated with OBE are the hallucinogens (such as LSD, mescaline, and PCP). Hypnosis is another method that some have used to have out-of-body experiences. OBE's can also be obtained by deep meditation, yoga exercises, incantations, and mantra recitations.

Most people who use hallucinogens or who undergo hypnosis desiring to have an out-of-body experience do so in the hopes of "seeing" something. The shamans of the American Indians, for example, chewed peyote to visualize sacred desert coyotes. Some Christians have tried to visualize the Virgin Mary or Jesus. Today, it appears that some are trying to see angels.

The Scriptures tell us to think of Christ and to come to know him, but not to visualize him. Our desire should be to obey Christ, not visualize. (See 2 Corinthians 10:5.)

Ancient witchcraft and modern shamanism are very similar. They attempt to put a person in contact with information that has been forbidden to them by God.

One of the most common forms of out-of-body experience is called "astral travel." This is not unlike the "beam-me-up-Scotty" approach taken on Star Trek television programs.

In astral travel, however, one's destination is unknown, and is at the whim of the drug involved or the spirit guide evoked. Both good and bad trips are possible.

Astral travel is not a new phenomenon. Shamans throughout the Indian religions claim to have the ability to fly out of their bodies when they are in a state of trance. Witches have long been thought to "fly" astride broomsticks. Medieval men and women considered the mandrake to be a magical root because it caused some people to have an illusion of flight. (Mandrake does contain the hallucinogenic substance *hyoscyamine*.) Buddhist monks in Tibet still subject themselves to intense cold or fasting in hopes of achieving a mental state in which their spirits leave their bodies. During out-of-body experiences, the New Age teaches that the "astral body" is actually connected to the physical body by a silver cord that emerges from the person's third eye, which is thought to be the spiritual center of the body. As part of a twisting of the truth, the New Agers have taken this idea from Ecclesiastes, in which the transition from life to death is described as a time when *the silver cord is loosed . . .then the dust will return to the earth as it was, and the spirit will return to God who gave it* (Ecclesiastes 12:6-7).

The Influence of Jung

One of the people quoted often by the New Age writers is Carl Jung, the Swiss psychologist who first introduced the idea of the collective unconscious. Jung believed that, at a conscious level, our individual minds are separated, but that our unconscious minds are merged and linked therefore to those who have lived before us. His idea supports the theory of a "collective memory," into which those who seek psychic energy and ideas often attempt to submerge themselves.

Even in his time, Jung was called the Hexenmeister (warlock or male witch) of Zurich. He claimed to have had psychic visions from childhood, and that he regularly saw ghosts and consorted with astrologers. For a five year period (1912-1917), he went through an ". . . intense period of experience which involved a tremendous flooding of his consciousness from within by forces which he called archetypal but which previous ages would have declared to be divine and demonic."[12]

He wrote of these experiences in 1,330 pages of handwritten text using a style of handwriting related to the fourteenth century. He called this work *Jung's Red Book* and only allowed one portion of it, called *Seven Sermons to the Dead* to be published, primarily for his friends and associates. In his later years, Jung stated that all of his work and all of his creative activity stemmed from the visions and dreams in his book.

Jung described other instances of paranormal experiences—including out-of-body experiences—in a book titled *Memories, Dreams, and Reflections.*

He is a major proponent of out-of-body realities, and much of his teaching has been adopted by the New Age writers.

It is very likely that a great number of people are first introduced to the possibility of OBE by Jungian psychologists when they go for counseling or therapy. Jung has enjoyed a resurgence of popularity in the psychology profession in recent years.

What Does Science Say?

Various scientific views have been taken about out-of-body experiences. Some hold to the theory that this is a form of lucid dreaming in which the person is asleep but is conscious of dreaming. Others think out-of-body experiences could be the type of image that people have just at the point of falling asleep. Still others think they involve an altered state of consciousness.

There's one main difference however, between out-of-body experiences and near-death experiences. Out-of-body experiences are nearly always *desired*, with the person who has the OBE doing something or taking something in order to have the experience.

Out-Of-Body Experiences and the Bible?

One of the troubling practices I see in Christian circles today is a desire among some to conduct "astral travel" in order to go to other parts of the world to pray for or to minister directly to people in need. Some see this as a form of "sending their spirits" to unite with those in need. The practice is not biblical.

Anytime a person is translated for a spiritual purpose in the Bible, his body goes with him!

In Acts 8 we have the story of Philip's ministry. An angel of the Lord directed him to go to the Gaza road, which he did, and there, Philip saw a man from Ethiopia. Philip overheard him reading the prophet Isaiah and asked the man if he understood what he was reading. The Ethiopian responded, "How can I, unless someone guide me?" He then invited Philip to sit with him in his chariot and explain Isaiah 53:7–8 to him. Philip preached Jesus to the man and then upon his confession of faith, baptized him in water. (See Acts 8:26–37.)

The Scriptures then tell us:

> *Now when they came up out of the water, the Spirit of the*
> *Lord caught Philip away, so that the eunuch saw him no*

more; and he went on his way rejoicing. But Philip was
found at Azotus. And passing through, he preached in all
the cities till he came to Caesarea (Acts 8:39–40).

In this passage, we find the work of both angels and the Holy
Spirit. It is an angel who tells Philip to go south along the road that
runs from Jerusalem to Gaza. Once there, it is the Spirit who says
to Philip, "Go near and overtake this chariot." It is also the Spirit
that catches Philip away from the Ethiopian's sight.

Two main truths need to be drawn from this passage. First,
Philip may have been translated by the power of the Holy Spirit
from the baptismal waters to Azotus, but he remained in his
body. This was a literal event. The Scriptures tell us that he was
"found" at Azotus, and that he passed through there, preaching in
all the cities till he came to Caesarea. This was not an out-of-body
event. The Spirit of God relocated Philip—mind, body, and spirit.

Second, *Philip did not initiate this event.* He was not praying
for it, expecting it, desiring it, or believing for it. The events of
this story are God-centered, not Philip-centered. Philip actually
had little to do with the Ethiopian's conversion, other than to do
what God directed him to do and say what he knew to be true
about Jesus. The event was initiated by God—speaking first
through an angel and then through His Spirit.

Subject to Interpretation

What are we to conclude then about near-death experiences?
Our conclusion must be that there can be no conclusion. The
views regarding the dying process differ *according to what one*
believes. Different experiences have different interpretations.

The medical world and the metaphysical world have entirely
different takes on what it means to die.

The Medical Perspective

A book that spent several months on the *New York Times* best
seller list was *Closer to the Light* by Melvin Morse, M.D. This book
details near-death experiences of children.

Dr. Morse felt compelled to do research into near-death expe-
riences after a drowning victim named Katie told him of seeing
God, a man of bright light who filled her with love and kindness.
She also talked of a guardian angel named Elizabeth who showed

her heaven and allowed her to return home once to see her family. She saw her grandfather and met two young boys—Andy and Mark—who were "souls waiting to be born." Elizabeth supposedly told Katie that she had the option of staying in heaven or returning to her mother, and she chose to return.

In the hospital room, Katie's family held hands around her bed and prayed aloud during this experience.

Dr. Morse probed the religious beliefs of Katie's family and was told that no one in the family espoused a belief in spirit guides or tunnels to heaven. They did claim, however, to be Mormons who believed in the afterlife and attended Sunday school regularly.[13]

In his subsequent research, Dr. Morse claims that his research team has proven that a person actually needs to be near death in order to *have* a near-death experience. He studied 121 children who had been critically ill, but not near death, as well as 37 children who had been given mind-altering drugs for various reasons. He compared them to a study group of 12 children who would probably have died or faced severe handicaps had it not been for intensive medical intervention. None of the seriously ill or drug-treated children reported near-death experiences, while most of the children who had been near death described at least one of the NDE phenomena.

A Brain Center for NDE?

Dr. Morse's researcher team also believes they have isolated the area in the brain where near-death experiences occur—the right temporal lobe, which the researchers say could be the "seat of the soul." This area is connected to the hippocampus, which is the brain's master control, sorting out thousands of pieces of sensory input at any given time and deciding which of them should be acted upon. This is the area of unconscious desires and the ability to dream. It is directly connected to areas in the right temporal and occipital lobes that have the neuronal circuitry to create near-death experiences. The collapse of visual fields to create the tunnel experience occurs in the occipital lobes.

Wilder Penfield is the widely recognized father of neurosurgery and even though he made his extensive "brain maps" in the 1930s and 1940s, he is still considered responsible for much of the current understanding of brain function. His maps of the brain were made by putting patients under local anesthetic and then prodding different areas of the brain electrically. He carefully documented what happened.

Penfield's noted that light was often seen by those whose right temporal lobes were stimulated by a lack of oxygen.

There are those who see the map of the brain as being something that is genetically printed at birth. Birds, for example, seem to have a genetically coded map of the night sky imprinted on their brains. Even birds raised in laboratories and never exposed to the night sky are able to navigate within planetariums.[14]

Morse writes, "The sensations of leaving the body, seeing dead relatives, hearing heavenly music, speaking with God, and reviewing one's own life are part of our genetic makeup, 'hard-wired into each of us.'"[15]

The Sequence in Brain Death

From a biological and anatomical standpoint, there are physicians who explain a near-death experience as a sequence of dying in the brain. Dr. Susan Blackmore, of the Brain and Perception Laboratory at Bristol University in England, believes that the tunnel of light appears because:

> "The vital cells that normally regulate the activity in the visual sector of the brain—the visual cortex—are seriously inhibited by the increasing lack of sensory information. This destabilizes the normal visual controls, producing stripes of irregular activity. As this information travels between the retina of the eye and the brain, the stripes are interpreted as being concentric rings, tunnels, or undulating spirals, light in the center and darker at the edges. . . .The mind latches onto these tunnel images and accepts them as a new actuality."[16]

Brain scans have shown that the visual cortex of the brain is one of the last areas to die.

What about those who see their bodies from the ceilings of emergency rooms? Dr. Blackmore suggests that when the mind is deprived of its usual kinds of sensory input, it starts seeking input from memory or other sources. She also notes a discrepancy among those of differing cultures. For example, near-death subjects in India often encounter a messenger who looks at a list of names and then concludes the person is not ready for death. Christians in the West tend to identify various beings as Jesus, Gabriel, or St. Peter.

Drugs and Death

One of the things we apparently can rule out is that these near-death experiences are not *entirely* drug related. For a number of years, many people seemed to dismiss NDE, saying, "They were on drugs," or, "they were hallucinating." The role that medications may play in near-death experiences is just now being explored.

According to a number of researchers, hallucinations, visions, and psychic phenomena produce results that are different than near-death experiences. Marijuana, psychedelics, alcohol, narcotics, anesthetic agents, Valium, lack of oxygen, and even severe psychological stress apparently do not cause near-death experiences, unless the person is actually *near death*.

It should be pointed out, however, that many people who are near death are given drug injections as one means of attempted resuscitation. The influence of these drugs at the time of death has not been determined fully.

Comatose States

The exact depths of the "coma" state are still not known. It is interesting, however, to note that very few near-death experiences have been reported by people who have been in comas for long periods of time.

In a coma, a person's heart and breathing rates often slow to near imperceptible rates.

There are yet others who might regard near-death experiences as some type of "life suspension." Perhaps the most famous story in this area involves an Indian yogi called Haridas. In 1835 he allowed himself to be buried alive for forty days.

In preparation for this, he drank only milk and ate yogurt for days before his burial, bathed in hot water, swallowed a long strip of linen and regurgitated it to clean his alimentary canal, and then went on a total fast. He closed his nose and ears with wax, had his tongue muscles cut so his tongue could be folded back to close his nasal passages at the back of the throat, and sat down in a cross-legged pose. Doctors found that his pulse had virtually stopped.

Haridas was wrapped in linen, put in a padlocked chest and buried. A wall was built around the burial site and guards were posted. Forty days later, the chest was unearthed. The locks on it were intact. The shrouded yogi was inside, still in the same pose. He had no detectable pulse and his arms and legs had atrophied and were stiff. The attending doctors began to massage Haridas, pulled back his tongue, emptied his ears of wax, and inflated his lungs with bellows. Eventually signs of life began to reappear. Within a few hours, he was fully restored to the land of the living.

Did Haridas go beyond the stage of clinical death? Apparently not, even after forty days. The incident is an example of how much self-control can play in biological functions. It also shows the resiliency of the body to "fight" or resist death.

The Will to Live

The will to live is a powerful force. Most physicians and nurses are quick to point to the will to live as a key ingredient in the recovery of their patients.

There is no telling how much the will to live plays in near-death experiences. But where there is still a very strong will to live, it surely must be concluded that there *may* be a greater likelihood for a person to return from a near-death visit to the afterlife.

The Metaphysical Perspective

The approach of the Eastern religions, and thus much of the New Age, is that man doesn't truly "die." Rather, man evolves . . . progresses . . . enters a new stage . . . moves forward . . . takes on a higher consciousness . . . but whatever the terminology, continues to exist. Death is seen as a transition to a higher state of the Self, or at least, death holds out that possibility.

Buddhism advocates reincarnation, something of a cosmic "recycling" of the spirit upon death. The Tibetan Buddhists believe their spiritual leader, "dalai lama" is the embodiment of Chenrez, the Buddhist god of grace, who has been appearing in different incarnations since 1391. When one mortal body dies, he chooses a new one and his followers then have to search to find the infant he has become. At present, of course, two boys are in contention to be the next dalai lama. Apparently the dalai lama doesn't make it known for certain where and when he reappears.

Hebrews 9:27 tells us plainly, *It is appointed for men to die once, but after this the judgment.* The Bible leaves no room for reincarnation.

An Ascent at Death

Most of the New Age writers teach that when man "dies," he is actually ascending to a higher level of being. This has nothing to do with going to be with God, but rather, that man has evolved one degree closer to *being* god.

Channeled spirits claim not to have died in the past, but to have ascended. The spirit Ramtha told J.Z. Knight, "I learned to harness the power of my mind and to take my body with me into an unseen dimension of life."[17]

Underlying this belief is a belief that, at death, mankind somehow "pulls himself together" spiritually. He achieves a greater unity, or personal "wholeness."

New Age psychology teaches at its core that man's interior being is a collection of fragments, a cluster of disjointed entities, and that these entities only come together fully at death, or prior to death, through various enlightenment exercises.

The person who is considered sane or mentally healthy is a person who has figured out a suitable integration for his various mental, emotional, and spiritual parts. The person who is mentally ill, schizophrenic, or who has "multiple personalities" is perceived to be a person who doesn't have a means, either chemical or psychological, of putting all the pieces together or of holding them together in a consistent manner.

In the New Age philosophy, the actual term "fragmentation" is something of a dirty word. And yet, the philosophy is based on the ability of a person to pull together a wholeness entirely through an interior spiritual or mental process.

The fact that people need to be made whole is an admission that people start out being fragmented or disjointed spiritually. Many gurus and Eastern mystics insist that Jesus' words in the Bible, *In My Father's house are many mansions* (John 14:2) should actually be interpreted "in *your* house" there are many rooms. It is the exploration of these rooms and the attempt to put them together into a house, of sorts, that is the goal of most Eastern-religion techniques.

A number of New Age writers have discussed at length the various levels of the soul. Some claim there are four levels above the one most of us live at, and four levels below. Other say nine levels above and nine below. Some claim to have visited the bottomless hell of the lowest level during bad LSD trips. Some claim to have reached upper levels through drugs, meditation, or hypnosis, and at that level, to have gained a glimpse of heaven.

From this perspective, not only do angels reside within us to help us pull these various areas of our psyche or soul together, but the entire range of existence lies within our being. Heaven and hell are inside us! The depths of a soul are a ghoulish place to be. The heights of the soul are glorious beyond measure. The individual human being is the universe.

If you believe that you contain the universe within and that you can elevate yourself to higher states of reality, it is only one small step to reach the conclusion that you are capable, at some point, to name your own death point. In other words, you can decide as an individual when you are actually going to die, or if you should return to this life.

The Omega Point

New Age philosophy speaks of an "Omega Point." This is the point at which a person faces a decision to return to earth after a near-death experience, or to buck the desires of the eternal host and remain in the afterlife. All those who buy into the Omega philosophy see the afterlife as a heavenly place, and view those who are returned to earth as ones sent back with a mission of bringing the world toward greater peace and brotherly love.

Very often, this mission on earth has to do with the ability to work miracles, help others, or be an agent of healing.

One New Age writer, Paul Pearsall, has written an entire book from this perspective. It is titled *Making Miracles.*

From the first few words of the dedication of Pearsall's book one might think he is a Christian since he begins, "For everyone who prayed for me." He also dedicates the book to the "spirit" of his father, and then concludes, "Thank you for my miracle."[18]

In some ways, this book is more subtle than many New Age books. Pearsall writes:

"The book you are about to read will document that you do not have to accept bizarre beliefs about astral projection, hauntings, channeling, psychic energy, or the Bermuda Triangle to discover as I did that every aspect of our own existence is miraculous. You will see that within our very nature is a wonderful and wondrous capacity to create the miraculous. . . . I will show you that *we can all be miracle makers because we are at the center of the universe where science and spirit meet.* Each of us represents the merging of these two systems of explaining life. . . . Where science and spirit meet is where miracles explode into being. . . . I will also describe the science behind the facts of levitation, traveling through time, seeing without looking with the eyes, altering the past, remote viewing, sharing consciousness with animals and plants, miracle healings, the power of prayer, and research findings on the right and wrong and effective and ineffective way to pray."[19]

Pearsall states that "we are all a part of God, we are all everywhere and a part of everything."[20] He also advocates that we all lead a divine life and that when we discover the godlike characteristics in ourselves that transcend our here-and-now bodies, we become a co-creator with God.

Some Christian teachers, of course, take a position very close to this—that we are part of God's ongoing creative process.

We use the word create a great deal, but man does not actually create—not in the truest meaning of the word. To create is to make something from nothing. Man does not have that power or ability, regardless of what Pearsall may claim. Man *makes*. We are bound to the tangible, physical world in our ability to make. God's words to Adam and Eve, and then again to Noah and his family, were words of "management," not creation. He said that mankind was to *have dominion over the fish of the sea, over the birds of the air, and over the cattle, over all the earth and over every creeping thing that creeps on the earth.* God blessed man and said, *Be fruitful and multiply; fill the earth and subdue it; have dominion over the fish of the sea, over the birds of the air, and over every living thing that moves on the earth.* (See Genesis 1:26, 28 and 9:1.)

Through the eons of time, man's heart hasn't changed. The nature of man is no different now than it ever was. Despite what Hinduism might claim, man has done nothing to create a better heart for himself, individually or collectively. Our cruelty to one another is only more subtle on the one hand, and more globally devastating on the other.

Through the eons of time, man has, however, "made" things. We call mankind's inventions music, technology, poems, science, language, and so forth. These are not creations, but manipulations and "makings" that spring out of natural law.

Pearsall advocates that believing results in seeing. Again, that may sound like Scripture. Hebrews 11:1 states that *faith is the substance of things hoped for, the evidence of things unseen.* The believing that Pearsall writes about, however, is a believing that has nothing to do with faith in God. It stems from Carl Jung's concept of "synchronicities," bridges between the worlds of matter and mind and science and spirit.[21] In synchronicity, seemingly accidental meetings of two unrelated causal chains cause a new reality. When we see meaning, or *believe* in the meaning we attribute to an event, experience, or activity, we adapt, learn, or evolve in some way. Thus, the sick person might believe in a hocus-pocus chant, and because he believes this chant has meaning, he has opened himself up to "evolve" or "adapt"—ideally, toward a more healthful state according to the New Age.

Pearsall claims that guilt is the number one block to making miracles. Thus, it is better for a person not to have a concept of sin since that can lead to guilt.

He quotes Jesus saying, "Thy will be done"—but "Thy will" is *not* the will of the Heavenly Father, but rather, the collective-consciousness will of all humanity. The individual must yield to the whole. This includes, the will of all nature. Pearsall says, "Don't give orders to the universe: let the universe order you."

The Near-Death Connection

What does all this have to do with a near-death experience?

Pearsall became sick in 1988—at 8 p.m. on the eighth day of the eighth month, to be precise—a time when he claims spiritists around the world were in eager anticipation that they would be able to unite their consciousness to create more peace, love, and ecological wholeness on the planet. Pearsall, however, had pain, which eventually was so severe that he was unable to lift folders out of his file cabinets. He eventually was diagnosed with cancer and had not only whole-body radiation and intensive chemotherapy, but a bone-marrow transplant. One physician told him, "This is the sickest anyone can be and still be alive. Everything is wrong with you and nothing is right. We have almost, but not quite, killed you."[22]

While recovering from the bone-marrow transplant, he suffered a viral infection and was rushed into emergency surgery. He reported that while coming out of the anesthesia, he made a conscious decision to return to life. He writes:

> "I chose to come back from death. The peacefulness, safety, and seductive feeling of freedom . . . common to most near-death experiences was strong, but something told me that I had to come back. I felt myself being 'returned' and reassembled. I felt the energy fields around me doing their healing work, and like the regenerative gecko syndrome, I was becoming whole again. I could actually feel the vibrations of healing like the tingling you feel when your foot becomes numb because of poor circulation. I felt the power of my family's energy transfusions and the power of my friends' prayers. I was being vibrated back to physical life. At long last, I felt my spirit merging with my body."[23]

It should be noted that Pearsall also states that the doctors were responding to his condition with Life-Pak, electrical paddles, and oxygen.

Pearsall's main concern is not with death and what he experiences, but about the "miracles" that he claims helped him return to a fullness of life and health. Those forces are ones that he roots in everything from the laws of thermodynamic medicine (the flow of energy through a system to bring order to the system) to the good chants of the Hawaiian *kahunas,* or healers, whom he visits.

Fuzzy Lines

Again, Pearsall speaks at times in language that a Christian might find familiar. While Christians might believe strongly that they are called to pray and believe in God for miracles—and thus, that they participate in some way in the miraculous process of healing—Pearsall defines miracle-working in a different way. He claims that every person has a birthright as a miracle maker. He sites the characteristics of a miracle-worker as being six-fold:

- You must choose between being creative, open, and vulnerable to the unpredictable energy of spiritual growth or accepting the more predictable local life of the here and now.

(The Bible teaches that while we might be creative, open, and vulnerable, it is to be toward God, not some energy flow. Above all, we are to be steadfastly faithful and obedient to follow God's commandments. We aren't to seek out an unpredictable life, but rather, to trust in God who changes not.)

- You must choose between accepting transitional life crises as psychic toughening exercises and a necessary part of attending soul school here on earth or viewing the transitions and tragedies of daily living as punishment or as proof of the bumper sticker axiom that reads "Life's a bitch and then you die."

(The Bible teaches that our life here is, indeed, a soul exercise, but it is one that prepares us for eternity. Life is not a toughening exercise, but a matter of softening our already hardened hearts toward a loving God, and of accepting His offer of forgiveness through the shed blood of Jesus Christ.)

- You must choose between pursuing your yearning for a spiritual life that connects you with everyone and everything, and being teased by a sense that there is more to life than your local existence.

(The Holy Spirit doesn't "tease" us into turning to the Heavenly Father. The Holy Spirit seeks to connect us with the Father, to reunite us into a close fellowship with Him, and in that, to open us up not only to the possibility of developing a loving relationship with others, but equipping us with the love that can truly bring us into a union with other people.)

- You must choose between a view of life that emphasizes simplicity: freedom from acquiring things, good, and money, or an outlook on life that stresses doing and getting more

and more until the things of your life become the focus of
your living.

(The Scriptures also point man toward a life that is "free" from
placing primary importance on things, goods, and money . . . but
it is not an outlook that is necessarily one of simplicity. Simplicity,
in my thinking, is equated here with "easy" or "simple." Jesus did
not promise us an easy road, but one of constant spiritual warfare
and growth in faith. He didn't promise us peace and love with
everyone, but rather, said that in our pursuit of a relationship with
the Father, we were likely to suffer painful separation and aliena-
tion from beloved others who neither understood our relationship
with the Savior nor desired to have such a relationship of their
own. Priorities shift when we come to know Christ and to follow
Him, but they do not shift toward a simple peace-and-love-oneself-
and-everybody existence.)

- You must choose to utilize as a source of learning the energy
  released at times of personal decision and development,
  challenges, changes, and transitions of your life rather than
  adopt the view that things happen randomly to us and have
  little meaning other than as aggravations and threats to our
  survival and happiness.

(The Scriptures also tell us that our will is involved in our life
choices. Nothing is random according to God's plan. But our focus is not to be upon energy flows. Rather, it is to be upon the
Lord Almighty, and the unfolding of His plan and purpose in our
lives.)

- If you are to make your own miracles, you must choose to
  be a gambler . . . .You must choose to put yourself in the
  miracle position, opening the way for the coincidence
  clusters that fuel miracles.

(Bible miracles were never based on coincidence clusters.
They were interventions by God in the affairs of men. The Bible
does not teach that we are to gamble with our lives, but rather,
that we make a conscious and conscientious decision with our
will to pursue a relationship with Almighty God, and to obey His
commandments in our life. We are to pray and believe for miracles,

putting our faith squarely in God's love and faithfulness, not in "coincidence clusters.")

Pearsall also concludes that there is a seventh characteristic, and that is that miracle makers choose to show patience, forgiveness, generosity, truthfulness, and equanimity in what he terms "loving kindness." The Bible states that this loving kindness, or *chesed* in the Hebrew, is a quality of God—it is the very nature of His love and it is equated with steadfastness throughout the Bible. The only way we can express that love consistently and continually is to have a relationship with God and to draw from that relationship the ability to be genuinely patient, forgiving, generous, and truthful in our relationship with others. To try to do it in our own strength—over time and in all situations to all people—is a nice idea, but futile.

Passive and Beautiful

Nearly all of the New Age writers speak of death as being passive and beautiful. Goldman writes, for example:

- "The arms of death are gentle and magnificent, ready to express the love we have not yet found in one final embrace."
- "Our souls, like angels, are immortal. If we could only realize this, death would bother us no more."
- "To an angel, death is not an enemy, but a trip to a new country filled with friends, harmony, and comfort. It is a journey with wondrous visions that fill one with love."[24]
- "Death is only a resting period before the shoots of life sprout up through Consciousness reaching for the sun again."[25]

Again, we see the "oneness" and transitional elements of reincarnation philosophy.

The Bible Perspective

The Bible speaks of death in far different terms than those offered by the New Age.

Death is called "the last enemy" that will be destroyed by Christ Jesus. In the Revelation of John, we find death and hell both being cast into the lake of fire (Revelation 20:14). There is nothing passive about death in the spiritual realm. It is a blow of Satan. It is a wrenching of life from physical body. Often it is accompanied by pain, great discomfort, and sickness. In Revelation, it is associated with tears, sorrow, crying, and pain—one of the great joys of Heaven is that death will be no more! (See Revelation 21:4.)

That does not mean that we cannot look beyond the pain and sorrow of death and experience God's comfort. He is present in the moment of death to bring about a total and complete victory for our selves and our loved ones. But this is not an automatic peace or joyful bliss known to all human beings at death. It is a gift of God's mercy and a work of His grace.

Out-of-Body Experience?

Does the Bible have any mention at all of near-death or out-of-body experiences? The apostle Paul *may* have had one. In 2 Corinthians 12:2–4 we read:

> *I know a man in Christ who fourteen years ago—whether in the body I do not know, or whether out of the body I do not know, God knows—such a one was caught up to the third heaven. And I know such a man—whether in the body or out of the body, I do not know, God knows—how he was caught up into Paradise and heard inexpressible words, which is not lawful for a man to utter.*

Given the great list of highly traumatic experiences Paul went through—from stoning to torture—it seems very likely that Paul may have been "clinically dead" on more than one occasion.

A Transition

The Bible presents the view that death is a transition into God's direct presence. As the Apostle Paul said, we should look forward to that day when we will know what it means *to be absent from the body and to be present with the Lord* (2 Corinthians 5:8).

The Bible speaks of two "means" of transition. One is death. The other has come to be called the "rapture" of the Church.

This is described by the apostle Paul in 1 Thessalonians 4:16–17:

> *For the Lord Himself will descend from heaven with a shout, with the voice of an archangel, and with the trumpet of God. And the dead in Christ will rise first. Then we who are alive and remain shall be caught up together with them in the clouds to meet the Lord in the air. And thus we shall always be with the Lord.*

Note that angels will be present to help human beings in this transitional moment when the very elect of God are caught up to be with the Lord. In Mark 13:23–27 we have these words of Jesus:

But in those days, after that tribulation, the sun will be darkened, and the moon will not give its light, the stars of heaven will fall, and the powers in the heavens will be shaken. Then they will see the Son of Man coming in the clouds with great power and glory. And then He will send His angels, and gather together His elect from the four winds, from the farthest part of earth to the farthest part of heaven.

As mentioned earlier in Chapter 2, the Bible tells us that angels escort us at death, too. Apparently angels are our escorts into God's presence either in death or in the "gathering" of the elect.

One of the most interesting accounts I have read about angelic escorts is told in a book titled *Angels of Mercy.*

A nurse in England by the name of Joy Snell is reported to have seen many take-away apparitions as she worked with the dying in hospitals. After she retired she wrote about these experiences in a book titled *The Ministry of Angels.* Sometimes she saw angels arrive at the bedside of a dying person, standing in readiness for the moment of transition. Upon the person's death, she would see the soul leave the body and coalesce into a spirit body just above the corpse. The new spirit body had the same radiance as that of the angels. Once that body had formed, the angels would take it away. Snell desired to see the place where they went but was told by an authoritative voice that she could not, since the true Other Side was not intended to be glimpsed by the living.[26]

Snell saw other forms of angels—one who appeared very human, and who walked the halls of the hospital at night, touching sleeping or unconscious patients who had been in great pain or distress. She also saw apparitions she described as the Angel of Death—a dark, shadowy, veiled figure. If this figure appeared, the patient always died within two or three days, no matter how well the patient might have appeared to be recovering. The Angel of Renewed Life, by contrast, was a bright figure in luminous array with a youthful happy face. If he appeared, the patient always recovered, regardless of a physicians' prognosis of death.[27]

Healing in Death

The Bible clearly presents the image that those who die in the Lord are free of earthly pain, sorrow, and suffering. The righteous dead live in bodies that are not bound to the elements, diseases, and trauma of this earth.

The Bible does not say, however, that people come close to death in order that they might become healers.

Neither does the Bible state that man's "mental processes" can heal man.

In agreement with the New Age, the Bible does state that man is fragmented! The Bible perspective, however, is that only Jesus Christ can make man whole. One of the phrases used frequently by Jesus during His earthly ministry was, "Be made whole."

The Hebrew concept of the human being is one of wholeness. A person is not seen from the Hebrew point of view as having an interior and an exterior being. Rather, the whole of the person is the whole of the person. What effects one aspect of a person's life inevitably effects the entire person. A person isn't sick in "one area." He is sick if he is sick in any area.

In our Western mind, we tend to say, "I *have* an upset stomach." The Hebrew mind would say, "I *am* ill."

The entire ministry of Jesus was not directed toward the "cure" of particular diseases or ailments, but rather to make people whole, spiritually, mentally, emotionally, physically, and in their relationships with others. His ministry was one of total reconciliation to the Father of all aspects of humanity.

Jesus taught that those who are sick need a Physician. (See Matthew 9:12.) A physician was not a doctor as we know doctors today, nearly all of whom have now specialized into one area of the human body. A physician was someone who could bring a person to wholeness. Jesus was clearly stating that such a person must exist *outside* the individual who is ill. Jesus didn't say, "Be your own physician," or "Those who are sick, be your own physician."

The Bible approach to healing is that God is the one who brings healing and wholeness to an individual.

Most certainly the Bible approach is that heaven and hell are places external to the troubled mind of man. While we might *think* ourselves to be in heaven or hell at certain moments of our existence, we are only thinking that this is how it must feel to be in heaven or hell. The Bible links the afterlife to specific places—not a place, but two places. One of them is hell. The other is heaven.

The Certainty of Death

On one point the Bible is very clear: man must die.

The New Age teaches that man doesn't truly die. This teaching is straight from the devil. In fact it is part of the devil's initial lie to mankind.

The promises of Satan in the Garden of Eden are fourfold, as given in Genesis 3:4-5—*You will not surely die. For God knows that in the day you eat of it your eyes will be opened, and you will be like God, knowing good and evil.* Note the relationship of these four lies to the beliefs undergirding near-death experiences as viewed from the New Age philosophy:

(1) *You will not die.* Nearly all in the New Age believe either in reincarnation or in an eternal afterlife for everybody. They accept no judgment of final death.

(2) *Your eyes will be opened.* Enlightenment is the goal of the New Age. Those who have near-death experiences and angelic encounters frequently claim that they suddenly were able to "see with new eyes." Many of the attempts at conjuring angels, including the manipulation of mandalas, use spiritual visualization techniques.

(3) *You will be like God.* New Agers have taken the Scriptural statement that man is to be "like," as in similar to, God to mean that man is to be "as" God, equal to, synonymous with, and one and the same as!

Dave Hunt has a good comment related to this: "If I am God, then why don't I know it? And if I know it, then why don't I act like it?"[28]

The Bible is a monotheistic book, proclaiming one God, who is omnipotent, infinite, omnipresent, eternal, and omniscient. Man, by comparison, is limited in power, space, time, and knowledge.

The New Age buys into pantheism—that there are many gods, including people as gods. They hold to the opinion that "everything is god and god is in everything."

(4) *You will know good and evil.* The New Age philosophy contends that god has two sides: dark and light. Evil does not exist as a separate entity. The two are part of the same whole.

The Bible states that good and evil have different sources. God's highest desire was that Adam and Eve *not* know evil and have no experience with it. Satan held out the idea that the knowledge of evil was important for Eve's spiritual growth. In the end, it was the lie that led to her spiritual downfall.

We are *not* to know evil today as Christians. Although we are surrounded by evil, we are to seek good, pursue only what has virtue, and resist evil at every turn.

We'll Know *Someday!*

Ultimately, we don't know the fullness of God's plan. We don't know anything about the hereafter with certainty. The hereafter lies in the realm of "believing." We know with certainty only that the Lord Jesus Christ tells us to prepare for the hereafter and those who believe in Him and confess His name have been given eternal life.

We are also admonished in God's Word to leave the judging of other people up to God. We are to discern good from evil, make wise choices regarding our own lives, confess our own sins and turn from them, embrace Jesus Christ as our personal Savior and Lord, and extend loving-kindness to others. The consequences of another person's life and the true nature of another person's heart are for God alone to judge.

16

Heaven and Hell

ONE of the best known visions of the afterlife through the years has been that of Rebecca Springer. Her vision was originally titled *Intra Muros* and later *Within the Gates*. It was first published at the turn of the century by a publishing house associated with the Methodist Church. By all accounts, she was an earnest and devout Christian lady.

She said this in response to those who asked her about her experience, "I can only say . . . that I gave it as it came to me, and everyone must draw his own inference concerning it. I can be a guide to no one."[1]

Her vision has these two overriding qualities about it:

- she sees life as a continuity—that people are building for eternity during their earthly lives; she sees human friendships as enduring from this world into paradise
- she exalts Jesus Christ as the Redeemer of the world throughout her vision

Rebecca Springer did not have a tunnel experience. Rather, her brother Frank appeared and helped escort her through a window, out onto a veranda, and down the street from the hospital where she had been ill. He walked with her, carrying her part of the way, until they arrived at a beautiful garden.

Her vision includes a description of the homes and gardens of paradise, the river of life, craftsmen at work beautifying the structures in paradise, and the "shores of eternity."

She encounters her parents, loved ones, loving strangers, and Jesus Christ the Savior in her vision. She does not encounter Jesus immediately upon her arrival in Heaven, but some time later.

She visits a great city in paradise and enters the Temple there, which is the only place in which she encounters angels.

She has no life review or judgment encounter.

Rebecca Springer believed, and so do many others, that her vision was about a place called "paradise." She regards this as the place where all Christians go prior to the great judgment. The life that exists beyond the great judgment is one unknown and unknowable.

Is There Christian Consensus About Heaven?

On the surface, you may be tempted to say, "Of course! Golden streets and pearly gates."

The Bible revelation many people think of as a description of heaven is more likely a vision about the Church. Regardless of how you read and interpret that passage in Revelation, the conclusion must be drawn that there is no decidedly Christian consensus about what heaven is like, where it is located, or when a person enters its domain.

The best term to use in describing the afterlife, indeed, is the word "paradise." That is the word Jesus used to describe the place of the righteous dead. He said to one of those who was crucified at the time He was, *Today, you will be with Me in paradise* (Luke 23:43).

The word "paradise" is a word used in literature of that time to describe a beautiful garden-like courtyard of a king's home. Such a place in the ancient world—which tended *not* to be a place of cleanliness, beauty, or comfort—was likely to be regarded as the place of *greatest* beauty and serenity known to man. It was a place of total protection—against wild beasts, the elements of nature, and evil people—since the king provided maximum protection to those who were inside his gates. A king's dwelling was regarded as a place of comfort and provision. Any person privileged to be in the "paradise" of a king would know joy without bounds.

There are those who interpret paradise as being some type of intermediate step to heaven that has since been abolished with the resurrection of Christ—almost a pleasant purgatory. I believe

Jesus was saying to this man precisely what he meant. The man, through his acknowledgement of Jesus as the sinless Son of God, was going to be with Jesus in a place that was:

* beautiful
* peaceful
* comforting and comfortable
* with total provision
* with total protection
* marked by exceedingly great joy.

The vision of John in the Bible regarding heaven as a place of gold streets, pearl gates and jeweled walls is labeled "The New Jerusalem," a holy city. (See Revelation 21.) John describes the "nature" of heaven this way:

> *And God will wipe away every tear from their eyes; there shall be no more death, nor sorrow, nor crying. There shall be no more pain, for the former things have passed away.*

The details about heaven are not given to us in the Bible—only the characteristics of man's life once He is with the Lord in the afterlife.

Frankly, I think our finite minds are incapable of grasping fully the glory of heaven. Anything that we can imagine or "think" will fall so far short of the glory of being with the Lord that there is little use in our attempting to envision heaven or describe our life there.

Rather than search for a full-blown description of a place we cannot fully describe, we are to comfort one another with the fact that Jesus has gone to prepare a place for us, and He will either come again to escort us there, or we will go to be with Him there in our death. Either way, we will be with the Lord and the details of that existence will be revealed to us at that time.

Whatever it is that Jesus is preparing for us is going to be exceedingly abundantly beyond anything we can envision.

A Parable About Paradise

One of the parables of Jesus deals specifically with two types of afterlife. It is found in Luke 16:19-31:

> *There was a certain rich man who was clothed in purple and fine linen and fared sumptuously every day. But there*

was a certain beggar named Lazarus, full of sores, who was laid at his gate, desiring to be fed with the crumbs which fell from the rich man's table. Moreover the dogs came and licked his sores. So it was that the beggar died, and was carried by the angels to Abraham's bosom. The rich man also died and was buried. And being in torment in Hades, he lifted up his eyes and saw Abraham afar off, and Lazarus in his bosom.

Then he cried and said, "Father Abraham, have mercy on me, and send Lazarus that he may dip the tip of his finger in water and cool my tongue; for I am tormented in this flame." But Abraham said, "Son, remember that in your lifetime you received your good things, and likewise Lazarus evil things; but now he is comforted and you are tormented. And besides all this, between us and you there is a great gulf fixed, so that those who want to pass from here to you cannot, nor can those from there pass to us."

Then he said, "I beg you therefore, father, that you would send him to my father's house, for I have five brothers, that he may testify to them, lest they also come to this place of torment." Abraham said to him, "They have Moses and the prophets; let them hear them." And he said, "No, father Abraham; but if one goes to them from the dead, they will repent." But he said to him, "If they do not hear Moses and the prophets, neither will they be persuaded though one rise from the dead."

Jesus does not describe just one afterlife for all who die, but two. One is a place of comfort, the other of torment.

Jesus makes it clear that there is a chasm between the two places that cannot be crossed. Those who are in comfort cannot travel to the place of torment, and those in torment cannot pass over into comfort, even though they can "see" the place of comfort. (No doubt that is part of their torment!)

In this story, Jesus also dismisses the testimony of those who rise from the dead. He doesn't say that people don't rise. Nor does he discount what they may have experienced. He simply states that their experiences ultimately have little impact on persuading others about the afterlife. Ultimately, what one believes about the afterlife is *what one believes*. We have no way of determining with certainty the nature or characteristics of the afterlife. We each must approach our death and hereafter with faith. And Jesus tells us that we are far better off to place our faith in what Moses and the prophets have had to say, rather than what a person says who has been "raised from the dead."

Descriptions of Heaven

Elsewhere in God's word heaven is described as a place of:

- great beauty (Revelation 21:1-22:7)
- life (1 Timothy 4:8)
- holiness (Revelation 21:27)
- service (Revelation 22:3)
- worship (Revelation 19:1-3)
- fellowship with God (2 Timothy 4:8)
- glory (2 Corinthians 4:17)

Those who enter Heaven are called to be like Christ in standing and state (Romans 8:29, 1 John 3:2).

Entry Requirements

The biggest difference between those who are in the New Age movement and Bible-believing Christianity is *not* related to the glory and beauty of a heavenly afterlife. The difference is in what it takes to get to heaven.

To New-Age writer Karen Goldman, the only prerequisite for heaven is "purity of intention alone, the deepest sincerity of the heart."[2] No . . . the Bible says that a person must be born anew of the Holy Spirit. (See John 3:16.)

Prevailing Belief in the Afterlife

The prevailing opinion in the world today is that man has an afterlife.

That wasn't necessarily true just a couple of decades ago. Then, many people thought that death was an oblivion, a cessation of life and all consciousness. A significant number of people held the opinion that "when you die, you die, and you are no more." The no-afterlife viewpoint has almost universally been replaced with a good-afterlife philosophy. Very few of those who did not believe in an afterlife, and now do believe, think there is a hell.

Polls have indicated that seventy to eighty percent of Americans believe in heaven, while only fifty to sixty percent believe in hell. Most people seem to think that all Christians believe in hell. Actually, a declining number of ministers do and an increasing number of laymen! Recent polls have indicated that only thirty to forty percent of Christian ministers believe in hell or preach about it publicly. A Gallup Poll in 1990 showed that a greater percentage of Americans believe in hell today than they did in the 1950s.[3]

In the Second Vatican Council in the 1960s, the Catholic Church adopted a position that all souls have the potential to make it to heaven, although purgatory might be a "temporary requirement" for some.[4]

The Bible, however, has more to say about hell than it does about heaven.

The Bible presents hell as a place of everlasting torment. It is eternal, intended for the devil and all who follow him. It is portrayed as a place to be avoided at all costs!

The images associated with hell include:

- torment (Luke 16:28)
- undying worms and unquenched fire (Mark 9:44)
- a lake with fire and brimstone (Revelation 21:8)
- bottomless pit (Revelation 9:2)
- weeping and gnashing of teeth (Matthew 8:12)
- blackness of darkness (Jude 1:13)
- no rest (Revelation 13:11)

Jesus spoke more about hell than he did about heaven. He often used the term "Gehenna" to describe it—Gehenna being the name given to the valley of Hinnon at the southwest edge of Jerusalem, a valley that had become a trash heap and one where pagans had once burned their children alive.

Hell, as described by Jesus, is an everlasting fire prepared for the devil and his angels. (See Matthew 25:41.)

What happened to this view of hell through the centuries?

For the most part, it remained the same as the Bible portrayal. This image was certainly intact when John Milton gave this description of hell in *Paradise Lost:*

> A Dungeon horrible, on all sides round
> As one great Furnace flam'd, yet from those flames
> No light, but rather darkness visible
> Serv'd only to discover sights of woe
> Regions of Sorrow, doleful shades . . . with ever-
> burning Sulpher, unconsum'd.[5]

In Dante's version of hell, titled *Inferno*, Satan is clearly identified as being part of hell. He is called Lucifer or Dis. Hell is not a fiery pit to Dante, however, but frozen in a lake of ice. Ice is considered by many to be a metaphor for the cold heart, one incapable of love.

Still, it is a place to be avoided. Images of hell through the art of the centuries is laden with images of bizarre and frightening torture.

It was only fairly recently that this view of hell changed. In fact, it is only in the last two centuries that we have seen a widespread belief that hell doesn't exist.

Consider the opinions of these nineteenth and twentieth century cults and cult leaders.

- Mary Baker Eddy, spiritist founder of Christian Science, taught that "there is no death." Heaven and hell are considered to be states of thought.
- Edgar Cayce, spiritist whom some consider the founder of the New Age Movement, taught that all souls become "One with the Creator" and no soul is ever lost.
- Sun Myung Moon of The Unification Church believes that God does not depart from any person eternally and all people are restored to God eventually.
- Mormonism teaches that the idea of endless punishment is unscriptural, unreasonable, and revolting.
- Jehovah's Witnesses says that the teaching of hell is a "teaching of demons."
- The Rosicrucians, an occultic group, redefine the terms and state that "eternal damnation" doesn't mean destruction or endless torture.
- Unitarian Universalism holds to a position that there is no resurrection of the body, no literal heaven or hell, and no kind of eternal punishment.

- "Ramtha," the spirit who speaks through medium J. Z. Knight, says, "God has never judged you or anyone" and "there is no hell and there is no devil."[6]

Actually these cultists and New Age teachers depart from the Eastern religions on the point of hell.

Buddhists believe that there are "eight cold hells" for the wicked. These are the major hells and there are 128 lesser hells. Jainism and Taoism, which are variants of Buddhism and Hinduism, also contend that hell exists.

Do Any Near-Death Survivors Go to Hell?

So much has been written by New Age writers about near-death and death experiences resulting in a beautiful afterlife that we sometimes forget that not all people who supposedly have these experiences go to a place of comfort and beauty.

A book about such experiences has been written by Maurice S. Rawlings, M.D. In his own words his book was written:

"To expose the negative cases, those secreted, embarrassing cases found primarily during resuscitative procedures, during the heat of the battle for survival, the time when nothing is concealed, the time when the psychologists and psychiatrists who write most of the books on the subject are absent from the scene."[7]

One researcher cited by Rawlings, Dr. Charles Garfield, has noted, "Not everyone dies a blissful, accepting death. . . . Almost as many of the dying patients interviewed reported negative visions (demons and so forth) as reported blissful experiences, while some reported both."[8]

In 1977, Dr. Rawlings described one of his resuscitated patients this way:

"He had a grotesque grimace expressing sheer horror! His pupils were dilated, and he was perspiring and trembling—he looked as if his hair was standing on end. 'Don't stop. Don't let me go back to hell!' he pleaded desperately."

The hell that Dr. Rawlings' patients describe is often desolate, windy, arid, superheated, empty, "full of eyes," and is filled with a sound of moaning. The ground is rocky or gritty and the air dark or sulfurous. Shadowy figures may lurk in the background, but they seem oblivious to the newcomer. The overwhelming feeling is one of despair and isolation.

Others who claim to have gone to hell as part of a near-death experience recall:

- cramped quarters or a feeling of being stifled
- screaming
- being totally alone
- frightening voids
- menacing voices
- violence
- a feeling of being trapped
- blackness
- a heavy "pressurized" feeling of crushing
- great despondency
- dry, dehydrating heat and scorching
- overwhelming loneliness
- moving through a vacuum
- themselves shrieking and crying in great fear

The negative sequences, apart from ravaging scenery, seem to move more rapidly and cover a shorter time period than the blissful heavenly experiences.

Almost without exception, those who report going to hell believe that "no mistake was made."

Some of those who go to hell *seem* to see familiar people, only to have those images transform into hideous visages of demons.

No report from those who have been to hell and back, includes a visage of Satan or Lucifer. This is because he is not yet there, according to Revelation 20:10. The day has not yet arrived when the devil is cast into the lake of fire.

Is Hell Really Down Under?

A dark nether world has been believed since the earliest known writings of man. Some speculate that early cave dwellers often had to battle ferocious animals who lived at the back of their caves and they thus identified the darkness with fierce beasts and evil moments. The same theory is proposed by some for sea-faring people, who saw the deep of the ocean as a scary place filled with monsters.

Hidden worlds beneath the surface of the earth figured prominently in ancient beliefs. Central Asian Buddhists had a belief in the kingdom of Agartha, a labyrinth of subterranean passages that were a haven for the populations of vanished continents. King Gilgamesh, the legendary Assyro-Babylonian king, was said to have had a long conversation with the ghost of a dead companion about the underworld. The Greeks speculated about the depths of the earth—Orpheus tried to rescue his wife Eurydice from Hades, for example. Homer imagined an underworld and Plato wrote that a god sat at the navel of the earth and emanating from him were tunnels that were both broad and narrow. The Egyptians believed in an infernal underground kingdom. The Incas supposedly escaped with their treasures into deep tunnels that led to the earth's interior.

Edmond Halley, the British astronomer whose name has been given to a comet, found that the magnetic north was not always in the same place. By studying compass readings, he concluded that the earth had more than one magnetic field. He theorized that the earth had a "twin," an outer shell with a similarly shaped inner core. Later he added a couple of more "interiors," finally envisioning an earth that looks a little bit like a set of nesting boxes. The lower cores he believed to be populated by creatures that God had created.

Others have theorized that the earth's inner core contains a paradise, with the earth having an interior sun or suns that give light to an ideal world.

Modern-day occultists have also had a fascination with under-the-earth empires and lost civilizations. Edgar Cayce, who often spent long periods in deep trances, described a supposedly former life in "Atlantean land." In more than 650 readings that he gave while "sleeping," he painted a vivid picture of the ancient world of Atlantis.

The Biblical Location of Hell

The Bible does not give us a "location" for hell. Jesus spoke of its characteristics as being a place of burning, torture, and separation from God.

The idea of hell being a place "down under" comes from Christian church tradition—the idea that Jesus "descended into hell" following His resurrection is not in the Bible, but in church writings.

Different Aftermaths

The biggest difference between Hell and Heaven near-death experiences seems to be in the influence the experiences have on those who have them. Those who report going to Heaven rarely change anything about their lives. They are quite content to continue their life as it was prior to their "Death."

Those who have negative events redirect their lives. Their brush with hell causes conviction, conversion, and a new lifestyle.

We should note, too, that just as near-death images of heaven may not be at all an accurate description of the afterlife, so, too, the descriptions that near-death patients give about hell may not be accurate. One writer, D. Scott Rogo has argued that "these hellish experiences may be hallucinations produced . . . as a reaction to the violent physical ordeals which are part and parcel of normal resuscitation techniques."[9] In other words, they may be linked to the shock treatments and drugs used in treating cardiac arrest.

Baxter's Revelation is a Hellish One

One of the hottest books on the market *among Christians* in recent months has been *A Divine Revelation of Hell* by Mary K. Baxter.

Mary, who is ordained in the Church of God, claims to have had a series of dreams, visions, revelations, and encounters with Jesus beginning in 1976. She claims that for a period of forty days in 1976, Jesus took her into hell, night after night. Six years later she wrote about her experience, which was just published in 1993. The Lord supposedly told her, "Your soul will be taken out of your body, by me, the Lord Jesus Christ, and transmitted into hell and other places that I want you to see. I will also show you visions of heaven and other places and give you many revelations." The bulk of the book is devoted to a vivid description of various people and situations she encountered in hell.

This experience happened to Mary Baxter after she had been praying in the Spirit for several days. The vision that Baxter paints is of a "body" of hell—with legs, arms, and so forth—deep within the earth. The beings she encounters there are grotesque, and tortured for the most part, by fire, worms, and decay.

I will not attempt to diagnose what happened to Mary Baxter, but the vision of hell is one that she claims was given to her as a Christian, by Jesus, under the inspiration of the Holy Spirit, and for the body of Christ on earth. On that basis, I believe her revelation of hell should be subject to even *more* scrutiny against the criterion of the Bible than a near-death experience reported by someone such as Betty Eadie.

Mary Baxter is making a claim that her revelation of hell is something which I, as a Christian, should believe. Her character and her revelation is endorsed by her pastor, Dr. T. L. Lowery of the National Church of God in Washington, D.C. (Lowery, by the way, holds the copyright to her book.) As Christians, we are to judge such words and revelations against the Holy Bible. Just because a person claims to be a Christian does not exempt him from this scrutiny.

I reject this revelation as being from God because of five major discrepancies I see between Baxter's experience and the Holy Bible.

Discrepancy #1: The people Baxter encounters in hell are there primarily because of bad behavior, not because they have failed to receive the atonement offered by Jesus Christ.

One particular preacher is in hell because he was racially prejudiced, made up his own rules about heaven, took money from the poor, and compromised the truth.[10] To another, Jesus supposedly says, "You were given many opportunities to repent, but you hardened your heart and would not . . . And you knew My Word said that all whoremongers will have their part in the lake of fire."[11]

To one woman Jesus is reported as saying, "You loved darkness rather than light, and your deeds were evil. If you had repented with your heart, My Father would have forgiven you. But now, it is too late."[12]

People are irreversibly in hell for lying, occultic activity, strong drink, adultery, and failing to forgive a spouse. Some of them cry out to Jesus for forgiveness when they see Him. He turns a deaf ear.

Throughout the book, Baxter calls repeatedly for people to repent. Her entire focus is on the repentance of man, rather than upon the forgiveness of God.

Repentance and Forgiveness

Repentance means to turn from one's sins. Indeed, as Christians we are to repent of our former sinful ways and live according to the commandments of God.

But Baxter makes repentance a "work," and we are *not* saved by works, but rather by faith (Ephesians 2:8).

The stance of the sinner before God is one of remorse and sorrow as the sinner recognizes and acknowledges that he or she is, indeed, a sinner—one who has lived apart from the commandments of God and who has spurned a relationship with God. The sinner acknowledges sinful behavior, but more than that, a sinful nature. "Have mercy on me, a sinner," is the plea of the one who stands at the foot of the Cross.

God responds to such a person with forgiveness, which the sinner receives *by faith.* The Word of God clearly states that those who confess Jesus Christ as Lord *are* saved. Romans 10:9-10 tells us:

If you confess with your mouth the Lord Jesus and believe in your heart that God has raised Him from the dead, you will be saved. For with the heart one believes unto righteousness, and with the mouth confession is made unto salvation.

Believing and confessing Christ are at the core of the salvation experience.

Upon believing and confessing, the Holy Spirit of God is imparted to the person—formerly a sinner and now a saved believer—and it is the Holy Spirit who enables the person to live in the freedom of righteousness. (See Romans 8:9-17.) Romans 8:26 tells us that it is the Holy Spirit who "helps in our weaknesses." It is the Holy Spirit who enables us to repent and turn away from sin and live a holy, righteous, and acceptable life before God.

Prior to the impartation of the Holy Spirit into a person's life, it is virtually impossible for a person to repent of his ways, or "clean up his act." To repent prior to receiving forgiveness and the presence of the Holy Spirit in one's life makes repentance something we must *do* as a prerequisite to salvation. It's the old "get good and then you can get God" philosophy. That isn't the Gospel of Jesus Christ!

The Gospel states that while we were *yet sinners*, Christ died for us. While we were unworthy, He gave His life for us. And it is while we are unworthy, that He offers us His forgiveness. (See Romans 5:8.)

I did not find one place in her revelation of hell where Jesus says to a person, "I loved you. You rejected my love and refused the forgiveness I offered you. You wouldn't receive the salvation I so freely offered you."

No, quite on the contrary, the people in Baxter's hell are there because they did not do the right works of repentance.

Hell is a punishment for human bad behavior, not the automatic outcome of separation and torment for those who find themselves separated from God's presence because they refused to accept God's offer of forgiveness.

Discrepancy #2: Jesus is punitive, condemning, and callous, and downright mean to those He meets in hell.

Baxter quotes Jesus as saying, "I came to save all men. I desire that all who are lost will repent and call upon My name. It is not My will that any should perish, but have everlasting life. Sad to say, most will not repent of their sins before they die, and they will go to hell." Jesus hardly sounds sad about this fact!

Throughout Baxter's vision, she and Jesus walk through hell and encounter various people who are experiencing various kinds of torment. Jesus supposedly tells one man, "You should have told the truth . . . You knew the way of the cross . . . and now it is too late, too late." Throughout the book, Jesus tells people that it is "too late" for them.

One woman encounters Jesus and says, "I can change . . . I will serve You." Jesus ignores her.

To her and to many others who cry out in torment, Jesus says what appear to be highly absurd words, "Peace, be still!"

How can a person have peace or be still if he or she is being tormented in hell? Why would Jesus tell people to have something they cannot have and to do something they cannot do?

Abandoned in Hell?

Baxter writes, "For the first time since Jesus had left me, I began to realize that I was lost without any hope at all. I sobbed and called out to Jesus over and over again. Then I heard a voice in the darkness saying, 'It will do you no good to call for Jesus. He is not here.'"[13]

This apparently happens during one of at least two times that Jesus abandons Baxter in hell. A roaring fire springs up in front of her, she feels as though her flesh is being ripped off her body, she hurts with pain beyond belief, and feels that evil spirits in the form of bats are biting her all over her body. She is dragged before Lord Satan and fire burns her body and worms crawl over and through her. She begs to die.

Then Jesus appears and "tenderly" speaks to Baxter, "My child, hell is real. But you could never know for sure until you had experienced it for yourself. Now you know the truth and what it is really like to be lost in hell."[14]

Frankly, my response at that point would have been to say, "Thank you for this revelation, Jesus, but I don't intend to go back to hell with you again."

Jesus is hardly a person one can trust, much less trust with one's very life and eternal soul, if He rather casually leaves a person to suffer hell for no stated reason other than "I wanted you to know *for sure* that hell is real."

At no time in the Word of God do we find Jesus, the Holy Spirit, or the Father torturing people so that they will believe more strongly something they already believe! In fact, the righteous throughout the Word of God are portrayed as being rewarded and blessed with peace, joy, and the steadfast presence of God. At no time do we find the righteous being abandoned, much less abandoned in hell.

In fact, the only time we see any righteous person in Scripture who is "separated" from God, it is at the time Jesus takes on the sins of the world and becomes our Sacrifice on the Cross. Jesus cries out that God has forsaken Him. In that moment on the Cross, when Jesus embodied the sins of the world, He *was* no longer righteousness before God. God could not look upon Him because He could not look upon His sin. The death on the cross was pure agony for Jesus because of His feeling forsaken.

God did not abandon Jesus to the torture of crucifixion, but rather, God abandoned our sinful natures to that torture. The more important fact, however, is that Jesus died so that *we wouldn't have to.* He experienced the torture of the cross and the agony of a death laden with sin so that *we would never have to experience such a thing.*

It would have been one thing had Baxter said Jesus took her to the brink of hell where she could see torture. It's quite another for her to say that Jesus took her to hell and left her there . . . twice!

The picture given in God's Word is that the Lord rescues His people from situations such as that described by Baxter. He doesn't *put* them in such situations!

Discrepancy #3: Demons come to earth and live as human beings.

Baxter claims to have seen beautiful dancing women who were actually demons that had been given beautiful bodies. As if watching a movie, she sees these women go to earth at Satan's command and there they appear on a city street, in a nightclub, a store, a bakery shop, a department store, a bank, a wedding, a rummage sale, a church, and a city hall. They use their beauty to seduce men, and Baxter labels them "seducing spirits."

At no time does the Bible say that human beings are demons in disguise. Human beings may be "possessed" by spirits, but they always retain their identity as human beings. Demons may take control of a body by overriding the human spirit, but never do they take on a human body that does not have a human spirit. It is always possible in Scripture for a demon-possessed person to be restored to their right mind. The figures Baxter describes would have no such restoration possible because they have no such mind!

Discrepancy #4: The overriding emotion of this revelation is one of fear.

Baxter says, "Fear—the most awesome fear—gripped my soul."[15] She refers repeatedly to an awesome fear.

Frankly, I believe that is the purpose of this book—to instill people with such a fear of hell that they won't want to go there.

Fear is a poor motivator.

Fear destroys trust . . . it doesn't build trust.

Fear kills relationships . . . it doesn't build them.

Fear leads a person to doubt God's love . . . it doesn't cause a person to embrace more of God's presence.

The Bible teaches that deep fear of the spirit is of the devil, not of God. Such fear is the very opposite of faith.

Furthermore, fear is an emotion and emotions are transitory.

A person is to base their relationship with God upon faith, and upon an act of the will . . . not on how they "feel" about anything, including how they feel about hell.

Our response is to always be *to* Jesus and *to* His Word. Choosing Jesus just to avoid hell is not truly choosing Jesus. It's choosing not to be punished.

A Despairing Aftermath

Baxter's response to her own revelation was one of despair. She exhibited many signs of clinical depression. She states, in her own writing:

"I was sick for many days after I was left in the jaws of hell. I had to have the lights left on when I slept. I needed the Bible with me at all times, and I read it constantly. My soul was in severe shock. I knew now what the lost endured when they went to hell to stay. Jesus would say, 'Peace, be still,' and peace would flood my soul. But a few minutes after I would wake up screaming, hysterical with fear. During this time, I knew I was never alone—Jesus was always there. But even with that knowledge, I sometimes could not feel His presence."

She concludes, "I was so afraid of having to go back to hell that I was fearful to even have Jesus near me sometimes."[16]

Surely a loving all-powerful miracle-working Jesus would not leave his trusted revelator in such a state! Would the Jesus of the

New Testament say "Peace, be still" and not have it be so—would the peace He gives be so transient?

Would Jesus not only abandon one of his saints in hell, but then apparently abandon her as she struggled to regain her emotional and spiritual health after the experience? If so, why? That isn't the Jesus I see in the pages of the New Testament.

What would be the purpose of this great shock to her soul? Certainly, it had no redemptive purpose. It is difficult for me to square the Jesus of the Bible with a Jesus who would do such a thing to one of His own.

Discrepancy #5: The Day of Judgment is portrayed as the day a person dies.

Baxter reports Jesus saying to her:

"Here in hell there are different torments for different souls. Satan administers this torment until the day of judgment, till death and hell are cast into the lake of fire. Also, a lake of fire comes through hell at times."[17]

Her chronology of events related to judgment are out of line with God's Word.

The Bible tells us that when a righteous person dies he or she is immediately with the Lord. The Bible describes the place to which this person goes as "paradise." The Bible frankly doesn't say definitively what happens to a person who does not know the Lord at the time of his or her death. Some state that the Bible inference is that these souls "sleep." Others interpret Jesus' parable in Luke 16:20-31 to say that they go to a place called Hades, which is a place of torment and flames that is obviously separated from paradise. No bridge between the two exists.

Hades, however, is not the hell described in Revelation, with its abyss, lake of fire, and eternal damnation.

Furthermore, Hades has never been regarded by the Church to be a permanent place, but rather, a place that existed prior to the crucifixion and resurrection of Jesus Christ.

The Bible then speaks about a Great White Throne judgment day in which all of God's creatures—mankind, angels, demons, and Satan himself—are called into judgment. It is *later* that Satan is cast into the lake of fire along with the demons, and presumably all others who have chosen Satan over God.

In the Old Testament this judgment is called the Great Day of the Lord.

At no time does the Bible state that a person "dies and goes straight to hell." The only verse of Scripture with which I am familiar that *might* be used to construe that is Hebrews 9:27, which says, *It is appointed for men to die once, but after this the judgment.* The full meaning of this verse, however, when taken in context, is that men die once, not repeatedly (as stated by those who believe in reincarnation), and that we are judged on the basis of what we do in life. In other words, we don't get repeated chances. In no way should this verse be interpreted that we die and immediately face God's judgment and eternal damnation.

Other Questions About Baxter's Hell

Apart from those statements made in Baxter's revelation which I do not believe line up with God's Word, I have other questions about her revelation that are simply rooted in logic.

Why forty days? The torment of one such visit would have been enough to convince me.

What is Jesus doing in hell? Does he go there often? Did Satan know He was there? If so, I can't imagine that given what the Bible says about Satan's nature that Satan wouldn't have done all that he could do to detain Jesus or destroy Him during such a visit. If Jesus does frequent hell on occasion, for what purpose?

It also bothers me a great deal that everyone in Baxter's hell talk the same, regardless of their backgrounds or even the century in which they lived. Jesus talks the same as the people He encounters. Satan talks the same as Jesus, his victims, and Baxter. Everyone has the same voice. I don't sense that in John's Revelation, by comparison. There is a clear delineation of personhood and divinity in John's writing. In Baxter's writing, I come away with the sense that Jesus is pretty much like everybody else. Which leads me to wonder if perhaps, just perhaps, this escort of Baxter's was an imposter Jesus.

Finally, I question why, if Baxter's most important mission in life was to convey this vision to the world, she waited nearly eight years to get the word written and nearly twenty years to get it published.

I would have been at my typewriter the next day if the Lord had told me this was to be my major life's work.

Baxter Also Saw Heaven

Baxter also claims that she had a vision or revelation about Heaven. By comparison, it was a fleeting experience.

She sees two giant planets, beautiful and glorious. God is the light there. She encounters an angel who shows her around. The Heavenly Father speaks to her. She sees children in white robes and sandals who are being taught music from a golden book. She sees a profusion of color, and on the second planet, two mountains of gold, which have golden gates embedded with diamonds and other precious stones. And then suddenly she is back on earth.

In later visions, she sees the building of a mansion and a great "file room" filled with books that detail every person's life.

I think I would have asked for equal time had I been her. Surely forty trips to hell must be worth more than a few moments in glory.

Other revelations in the book relate to false religions, the mark of the beast, and ladders connecting heaven and earth.

How is this Book Being Used?

As in the case of Betty Eadie's book, my concern about this book does not lie solely in its contents, but in the fact that a good many Christians are reading it, and even recommending it to others or using it as a basis of study. I know of one church in which the youth pastor is using it as the basis of discussion with the young people.

I can't help but ask, "Why?"

Why not go directly to the Bible to see what God says about judgment and the hereafter?

Why rely on Mary K. Baxter for this information?

A number of churches are apparently using Baxter's book. I fear they and many others may do so in hopes of "scaring the hell" out of those who attend their Bible studies and discussion groups. Many preachers through the centuries have attempted to frighten people into accepting and following Jesus Christ as their Savior and Lord.

As I stated earlier, I believe fear is a lousy motivator. I recall hearing several sermons when I was a child that were very frightening to me. They did not make me love Jesus. In fact, they had just the opposite effect on me. I figured if God was that vengeful and hateful, I needed to remove myself as far as possible from Him as I could. I soon returned to the Lord, but not out of fear. I returned in response to a message of the Lord's loving forgiveness.

Intrigued by Horror

I suspect that some of the popularity of Baxter's book is related to our general fascination as human beings with horror and violence. We find it very difficult to avert our eyes from a bloody automobile accident. We likely find it intriguing to read about the grotesqueness and horror of hell.

After researching extensively for the book *Horror and Violence—The Deadly Duo in the Media,* authored by Phil Phillips and Joan Hake Robie, I have concluded that a general numbing of the spirit takes place the more we expose ourselves to messages that convey horror and violence. The younger we are when we encounter these messages, the more vivid the message, and the less protected we make ourselves spiritually before exposing ourselves to the message . . . the greater their impact. In essence, we "tune out" a portion of the violence in order to make it less scary and less troublesome to us. We dismiss some of the impact of the violence simply because we cannot accommodate horror in its rawest forms. Taken to the extreme, the numbed spirit begins to regard hell as a fantasy, or as a figment of the imagination. The reality of such a place would be too awful to believe.

We enter into dangerous territory if we totally dismiss the reality of hell and the possibility of eternal judgment. In so doing, a person is far more likely to live their life in any manner they choose, without self-control, self-judgment, or self-restraint. As individuals and as a society, the results of such an approach to living are psychologically and spiritually destructive.

If anything, we as Christians need to have highly sensitive spirits toward that which is evil, not numbed spirits. We need to be

268 Angels, Angels, Angels

acutely aware when something is not pure, innocent, truthful, righteous, or morally correct. Our ability to discern the spirits is based upon an unseared conscious that is able to accurately judge right from wrong.

You may say, "But what's so wrong about a 'little fear' if it turns someone away from hell and toward heaven, or calls someone to reevaluate the way he is living?"

Fear vs. Holy Awe

The Bible's references to the fear of God refer to a "holy awe," a healthy fear rooted in adoration, respect of the highest order, and worship born of love. Such a fear is our response to the knowledge that God is just and His judgments are true, and that He is omnipotent and we are not. My children have a respectful fear of me as their parent, not because I beat or abuse them—which I most definitely do not—but because they know that I am in authority over them and I have not only the ability but the responsibility to train them to follow God's laws.

The fear a person has about hell is not a "holy awe," in virtually all cases, but a fear of damnation. This fear is *not* rooted in a knowledge of God's justice and power to judge, but rather, a belief that God *desires* to condemn and punish. The Bible does not present that belief. One of Satan's most popular lies is the one that God is a fierce judge with a long white beard and piercing eyes, just waiting to squash somebody like a bug for a sin they commit. God's wrath is never exacted on those who have a holy awe of Him, but rather, those who willfully seek to overthrow God or do harm to God's people.

Furthermore, if fear is based on something less than one hundred percent truth, it is a fear that is *wrong*. In the case of Mary K. Baxter's book, I believe her portrayal of hell is less than one hundred percent truthful when held up to the criterion of God's Word. Any fear associated with her revelation, therefore, is also subject to being invalid. When fear and lies are mixed, any good that might be derived from such fear quickly vanishes away. Consider for a moment that you see a piece of lint on the floor that *looks* like a spider. If you are fearful of spiders, you are likely to find your palms growing sweaty and your heartbeat quickening, even though in reality the "spider" on the floor is only a leftover bit from the afternoon load of laundry. When you discover that the lint isn't moving and is, indeed, only lint, your heartbeat returns to normal and your palms dry quickly, and you go on with your day, probably calling yourself silly and laughing at lint. The next time you see lint, you *may* think of it as a spider but you may also think of it as lint. The effect of your initial fear has been reduced.

Hell is a place worthy to be considered frightening. It is a place nobody should want to go or see, even for a split second from a far-away vantage point. When we diminish hell by telling something that is not true about it, we lessen the impact of the reality of hell.

If a person finds out they have been believing something less than the whole truth about hell, what's to keep them from believing that they are hearing less than the whole truth about anything else they associate with the Bible?

Don't mess with imitation truth. If you want to study the truth about God's judgment, forgiveness, hell, and heaven, go directly to God's Word. Begin there. Don't resort to one person's supposed revelation about hell as a peg on which to hang the hat of your belief.

Angel Encounters

17

What About Angelic Encounters?

IN no way should what I have said about the New Age teachings concerning angels be interpreted to mean that I am categorically opposed to angelic visitations. I am convinced that angels do appear to men. They do so at God's initiative.

And, I suspect, the angels are at work in the affairs of men far more than many people recognize or acknowledge.

One reason for my writing this book is to explain that not *all* angelic visits are necessarily ones that line up with the Bible's teachings. What the New Age teaches about angels is far different than what the Bible teaches.

There is no reason to think, however, that God sent angels during the time of the Bible and then stopped sending them. The far more reasonable conclusion is that He is still sending angels on missions of mercy to mankind.

A number of books are presently on the market, or will be in the coming weeks and months, that detail "true-life" encounters that Christians have had with angels. Terry Law's book, *The Real Truth About Angels*, includes a number of stories, as do two books offered by *Guideposts* magazine: *A Rustle of Angels* and *Brush of an Angel's Wing*.

"Angels on Assignment"

Perhaps the grand-daddy of angel-experience books is one that is rather "old"—*Angels on Assignment*, which tells the experiences of Roland Buck as told to Charles and Frances Hunter.

Buck, a pastor in Boise, Idaho, supposedly was awakened by angels on a number of occasions and in all, spent some fifty hours in angelic conversation. The purpose of these visits, according to Buck, was to reveal certain things to him in the Word of God. He says that if he could put the substance of these messages from God into one simple phrase it would be, "I Care!"

In *Angels on Assignment*, Buck states that angels gave him messages such as these:

- God is a lot more interested in people than in procedures— He loves people!
- Regardless of an angel's function—as a praise angel, worship angel, ministering angel, warring angel—its highest purpose is to exalt the name of Jesus.
- God does not record the failures of believers in heaven. (Hebrews 10:17-18)
- The highest purpose of the Word of God is to reveal God's character.
- "There is an area between our permanent abiding place in heaven and this earth from which we can be brought back. People who have died and have been restored to life at God's prerogative, were still in this area. They had not yet reached the place of their final abode . . . I saw a type of hallway, which was something like a corridor or a tunnel between life and death, a waiting room from which individuals enter into the final dwelling place . . . . God told me that a person who dies and comes back has returned from this corridor."
- God's priorities for us are to be the Blood of Jesus, fellowship and communion with God, that Jesus is alive, the promise of the Holy Spirit, that we go tell the world the good news, that the atonement of Jesus is everlasting, and that Jesus will come again.[1]

In reading this book, I found nothing that contradicted God's Word. Rather, Buck is quick to give praise and glory to God, and to exalt Jesus as Lord. The final appearance recorded in the book is one in which Buck and angels joined together in worshiping God. Buck states that he has been able to corroborate every message given him by the angels in God's Word, and that he personally would have been content never to have had an encounter with an angel. Certainly, repeated visits were not his desire.

Buck claims to have seen the angel Gabriel—a creature of great power, size, and radiance.

On another occasion, he felt himself whisked directly into the throne room of God, where the Almighty revealed to him 120 events that would happen in Buck's life. Buck says:

> "It wasn't like you and I write; the information just suddenly appeared! I did not even need to read it, but right now, I can tell you *everything* that was on that paper, because it was instantly impressed on my mind like a printing press prints on paper."[2]

Buck denies that an angel being can come to him at his call. He states:

> "This is not possible! They do not respond to human beings, because they don't take orders from anyone except God . . . . Every single order comes from God, and that is why I know when they are speaking they are echoing words right out of God's heart."[3]

Not All Angel-Encounter Books are New Age

A number of other books on the market also tell of angel encounters, but do not attempt to teach New Age philosophy in the process.

The most in-depth stories are those in Don Fearheiley's book, *Angels Among Us*. Again, these are stories of "mysterious appearances" and occurrences involving benevolent strangers.

Joan Wester Anderson also tells stories of angelic intervention, beginning with the experience her son and a friend had after stalling out during a bitterly cold snowstorm. A tow-truck mysteriously appeared from nowhere and towed them home, only to disappear in the night without leaving tracks in the snow.

This experience led Anderson, a Catholic, to a study of angels. She also began to interview those who said they had experienced angelic intervention in their lives. Her book, *Where Angels Walk*, is a collection of those stories.

The angels nearly always appear in human form—as a lifeguard, a passing motorist, a "stranger" who appears from seemingly nowhere—and after they provide their help, they disappear without payment or an opportunity to say thank you. Other "angels" are felt as unseen hands providing help in times of danger.

The stories told in *There's An Angel on Your Shoulder—Angel Encounters in Everyday Life* by Kelsey Tyler are decidedly Christian in their orientation. The people in these accounts are followers of Christ Jesus and respond to the angelic intervention they perceive with thankfulness to God.

Truly Astounding Encounters

Some of the stories relayed in books such as these are truly astounding.

One of the most famous stories of World War I is about the Angel of Mons. In August 1914, British and French troops were retreating from a German assault. Casualties were heavy. One after another of the wounded who were taken to a field hospital told of seeing angels on the field. One particular angel on a white horse captured the attention of the soldiers. The French referred to him as Michael, the Archangel. The British saw him as St. George.

The soldiers later speculated that their exhaustion had brought on hallucinations. Some speculated that this was an instance of mass hysteria. Later, however, German soldiers told of the same images and said they found themselves absolutely powerless to move forward. Their horses turned around sharply and fled the scene after the angels appeared.

And Sometimes the Very Mundane . . .

I am amazed at the number of people who routinely credit angels with helping them remember or do the most mundane of tasks. In Sophy Burnham's book, *Angel Letters*, she prints letters from people who supposedly have had angelic visitations or received angelic help. Included in the letters are reports of angels:

- reminding a woman to pick up book matches (even though this particular angel was a man shopping with his wife and reminding *her* to get book matches)
- changing a flat tire on a car
- helping a woman decide to which building supply company she should send her son's resumé

I certainly am not saying that angels could *not* do these tasks, but I also question why these instances could not be interpreted as acts involving human insight or human effort.

The first international "Be An Angel Day" took place on August 22, 1993. It was organized by Jane M. Howard, a Maryland channeler of angels. The motto of the day was "Be an Angel, do one small act of service for someone, be a blessing in someone's life." According to the organizers, if a person did this, they would be taking on angelic energy for themselves.

That sounds like just good plain ol' human kindness to me.

Mysterious and Unexplainable

Most of these books tend to focus on mysterious, unexplainable events in which an unseen presence or a visible "unknown person" provides aid. The people always seem to attribute this help to God.

There is also no definitive explanation offered by the authors, other than that a loving God shows concern for His children and sends angels to their assistance.

I like the conclusion drawn by Joan Wester Anderson in *Where Angels Walk*. While not denying the supernatural intervention of God or the involvement of angels in many of the stories she relays, she writes:

"Why is it necessary to explain such occurrences? Why wouldn't a loving God, intimately concerned with His children, send angels *and* humans to do His work?

"For what is it that angels do? They bring us good news. They open our eyes to moments of wonder, to lovely possibilities, to exemplary people, to the idea that God is here in our midst. They lift our hearts and give us wings.

"We can do that for each other.

"Angels minister to us. They sit silently with us as we mourn. They offer us opportunities to turn our suffering into bridges of healing and hope. They challenge us toward new understanding, fresh perspective.

"We can do that for each other.

"Angels offer practical help. As we've seen (in the stories in her book), they furnish information, provide food, buffer the storms of life. Angels lead everyone in the same direction, although not everyone travels at the same speed. But angels are willing to stand by—and wait.

And we can do that for each other."[4]

Benevolent Results

Most of the angel encounter books also can be characterized as being "benevolent" in nature. The angels help, not hinder. They express love, not hate. They are good encounters that result in good feelings.

Many of these encounters result in a person feeling more kindly to God.

In the first few pages of *Brush of an Angel's Wing,* author Charlie Shedd writes:

"I believe that the God who created us did not go off and leave us. In his love he is constantly trying to reach us, lead us, guide us. Or maybe he wants to warn us, detour us, perhaps bring us to an abrupt stop for our own good. I believe that all around us, all the time, his angels are there wanting to direct us. And for what reason? Because he loves us."[5]

As an example of this type of story . . . .

A woman named Edith from North Carolina, a devout Christian who was struggling with serious family problems—including her husband's alcoholism and her mother's suicide—also claimed to see an angel in 1972. She awoke to find an angel hovering over, moving its hand across her forehead and speaking in a language she didn't understand. Another angel stood by her bed. She concluded:

"I knew that the Lord had sent those angels as a visible sign to me to let me know that he was sealing me with his Holy Spirit. I belonged to Him! And, he wanted me to be a witness to the sealing of his Holy Spirit upon me as an assurance to me, because he must have known that I needed that assurance."[6]

But Not All Are Christian or Neutral

The problem with angel-encounter experience collection books is that not *all* of them are Christian, or what I might term "neutral." Some of them are definitely slanted toward the New

Age, or include stories in them of people who are obviously followers of the New Age philosophy.

Eileen Elias Freeman's book is one such book that is *not* biblical or genuinely Christian in its orientation, although some of the
stories she tells sound very much like those in Christ-honoring
books. The main difference is in Freeman's personal experience
with angels, which she recounts in some detail.

Freeman is the founder of a newsletter called *AngelWatch,*
which is put out by The AngelWatch Network. Although she calls
herself a Catholic, Freeman has kept diaries of meditations since
she was eleven years old. As a child, she encountered an angel
who freed her from the fear of dying in the wake of her grand-
mother's death. This angel reportedly appeared to her later in her
life, saying, "I am Enniss, servant of God, and your guardian by
divine grace; and you are my ward in this world." Other angels,
named Asendar, Kennisha, and Tallithia also appeared to her. She
listened to these "inner voices" as they taught her, often with the
accompaniment of ethereal music. They gave her what Freeman
terms "inner visions." Enniss taught her "about the dimension
called heaven and the angelic beings who help us humans in our
quest to live in the fullness of that dimension."[7]

She prayed at Mass about her experiences, but at no time does
she mention ever going to the Bible to compare what is happening
to her with biblical teaching. Rather, she says that she often stayed
an hour after Mass to ask God for "enlightenment."

Her "inner lights and insights" continued to happen for nearly
three years, at which time Enniss told her that her initial work was
completed. By that time, Freeman had four volumes and twelve
hundred pages of writing that she titled *The Guardians of the
Earth.* The four volumes are ones she has subtitled:

- *The Pilot Program*—which describes "a new sort of relationship that is now beginning to develop between angels and
  humans"
- *The House of Healing*—"which shows how we can work
  with the angels through the medium of God's grace to heal
  our lives of evil and darkness"

- *The Rituals of God*—"which explores the ways heaven and earth are growing closer together as this present age winds down"
- *The Percivale Riddle*—"which envisions a world in which angels and humans cooperate in a new and stronger way than ever before to transform the world"

Freeman's book is a blend of Catholic and Bible imagery, with a very heavy dose of New Age philosophy. She quotes the Bible and Babylonian folklore with equal ease.

Some, although not all, of the stories she tells are from a New Age perspective. For example, one supposed angel repeatedly tells a man named Jack, "You know me, Jack, make room for me at your table." He finally concludes that the voice must be that of his guardian angel.

Another person is able to draw angels after experiencing a rush of energy in the middle of the night . . . even though she had no artistic talent by day.

Typical of a New Age story, although this one was told in another book, is one related by a mother who reported that her daughter was miraculously spared from the crash of a large tree limb. The mother states that the little girl told her:

" 'Mommy, a good god told me to sit down and not go under the tree, and I did just what she told me to do.' This 'good god' was a beautiful girl with long golden hair that flowed past her shoulders. She came from the sky and had wings. She had a light so bright about her, said my daughter, that it hurt her eyes, but, when she touched the light, she was surprised how cool it was. It did not burn. The angel had specific jewelry on, especially a necklace that was 'so shiny.' She wore, said my daughter, 'all colors.' "

When a story is told with the terminology of a "good god" full of light and color, you can be assured that the story is within the New Age philosophy.

A Desire to See Angels?

Many times I hear Christians pray that they might be allowed to see angels, or even to see Jesus.

The Bible tells us that we are to walk by faith, not sight (2Corinthians 5:7).

If seeing an angel, or having a vision of Jesus, is vitally important to the meeting of a need in our lives, then God may grant that dream, vision, or encounter. To insist, however, that the Holy Spirit give us such an experience is, very often, a request for God to meet our needs and desires *our way*.

In my personal experience, I find that sincere Bible-believing Christians who ardently desire and *seek* visions and angelic encounters are very often motivated by a desire to:

- earn some type of "spiritual badge"
- receive words of comfort or acceptance that they don't seem to be able to accept for themselves directly from God's Word
- have validation for their relationship with Jesus Christ.

If you are earnestly seeking a particular vision of angels or Christ, ask yourself, *Why is this so vitally important to me? What is it that I am hoping this vision or angelic encounter will do for me, or resolve for me? What do I hope to gain from this?*

Not a Spiritual Merit Badge

Seeing or encountering an angel is not some type of spiritual merit badge. In no place in God's Word is an angelic encounter equated with spiritual depth or as a "reward" for spiritual righteousness.

Rather, we have instances in which angelic visitations are associated with a lack of faith. In the case of Elisha and his servant, we find Elisha asking the Lord to open his servant's eyes so that his servant might see the host of God sent to deliver and protect them. There is no indication, however, that Elisha saw these angels . . . or that Elisha needed to see them. Elisha was strong in his faith that God was going to deliver them. It was the weak-faithed servant that needed to see the host so that he might have courage for the day's events!

Angelic visitations gave courage to most of those who had them in the Bible. The encounters with or visions of angels reinforced a wavering faith, or gave evidence that combatted doubt.

No, encounters with angels are not a sign of God's favor or a validation of a relationship with him.

"But," you may say, "what about the encounter between Gabriel and the Virgin Mary in which Gabriel says that Mary has found favor with God."

Gabriel wasn't sent to Mary as a "reward" for her purity or righteousness as a young woman. Mary's reward was that she was privileged to undertake the very difficult and reputation-destroying task of becoming the virgin mother of Jesus! Gabriel didn't say, "Mary, you have found favor with God and therefore, you are privileged to see and talk with me." He said, "You have found favor with God. And behold, you will conceive." (See Luke 1:26-38.)

Not a Spiritual Shortcut

Angels are not a spiritual shortcut to a relationship with Jesus Christ, or to healing work of the Holy Spirit, or to a renewing of a person's mind and heart so that they will think, act, and respond as Jesus would if He were living on the earth today. Some people seem to hope that in seeing an angel, they will feel closer to Jesus, or be stronger in their faith, or will have an aspect of their personhood healed.

That may happen. But not necessarily so. And furthermore, such an encounter is not necessary to the process of a person being transformed into the likeness of Christ Jesus.

The way to a renewed heart and mind is through accepting the cleansing work that Jesus Christ did on the Cross—truly appropriating the blood of Jesus Christ to your own life and experience—and then by building up yourself in the inner person. In Jude 20 we find an explanation as to how this inner work of edification is accomplished. We are to do three things, simultaneously and always:

- "praying in the Holy Spirit"
- "keeping yourselves in the love of God"
- "looking for the mercy of our Lord Jesus Christ unto eternal life."

Let's take a closer look at exactly what this verse means.

We are transformed as we pray in the Holy Spirit

This ultimately means that we pray according to God's will and in God's will. Our lives are transformed as we pray that God's will *will* be done in our lives. We don't merely pray that God's will *will* be done in a general sense, but that God's will *will* be done in *our* very specific circumstances, relationships, and opportunities.

Jesus gave us an outline for prayer. We often call it the "Lord's Prayer." That prayer begins with an acknowledgement of God's holiness and His absolute worthiness to be worshiped. The prayer requests that God's will be done and that as part of His will, our daily needs be met, our sins forgiven, and our lives be spared from evil and turned toward righteousness. The prayer ends with a praise to God's, recognizing that to Him belong all kingdoms, all power, and all glory. Jesus told his disciples to pray this way, and since they were men who were praying at least three times a day (in following the Jewish custom), we can assume that this prayer also is intended for our daily and frequent use.

As the Holy Spirit leads us, we are to pray for specific needs that we face personally, and which we face in our families, churches, and communities. We are to pray against evil and for the saints of God. We are to be in an attitude of prayer at all times and in all places.

Prayer such as this transforms us! But not by itself.

We are to keep ourselves in the love of God

We are transformed as we accept the fact that God loves us and we begin to live within God's love.

How can we live in God's love?

One way is by having loving relationships with other believers in Jesus Christ who are of like mind and purpose on this earth. We must stay in close fellowship with those who can give us a hug as if that hug comes from God himself, and those who will call us into accountability for our sins just as a loving parent would admonish a child to turn from sin and toward right behavior.

Another way is to read, study, and memorize God's Word. The Word of God expresses God's great love toward mankind. Over and over, in story after story, psalm after psalm, teaching after teaching, the Bible tells us that God loves us. It is out of His great love for us that He gave us commandments to live in a way that is for our good. It is out of love that He chastises us to bring us back into a way of living that is truly "designed" for our good. It is out of love that God rewards us . . . blesses us . . . gives to us. God's loving desire is to live with us forever. Toward that end, He forgives us. He indwells us with His Holy Spirit. Yes, God *loves* us. The more we read His word, the more assured of that fact we become.

But if we don't have that knowledge from God's Word and we are living apart from the loving fellowship of God's people, it will be very difficult for that love to renew and transform our lives.

And still, prayer and love aren't enough by themselves . . . .

We are to look for Christ's mercy to be at work in us . . . from now all the way to eternity.

Jude 20 tells us that we also must continually set our minds in "anticipation" of our future in Christ.

We must know and recognize that each action we take has the potential for eternal consequence. We must be constantly on our toes, eager for the Lord's return. We must live on this earth with one eye on earthly matters, and the other eye on Heaven, knowing that what we do here impacts the way we will live there.

And still there's more. "Looking for the mercy of our Lord Jesus Christ" might have been translated, "expecting the mercy of our Lord Jesus Christ."

Do you live in a state of expectation that Jesus is doing a work in you, that He is your Author and Finisher, and that He is the one who is preparing you for the life you are going to live with Him in eternity? Are you expecting a new miracle every day? Are you believing that God's purposes are being fulfilled in your life, regardless of outer difficult circumstances or the struggles you sometimes encounter? This level of hope and expectation does a transforming work.

Angelic visitations cannot, do not, and never will take the place of prayer, loving Christ-centered relationships, the loving presence of God, or the inspirational hope that we have of our "forever life" with our Heavenly Father.

Do you want to feel God's presence?

Spend time with God in prayer and in reading God's word. Find opportunities to pray, praise, and worship God with others who love Him.

Not a Validation of God's Acceptance

Should an angel appear to a person, they must *accept by faith* that the angelic visitation was real and was from God. It is by faith that we receive the forgiveness of Christ Jesus into our lives, and then do the things that Jesus directs us to do. Reread Hebrews 11. That chapter begins, *Faith is the substance of things hoped for, the evidence of things not seen.* Our believing God's Word to be true *for us* is the only evidence we have to go on! Time and again in Hebrews 11 you will see the little phrase, "by faith." It was by faith that Abel made his sacrifice, Enoch was transported to heaven, Noah prepared an ark, Abraham dwelt in the land of promise as if in a foreign country, Sarah received strength to conceive a child in her old age, Abraham offered up Isaac, Isaac blessed Jacob, and Jacob blessed each of the sons of Joseph. It was by faith that Joseph prophesied the departure of the Children of Israel from Egypt, that Moses' mother hid Moses, Moses chose to associate with the Israelites rather than enjoy the pleasures of sin. It was by faith that the Children of Israel crossed the Red Sea on dry land, the walls of Jericho fell, Rahab was spared. It was by faith that Gideon, Barak, Samson, Jephtha, David, Samuel, and all other heroes and heroines of the Bible did what they did!

They didn't live from one angelic visitation to the next. They lived by faith.

They didn't expect God to live out their lives for them. They walked into their destinies by faith.

Who are we to *expect* to do anything else?

Our lives and relationship with the Lord Jesus are not validated by spiritual experience, but rather by our confession of faith and our living out our lives in steadfast obedience to His word and His call on our lives.

Our Prayer for Experience

Every night my wife and I pray for our four children, "God, make Yourself *real* to them. Make Yourself known to them."

That, in my opinion, is an appropriate prayer regarding spiritual experience and God's revelation to man.

How God chooses to reveal Himself (in addition to the Holy Scriptures) to our children so that they know He exists and is real . . . is God's business. We have assurance in our hearts that God will answer that prayer and touch each of our children's lives in a way that is unique, powerful and meaningful to them—a way that will bring about a relationship that they will never want to mar or dismiss from their lives.

If we were to tell God how we want Him to manifest Himself to our children, we would no doubt greatly limit Him!

18

Blurring Lines:
How to Test the Spirits?

THOSE who think they are summoning angels . . . in all likelihood aren't.

Maurice Rawlings, in his book *To Hell and Back,* tells the
story of a woman named Johanna who went to a place called a
"center for problem-solving." There, she was advised that she
should identify a spirit counselor. She selected "Jesus" and was
also assigned to a female guide named "Sarah."

In order to summon her spirit guide, Johanna was taught to
relax in a comfortable position on the floor, devoid her mind of
all thought and control, and enter an Alpha level of brain activity.
In that state, she was advised that she could reach up and pull
down an imagined door and call the special mantra she was taught
to summon her spirit guides.

Sure enough, when summoned, "Jesus" appeared. She is reported as saying:

"As the door came down, the room was filled with a radiant
light that emanated from the figure standing behind it . . . .
Shimmering brown hair parted in the middle, a high forehead, dark skin; eyes brown, deep, and gentle. There! It was
Jesus! The door went down now of its own accord, revealing
the rest of the figure which was robed in a long white linen
garment. He was glowing with a holy radiance and smiling
softly. I stood, then fell at his feet."

In a subsequent encounter, "Sarah" appeared with Jesus, also in beautiful array. The faces rapidly changed, however, into horrible faces that reminded her of "growling werewolves." Johanna said:

> "They just stood there watching me . . . (and as I approached the faces changed again) . . . . The face of Jesus flashed on—shining and loving—then in a flash, the werewolf reappeared. The same was happening with Sarah."

Johanna was told that this was a "test of her faith" and that as frightening as the faces might be, she should not think of them as evil, but rather "learn to trust and accept them" regardless of the discrepant images they might present.

Until she experienced a genuine act of Christ-centered deliverance several years later, Johanna was a victim of these spirit guides.[1]

What happened to Johanna?

She encountered demons masquerading as benevolent forces—which, by the way, is the *usual* form demons take, initially presenting themselves to human beings. I believe they were what the Bible terms "familiar spirits."

Familiar Spirits Can Take Many Forms

As mentioned in an earlier chapter, familiar spirits are just what their name implies—they are capable of adopting "familiar" images and characteristics, coupled with knowledge that makes them seem extremely familiar with the victim and his past circumstances, so that the person who encounters them sees them as friend, rather than foe.

Familiar spirits present themselves in such a way, *initially* in a guise that is not frightening, demanding, nor in any way threatening. This is the major trick of their deception.

It is only later, because they are incapable of truth and are lying spirits, that their true natures are inevitably revealed.

Most people, unfortunately, do not have a solid understanding about demonic power and how familiar spirits work. They think that demons must appear as hideous, grotesque, frightening creatures at all times. If that were the case, few people would associate with them in various occultic practices! No . . . demons entice and ensnare because of their ability to *appear* extremely appealing, loving, and benevolent.

We must keep in mind always that this is only an appearance. Their true nature is to use this masquerade in order to delude and ultimately to destroy.

Familiar Terminology

New Age philosophy offers a very "user friendly divinity." Familiarity is a trait common to much of the literature.

Only the Names Have Changed . . .

In many cases, the practices of evil now appear to be acceptable in the eyes of many people because the "name" of the practice has been changed.

- Fortune-tellers are now called "futurists."
- Demon possession is politely termed "channeling."
- Crystal charms have replaced crystal balls.
- Meditation has become an acceptable form of self-hypnosis, even among those who would never allow themselves to be hypnotized by others.

In the past, various entities were known as enemies of destruction, including Satan, Shiva, Kali, Pan, and Baal. Now they are known as "god of forces."

. . . and Sometimes the Definitions

When the names haven't been changed, the definitions generally have been!

God in the New Age is an impersonal energy force, immanent in all things. He can be a mother or father, god or goddess. New Age teachers advocate the worship of Mother Earth, the sun, moon, and stars.

Christ is considered to be a reincarnated avatar, Messiah, or messenger sent from the Hierarchy to give advanced spiritual revelation. Buddha, Mohammed, Confucius, Jesus and many others were Christs, but one greater than all of them is expected to usher in the New Age.

Christ Spirit has nothing to do with Jesus Christ. New Agers routinely refer to "the Christ spirit," but they define this spirit as an energy force.

Angels are often called Ascended Masters, Masters of Wisdom, Ancient Masters, spirit guides, inner guides, spirit counselors, the Higher Self, Superbeings, muses, or simply The Self. When taken as a whole, they form the hierarchy, which sends out Christs.

Born Again refers to planetary transformation and healing, and also to personal transformation and healing. This is accomplished when a person "lets go" and allows his Higher Self to guide his life.

The Second Coming refers either to a time when the Christ consciousness will be exalted, or to when the New Age Messiah appears.

Heaven and the Kingdom of God refer to a spiritually-cleansed and purified earth—a time when all people have achieved "Christ consciousness" and the New Age, or Aquarian Age, is established on earth.

Hell does not exist in the New Age. Neither does sin and evil.

Forgiveness is something angels do for a person. Actually, I am always amazed when forgiveness is used by the New Age. The idea is always presented that angels or some divine force freely forgives man and allows him entrance into a new phase of existence, usually depicted as a beautiful afterlife. But, if there's no divine punishment, judgment day, or possibility of hell . . . why forgiveness?

I never said the definitions were consistent . . . only that they differ markedly from Christianity!

The Lines Are Disappearing

Do you recall the old style of bifocal glasses? You could always tell when a person was wearing bifocals or trifocals because of the lines that were visible in the lenses.

Today, however, bifocals and trifocals are manufactured in a way that eliminates those lines.

This is similar, in my opinion, to what has happened to the difference between good and evil in our culture.

We once had a very clear definition of where to draw the line between what was acceptable Christian thinking and behavior and what was decidedly non-Christian. Today, those lines are blurred.

Some Christians dabble in Hindu and Buddhist techniques and philosophy without even realizing it. They aren't even aware that they have muddied up the purity of their relationship with Jesus by worshipping false gods.

Recently, I watched a woman sitting near me in an airport. She was reading a book on angels, which caught my attention since I was in the midst of my research for this book and had recently read the same book. She smiled as she read it and nodded a couple of times in what seemed to be agreement.

A few minutes later, she moved her luggage to let another woman sit down next to her in the waiting area. She struck up a conversation with this woman that I couldn't help but overhear, since they were so close to me. I was surprised to hear her begin talking about her church and pastor, and about the good messages he preached that were based squarely on the Bible.

I couldn't help but ask myself as I boarded the flight, "Did that woman call herself a Christian? Did she believe what she was reading in the New Age book about angels? Why was she reading the book in the first place? Was she able to discern the difference between what the Bible says about angels and what the New Age says about them?"

New Pseudo-Christian Experiences

One of the things that seems to be happening at present is a major outcropping of seminars and workshops that "call" themselves Christian or which use traditional Christian sites (such as churches, camp grounds, and conference centers).

Consider several of these statements from New Age books or books attempting to expose the New Age . . . .

In his book titled *The Lucifer Connection*, Joseph Carr describes a trance medium in operation at what he terms a pseudo-Christian New Age retreat center. The medium called herself a "channeler." She claimed to be doing the work of God and to be a Christian. Carr writes:

> "The young woman medium asked all people present to be
> quiet while she began to recite a repetitious 'prayer' in an
> unknown (to me, at least) language . . . . She was seated
> between two assistants and all three of them prayed with their

hands laid face up on their laps. After two or three minutes her body noticeably stiffened, her facial expression changed and her voice became hoarser. The 'message' that followed the centering down process sounded a lot like prophecies heard in certain churches; a fact which should warn Christians to test all spirits in everything they say or do . . . . Satan can and does counterfeit the miraculous."[2]

Consider, too, the experience of a woman named Carol whose story is told in *Angels of Mercy*. She is published as saying that she went to an evening mass to pray but felt so tired that she couldn't seem to settle into her usual prayer, which was repeating the name of Jesus as a mantra:

"My concentration just wasn't there, so I started to say my mantra out loud. I was feeling down, not necessarily depressed, but world-weary. It seemed I couldn't do anything right at the time. I felt an urge to open Scripture. I had my little Gideon King James Bible with me in my purse, and I cracked it to Acts 4, verse 10. I was overjoyed when I read it (because the verse mentions the name of Jesus as healer). I felt approval at my efforts despite my weariness. I felt heard and acknowledged.

"I was able to just settle down and pray when all of a sudden the whole church appeared to be filled up with moving light, flashes, and singing. I felt like the angels, saints, seraphim, and cherubim were all rejoicing with me and that the very universe, even the stones, sings praise when the name of Jesus is said or spoken. Don't ask me how, but I felt like the very name of Jesus is a caress to the Father, like a whisper of a kiss to his cheek. I can't tell you how long it lasted, or whether I saw with my open eyes. It felt like I did see with my eyes—the church was completely full of color, sounds, and movement, like it was going to burst open."

This experience gave Carol a feeling of guidance. She was experiencing family problems and coping with the death of a friend at the time. This experience, she is reported to have said, has opened her up to many visions and insights, and she teaches others how to meditate.[3]

On the surface, this would seem like a true, biblically-sound Christian spiritual experience. The flaw, however, is that Carol was using the name of Jesus as a *mantra* . . . as if to "conjure" the presence of Jesus, and that once she had experienced the presence of angels, she chose to teach others how to meditate.

A very subtle line of difference exists between praising the name of Jesus, and evoking the name of Jesus in order to "produce" His presence or get in touch with Him. The biblical teaching is that Jesus is present wherever and whenever two or more people are gathered in His name—not when they speak His name. Simply coming together with an intent to pursue the Lord's purposes, to worship the Lord, and to share the Lord's blessings is an invitation to the Lord to be present in our midst.

An Order Devoted to Angels?

What is one to think when the Catholic Church openly supports an order designed to increase angel involvement?

On the one hand, it is not a new concept for the Catholic church to place an emphasis on the presence and work of angels. On the other, it *is* new that leaders in the Catholic church would advise praying to angels or establish an order intended to enhance contact with them.

Pope Pius XI is reported to have prayed to his guardian angel every morning and evening, and if the day was a tough one, at other times. Pope John XXIII reported that angels helped him in his delicate diplomatic dealings.

In 1968, Pope John Paul VI sanctioned the Opus Sanctorum Angelorum ("the work of the holy angels"), a movement that was designed to renew and bolster a belief in guardian angels in the church. There were three phases to this:

- In the first phase, initiates were to make a promise to God to love their guardian angels and respond to their instruction when they were heard "through the voice of conscience." (This phase lasts one year.)
- In the second phase, the initiates are to participate in a candlelight ceremony to consecrate themselves to their holy guardians. They pledge to become like angels and to venerate angels.
- In the third phase, the initiate participates in a ceremony directed to all in the angel kingdom.[4]

More Ahead Within the Church?

Juliet Hollister, founder of the Temple of Understanding (which some call a spiritual United Nations), tells of a huge column of light standing at the foot of her bed one night. The light communicated to her telepathically:

"You're going to be speaking at the cathedral, and angels have a lot to do with holy, sacred places. We guard them. Millions of people don't believe in us, but we are real entities. On behalf of the angelic kingdom, we would appreciate it if, when you make your speech, you would tell the people about us, that we are real, that we love the human race, and that we would like to work on behalf of it. But we can't unless we're invited to do so. We don't enter the life of a human unless we're asked. We are very eager to help."[5]

Again, we see a blending of truth and lie. While angels may guard or be present in sacred places—and there is no biblical reason to think otherwise—the angel who supposedly speaks to Juliet speaks on his own authority, invites people to communicate directly with angels, and claims that angels cannot act on behalf of human beings without an invitation. These are decidedly *unbiblical* messages.

As Christians, we are to ask *God* for help, in the Name of Jesus.

Frequent Use of Out-of-Context Scripture

New Age literature has numerous instances of Scriptures and Bible phrases used "out of context" or misused to support New Age teachings.

One New Age writer quoted Isaiah 9:2 in his work. This passage states, *The people who walked in darkness have seen a great light; those who dwelt in the land of the shadow of death, upon them a light has shined*. Theologians have for literally thousands of years interpreted this as a passage related to the Messiah. To this New Age writer, however, it is biblical evidence for near-death experiences![6]

Another example of the subtle interweaving of accepted Christian terms and practices with New Age philosophy is evident in Terry Lynn Taylor's writings. Consider this excerpt from *Creating with the Angels:*

1. Ask your angel to join with you as a prayer partner when you are praying for the resolution of a problem. Pray, and then spend time with your guardian angel simply thinking about God. You will feel an energy shift, and your answer will be forthcoming. Look for it in creative ways.
2. Write a prayer request on a card and keep it with you. Hold the card in your hand whenever you like, at least three times a day, and pray with your angel for creative guidance and the highest good . . . . (She goes on to suggest creating a prayer box decorated with angel-related art.)
3. When you pray, allow a linking of your mind, soul, and heart to God . . . . Have an angel experience with your prayer, then let it go.

Prayer of two or more people gathered together is scriptural. Prayer involving a human and an angel is not in God's Word.

Writing down prayer requests is an acceptable focus for prayer. Asking an angel to guide prayer is not.

Uniting our heart, mind, and soul to God is Scriptural. Having an "angel experience" in prayer is not.

In another section of *Creating with the Angels*, Taylor suggests we cry "hosanna" in adoration to God. Her reason for doing this, however, is to create an environment in which a person allows his true spiritual creativity to "come out and play with the angels." A few sentences later, she advocates that you "keep your inner light bright and your center strong and spiritual, and stay close to the angels. In this way, you will be a natural creative force for the glory and the light of the Creator."[7]

Hosanna is an expression of praise. We are not, however, to focus our praise for a purpose other than adoration of God. Staying close to the angels is *not* the way to be of use to God. Staying close to *God* is the way to be of greatest use to Him!

We Are Admonished to Test the Spirits!

A very popular movie in recent times has been *Forrest Gump*. A prevailing theme line in this movie is, "Stupid is as stupid does." The character Gump gives this line several times in the movie, always in response to someone calling him stupid or asking him, "Are you stupid?" We've all heard the predecessor of that line, of course—"Beauty is as beauty does."

In judging demons we should use a similar line of thinking: "Evil is as evil does"—not as evil appears. Evil nearly always appears to be beautiful, kind, generous, and acceptable. That's one of the things that makes it so insidiously powerful. Evil rarely appears to be evil at the outset. It is the *working* of evil that reveals its nature.

Spiritual beings—whether angels, spirit guides, or any other so-called supernatural manifestation—must be judged by what they *do* and *say*, and not how they appear. Their words and actions must be clearly discerned and put to the test of judgment against the criterion of God's Word.

The Criterion We Are to Use

We are told to prove, try, or test the spirits to see if they are of God. How do we do this? The criterion is given to us in 1 John 4:1–3:

> *Beloved, do not believe every spirit, but test the spirits, whether they are of God; because many false prophets have gone out into the world. By this you know the Spirit of God: Every spirit that confesses that Jesus Christ has come in the flesh is of God, and every spirit that does not confess that Jesus Christ has come in the flesh is not of God. And this is the spirit of the Antichrist, which you have heard was coming, and is now already in the world.*

The words of John have never been more appropriate or needed than they are today. We are to test the things of the spirit— in other words, to put them up against a divine criteria—and not to take everything we hear about the supernatural at face value. This includes angels, near-death experiences, and experiences related to spiritual guides.

The test given in the Scriptures is five-fold.

An authentic messenger from God will proclaim, and will never deny that Jesus is God's Son, and that He came to this earth in fleshly form.

It was as a flesh-and-blood human being that Jesus gave His life on the Cross, died, was buried, and then rose again in resurrection power, and after a period of forty days, ascended into heaven. This fact of Jesus as "God's son in the flesh" is at the core of every Christian confession. As 1 John 4:2–3 states it:

By this you know the Spirit of God: Every spirit that confesses that Jesus Christ has come in the flesh is of God, and every spirit that does not confess that Jesus Christ has come in the flesh is not of God.

A number of heresies through the centuries have proclaimed that Jesus was more divine than human, or that He was solely spiritual or divine, or that He didn't die a fleshly death on the cross.

Others have denied that He was God's Son in the flesh, calling Him just a good man, a moral teacher, or a fine example.

Those who hold to these positions have never been and are not now true messengers of God's Word.

The Spirit of Antichrist

The New Testament refers to those who deny the flesh-and-blood nature of Jesus as "God come in the flesh," and who deny His crucifixion and resurrection as the one final and lasting act of atonement necessary for the forgiveness of man . . . as possessing the "spirit of antichrist." This is not *the* person of Antichrist portrayed in John's Revelation, but rather, the very spirit that is one hundred percent *not like*, but *opposed to,* Jesus Christ.

Indeed, if you want to try the anger or evoke the disdain of New Agers, bring up the name of Jesus. They are likely to look at you with a smug you-poor-dear attitude and say, "Well, that's what you believe." The implication is that when you are able to handle a higher knowledge, you'll move away from faith in Jesus and embrace the cosmic whole.

The fact is, there is power in the Name of Jesus that far supersedes anything that the New Age can offer. Those who live, act, and speak in the Name of Jesus have no need for the New Age, and are its greatest potential enemies. New Agers may scoff at Christians, but in part, it is a "cover." It is part of Satan's delusion. The Bible speaks to those who have bought into lies as having "scales" over their spiritual eyes. They cannot see the bright truth of God's Word. Our prayer for them must be that the Holy Spirit will remove the scales from their eyes, and that they will come to know the truth. In order for them to hear truth, someone must be willing to speak it. That is our role—not to debate nor to condemn those in the New Age, but to be in a position always to speak the truth to them. To speak the truth, you must be thoroughly familiar with God's Word. To be ready for that challenge, you need to be in close relationship with Jesus Christ and to be wearing the whole armor of His presence every day in your life.

God's Word does not need our defense. It does require our proclamation. We are to speak God's Word without apology, and let the Holy Spirit do the convicting and the wooing of lost souls.

An authentic messenger from God will always exalt Jesus Christ and point toward His atonement for sin, which He made when He died on the Cross.

First John 2:22–23 tells us, *Who is a liar but he who denies that Jesus is the Christ? He is antichrist who denies the Father and the Son. Whoever denies the Son does not have the Father either; he who acknowledges the Son has the Father also.*

The New Age promises forgiveness to everyone.

It isn't at all specific whom you are to ask, or why. Consider this passage quoted in one New Age book. It is from Dostoyevski's *The Brothers Karamazov:*

> "My brother used to ask the birds to forgive him; that sounds senseless but it is right; for all is like the ocean, all things flow and touch each other; a disturbance in one place is felt at the other end of the world. It may be folly to beg forgiveness of the birds, but the birds would be happier at your side—a little happier anyway—and children and all animals, if yourself were nobler than you are now. It's all like an ocean, I tell you. Then you would pray to the birds, too, consumed by an all-embracing love in a sort of transport and pray that they will forgive you your sin. Prize this ecstasy, however senseless it may seem to men."[8]

The New Age has attempted to appropriate every benefit of God . . . but without the shed blood of Jesus Christ!

The Bible makes no provision for angels to be associated with redemption.

Redemption belongs to those who put their trust wholly and solely in the Lord God and who obey His commandments. One of these commandments is given about Jesus: *This is My beloved Son. Hear Him!* (Mark 9:7).

And one of the things that Jesus said:

For God so loved the world that He gave his only begotten Son, that whoever believes in Him should not perish but have everlasting life. For God did not send His son into the world to condemn the world, but that the world through Him might be saved. He who believes in Him is not condemned; but he who does not believe is condemned already, because he has not believed in the name of the only begotten Son of God. And this is the condemnation, that the light has come into the world, and men loved darkness rather than light, because there deeds were evil. For everyone practicing evil hates the light and does not come to the light, lest his deeds should be exposed. But he who does the truth comes to the light, that his deeds may be clearly seen, that they have been done in God (John 3:16–21).

Jesus clearly says in this passage that there are those who practice evil and refuse to come to the light of truth and goodness. Not because of something God has done, but as the result of their own willful disobedience and choice. Jesus came to bring salvation to the world, but those who refuse to believe in Him are described as being condemned.

This was also the message of the Angel of the Lord when he spoke to the children of Israel at Bochim:

Then the Angel of the Lord came up from Gilgal to Bochim, and said, "I led you up from Egypt and brought you to the land of which I swore to your father; and I said, 'I will never break My covenant with you. And you shall make no covenant with the inhabitants of this land; you shall tear down their altars.' But you have not obeyed My voice. Why have you done this? Therefore I also said, 'I will not drive them out before you; but they shall be thorns in your side, and their gods shall be a snare to you.'" So it was, when the Angel of the Lord spoke these words to the children of Israel, that the people lifted up their voices and wept (Judges 2:1–4).

No Fatalistic Predestination

The general pervasive doctrine we must guard ourselves against is a doctrine of "fatalistic predestination." On the one hand, there are those who believe that certain people are destined for heaven, while others are not, and that no matter what a person does or does not do, they will never make it to heaven. That is not a biblical point of view. The Bible clearly says, *The Son of Man has come to seek and to save that which was lost* (Luke 19:10).

We have a responsibility to respond to God's initiative. Our will is involved. Our eternal fate was not sealed at our birth. It is sealed only at the time of our "new birth" or at the time of our physical death. As long as we are alive and have not hardened our hearts to the point where we can no longer acknowledge the work of the Holy Spirit, we are capable of receiving God's gift of eternal salvation and of repenting of our sins and leading a new life.

At the opposite end of the fatalistic predestination scale we find those who believe that no matter what they do, they will end up in heaven. Their rationale is generally along these lines: "A loving God would never send a person to hell." The facts are, however, that God is a just God who gave mankind certain commandments about life, and God also gave man a free will, which gives man just as much freedom *not* to obey as to obey those commandments. To say that a loving God would never send a person to hell is like saying that a loving teacher will never give a student an F grade or a loving principal will never expel a student from school. If a student refuses to attend class, doesn't do any of his homework, and performs miserably on every exam, the "love" of the teacher does not override the will of the student. The teacher is not "giving" the student a failing grade, but rather, the student has chosen a failing grade through his own willful actions. By the same reasoning, a student who misbehaves continually in school "earns" expulsion from school. It has nothing to do with how the principal of that school feels about the student or what the principal desires for the student.

Again, refer to John 3:16–21. Jesus taught clearly that there are those who love darkness and their practice of evil, and who both hate the light and refuse to come to it.

The more realistic conclusion is that "some people send themselves to hell because they refuse to accept the love of God."

An authentic messenger from God never encourages divination or occultic practices.

Most of us are aware that the rockets and satellites we project into orbit around the earth have "guidance systems" that direct them to an intended location. God's Word is intended to be our guidance system in life in preparing us for everlasting life with Him in heaven.

The enemy has a number of guidance systems—horoscopes, mirrors, crystal balls, Tarot cards, I Ching, fortune-tellers, shamans, mediums, and so forth. They lead to a different destination.

God's Commands About Divination

The Scriptures clearly teach against divination. (See Deuteronomy 4:15-16 and 18:10-13.) Every time a true prophet of God comes up against sorcerers and magicians in the Bible, God's man wins. (See Exodus 7:11-12 as an example.)

The reason that we are to avoid divination is *not* because divination doesn't work at times. Rather, it is because divination is *always* based upon chance, man-initiated methods, and man-made interpretations. Divination turns a person away from trusting in God, who does not rule the universe according to chance, but rather, has a plan and purpose for every living creature.

The Scriptures call us to turn to God, and to Him alone, for wise counsel. The Holy Spirit is called the Spirit of Truth, our Counselor, our Comforter. It is in God that we are to live and move and have our being. He is the one who has given us our personalities and who orders our days—and furthermore, He sent His Son to redeem us from the negative aspects of our personalities and His Spirit to guide us into all truth and purpose for our lives. We are not the product of an alignment of the stars. We are not to plan our days based upon divination. We are to seek God first and foremost, and follow His commandments and the leading of the Holy Spirit as we encounter the situations and circumstances that each day brings us.

Ultimately, divination causes a person to follow after a false god—which may be the divination technique itself. Deuteronomy 13 has strong words about this entire process:

> If there arises among you a prophet or a dreamer of dreams, and he gives you a sign or a wonder, and the sign or the wonder comes to pass, of which he spoke to you, saying, Let us go after other gods—which you have not known—and let us serve them, you shall not listen to the words of that prophet or that dreamer of dreams . . . You shall walk after

*the Lord your God and fear Him, and keep His command-
ments and obey His voice; you shall serve Him and hold fast
to Him. But that prophet or that dreamer of dreams shall be
put to death, because he has spoken in order to turn you
away from the Lord your God, who brought you out of the
land of Egypt and redeemed you from the house of bondage,
to entice you from the way in which the Lord your God
commanded you to walk. So you shall put away the evil
from your midst* (Deuteronomy 13:1-5).

The apostle Paul wrote to the Romans, *I want you to be wise in
what is good, and simple (or innocent) in what is evil* (Romans
16:19).

**An authentic messenger from God never contradicts
Scripture or dismisses its importance.**

Prophecy stands in sharp contrast to divination. A genuine
prophecy includes an admonition (or rebuke of past or present
practices), exhortation (a strong appeal to change), and supernatural authorship. Prophecy never contradicts Scripture.

Prophets are to be tested. How? Their words are to be judged
against the Word of God, and their words must come to pass, or
they are to be killed! (See Deuteronomy 18:20-22.)

Furthermore, an authentic message from God will have two or
three witnesses. Matthew 18:16 tells us, *By the mouth of two or
three witnesses every word may be established.*

God does not give revelation to just one person regarding His
Body. His truth is intended for universal application to all in the
Church and He makes His will known through two or more wit-
nesses.

One of those witnesses is the Word of God itself, the Holy
Bible. A person who gives a message that is contrary to the Bible
is not a messenger from God. God is Truth and His Word is true,
and God will not contradict what has already been spoken to mankind. He changes not.

Knowing God's Word

In order to be able to verify a messenger's words as in line
with Scripture, of course, one must know the Scriptures!

One of the stories I found interesting in doing the research for
this book was told by Arterburn and Felton. It was originally

reported, interestingly enough, in a secular newspaper, the *Yucaipa & Calimesa News-Mirror*. They write:

Connie Elliot, a twenty-three-year-old, attractive woman, had learned a lot about spiritual things for her young years. Growing up, she was always curious about the occult. Experiencing quite a bit of pain in her family life, Connie battled depression and was on a quest to find a way to overcome her problems: "She said her deepening involvement with the occult coincided with a serious bout of depression." Although she got more and more involved in the occult, "she said the occult failed to give her the satisfaction in life she craved." Through the confrontation and perseverance of her aunt, Connie finally came to see how deceived she had been: "She said her aunt was able to demonstrate to her the Bible had all the answers she had been searching for. 'Four days later, an overwhelming peace came over me like peace I had never had in my life,' she said, 'The void was gone when I became a Christian.'"[9]

Connie Elliot's aunt gives all of us an example of what we need to be prepared to do to rescue those who will *not* find genuine satisfaction through New Age practices. She:

- confronted,
- persevered,
- used the Bible to give answers.

Unfortunately, we seem to be a people who are fairly Bible illiterate. As reported by George Barna in the book *The Frog in the Kettle*, a poll revealed that:

- 31 percent knew that the expression "God helps those who help themselves" is *not* in the Bible.
- 52 percent correctly stated that the book of Thomas is *not* part of the Bible.
- 45 percent knew that the book of Jonah is in the Bible.
- 58 percent did not know who preached the Sermon on the Mount.[10]

Furthermore, in a poll reported by George Gallup, Jr. and Sarah Jones, only 51 percent of Americans believe in the full authority of the Bible, and only 69 percent believe in the divinity of Jesus Christ.[11]

When asked what it means to be a Christian, Barna found that 22 percent didn't know. Only 19 percent (about one in five) thought it meant to "accept Christ as Savior, personally." The other answers were scattered among these opinions: be a good person, go to church, be religious, believe in God, love others, help other people, and live differently from other people.[12]

We are a nation that doesn't know the Bible, doesn't know what it means to be a Christian, and doesn't know in Whom Christians put their trust!

If you are going to do what the Bible commands you to do—test the spirits—then you need to be reading and studying your Bible on a regular basis. You need to be digging for the deep truths in God's Word.

An authentic messenger of God never undermines the majesty, glory, or holiness of Almighty God, King of the Universe.

Many of those who write about angels today seem to have almost a casual approach toward them, and advocate a casual relationship with them. That is not how the people of the Bible responded to angels. In Daniel 10:10–11 we see how Daniel responded to an angel:

> *Suddenly, a hand touched me, which made me tremble on my knees and on the palms of my hands. And he said to me, "O Daniel, man greatly beloved, understand the words that I speak to you, and stand upright, for I have now been sent to you." While he was speaking this word to me, I stood trembling.*

Daniel literally fell to the ground without strength. Two more times in this passage he describes how the angel, *one having the likeness of a man* touched him and strengthened him after he had turned his face toward the ground, speechless and without strength.

Daniel had truly encountered the supernatural.

We Do Get What We Believe

On one point, the New Age is correct: we get what we believe.

When it comes to angels and near-death experiences, there is a strong tendency toward the position, "we see what we expect to see." This opinion is held by quite a number of modern-day physicists and psychologists. The New Age version tends to be stated, "You create what you think."

From a Christian standpoint, the Bible admonishes us to have faith . . . even when we don't see with our natural eyes. We are to believe God is at work, and trust Him to bring forth His blessing in due season.

If this includes an encounter with an Angel of the Lord—so be it!

Reference Notes

Chapter 1 — no end notes

Chapter 2
1 Nancy Gray, *The Angelic Army,* (Tulsa, OK: Harrison House, 1993), p.21.
2 Gail Harvey, *On the Wings of Angels,* (New York: Gramercy Books, 1993), p.5.
3 Charlie W. Shedd, *Brush of an Angel's Wing,* (Ann Arbor, MI: Servant Publications, 1994), p.15.

Chapter 3 — no end notes

Chapter 4
1 Harvey, p.3.

Chapter 5
1 Harvey, p.51.

Chapter 6
1 Morris B. Margolies, *A Gathering of Angels—Angels in Jewish Life and Literature,* (New York: Ballantine Books, 1994), p.225.
2 Margolies, p.10.
3 Margolies, p.19.
4 Sophy Burnham, *A Book of Angels—Reflections on Angels Past and Present and True Stories of How They Touch Our Lives,* (New York: Ballantine Books, 1990), p.179.
5 David Connolly, *In Search of Angels—A Celestial Sourcebook for Beginning Your Journey,* (New York: Perigree Books, 1993), p.65.
6 Connolly, p.48.
7 Connolly, p.61.

Chapter 7 — no end notes

Chapter 8
1 Terry Lynn Taylor, *Creating with the Angels—An Angel-Guided Journey into Creativity,* (Tiburon, CA: H. J. Kramer, Inc. 1993), p.5.
2 Connolly, p.20.
3 Karen Goldman, *Angel Voices,* (New York: Simon & Schuster, 1993), p.143.
4 Alma Daniel, Timothy Wyllie, and Andrew Ramer, *Ask Your Angels,* (New York, Ballantine Books, 1992), p.27.
5 Daniel, Wyllie, and Ramer, p.69.
6 Rosemary Ellen Guiley, *Angels of Mercy,* (New York: Pocket Books, 1991), p.xiv.
7 Burnham, pp.113-114.
8 Daniel, Wyllie, and Ramer, pp.4-5.
9 Burnham, p.7.

10 Burnham, pp.13–15.
11 Burnham, pp.21–22.
12 Guiley, pp.63–64.
13 Goldman, *The Angel Book*, (New York: Simon & Schuster, 1992), pp.11–12.
14 Goldman, pp.13–16.
15 Goldman, pp.83–84.
16 Goldman, p.24.
17 Goldman, *Angel Voices*, p.68.
18 Goldman, *The Angel Book*, p.45.
19 Goldman, p.46.
20 Goldman, p.78.
21 Goldman, *Angel Voices*, p.17.
22 Goldman, p.18.
23 Goldman, p.21.
24 Goldman, p.32.
25 Goldman, pp.56–58.
26 Goldman, *The Angel Book*, p.51.
27 Goldman, p.54.
28 Goldman, *Angel Voices*, p.150.
29 Goldman, p.34.
30 Goldman, *The Angel Book*, p.70.
31 Goldman, *Angel Voices*, p.27.
32 Goldman, *The Angel Book*, pp.78–80.
33 Goldman, p.32.
34 Goldman, p.33.
35 Goldman, pp.93–95.
36 Goldman, *Angel Voices*, p.94.
37 Goldman, p.95.
38 Goldman, p.95.
39 Goldman, p.96.
40 Goldman, p.79.
41 Goldman, pp.81–83.
42 Goldman, p.133.
43 Goldman, p.149.
44 Goldman, p.21.
45 Goldman, p.38.
Chapter 9
  1 Taylor, xiii.
  2 Sophy Burnham, *Angel Letters*, (New York: Ballantine Books, 1991), p.vii.
  3 Daniel, Wyllie, and Ramer, p.82.
  4 Burnham, *A Book of Angels*, p.43.
  5 Daniel, Wyllie, and Ramer, p.3.

6 John Randolph Price, *The Angels Within Us—A Spiritual Guide to the Twenty-Two Angels that Govern Our Lives,* (New York: Fawcett Columbine, 1993), pp.192–193.

7 Taylor, p.xiii.

8 Taylor, pp.12–13.

9 Taylor, p.37.

10 Taylor, p.40.

11 Taylor, p.54.

12 Taylor, p.76.

13 Taylor, pp.162–163.

14 Guiley, pp.92–93.

15 Guiley, p.76.

16 Walter Martin, *Kingdom of the Cults,* p.363. (note: no publisher or year mentioned)

17 Burnham, *Angel Letters,* p.13.

18 A. W. Tozer, *That Incredible Christian,* pp.69–70. (note: no publisher or year mentioned)

19 Guiley, p.65.

20 Guiley, pp.65–66.

21 Daniel, Wyllie, and Ramer, p.69.

22 Burnham, *A Book of Angels,* p.120.

23 Maurice S. Rawlings, *To Hell and Back,* (Nashville, TN: Thomas Nelson Publishers, 1993), p.160.

Chapter 10

1 Phil Phillips & Joan Hake Robie, *Halloween and Satanism,* (Lancaster, PA: Starburst, Inc., 1987), pp.91–98.

2 Ingrid Broller, *Do You Believe in the Supernatural?* Parents, (October 1989), p.32.

3 Reader's Digest, *Quest for the Unknown—Life Beyond Death,* (Pleasantville, NY: The Reader's Digest Association, Inc., 1992), p.75.

4 Taylor, p.213.

5 Guiley, pp.98–105.

6 Margolies, pp.260–261.

7 Peter Elkind, *The Curse of the Black Lords,* Texas Monthly, (May 1990), pp.95–179.

8 Goldman, *The Angel Book,* p.85.

9 Larry Dossey, *Healing Words—The Power of Prayer and the Practice of Medicine,* (San Francisco, CA: Harper Collins, 1993), p.xix.

10 Dossey, p.7.

11 Dossey, p.8.

12 Texe Marrs, *Dark Secrets of the New Age—Satan's Plan for a One-World Religion,* (Westchester, IL: Crossway Books, 1987), pp.18–19.

13 Marrs, p.19.

14 Constance Cumbey, *The Hidden Dangers of the Rainbow,*
    (Shreveport, LA: Huntington House, Inc., 1983), pp.121–122.
15 Marrs, p.11.
16 Marrs, p.15.
17 Marrs, p.16.
18 C. S. Lewis, *Mere Christianity,* (London: Collins Clear-Type Press,
    1952), p.188.

Chapter 11
    1 Jane Mersky Leder, *Psychics at Work,* McCall's, (October 1987), p.159.
    2 Will Baron, *Deceived by the New Age,* (Boise, ID: Pacific Press
       Publishing Association, 1990), p.11.

Chapter 12 — no end notes

Chapter 13
    1 C. S. Lewis, *The Screwtape Letters,* (New York: MacMillan Co.,
       1961), preface.
    2 Phillips and Robie, pp.172–174
    3 Billy Graham, *Angels: God's Secret Agents,* (New York: Doubleday &
       Company, Inc., 1975), p.167.
    4 Price, p.101.
    5 Guiley, pp.216–217.
    6 Baron, p.39.
    7 David Spangler, *Reflections of the Christ,* (Scotland: Findhorn,
       1977), pp.36–39.
    8 Spangler, p.178.
    9 Daniel, Wyllie, and Ramer, p.28.
   10 Daniel, Wyllie, and Ramer, p.29.
   11 Baron, p.11.
   12 Baron, pp.11–12.
   13 Baron, p.157.

Chapter 14
    1 Betty J. Eadie, *Embraced by the Light,* (Placerville, CA:
       Gold Leaf Press, 1992), p.7.
    2 Eadie, p.5.
    3 Eadie, p.8.
    4 Eadie, p.10.
    5 Eadie, p.12.
    6 Eadie, p.18.
    7 Eadie, p.73.
    8 Eadie, pp.31–34.
    9 Eadie, pp.37–38.
   10 Eadie, pp.41–42.
   11 Eadie, p.44.
   12 Eadie, pp.47–48.
   13 Eadie, pp.48–49.

14 Eadie, pp.83–84.
15 Eadie, p113.
16 Eadie, p.50.
17 Eadie, p.35.
18 Eadie, pp.84–85.
19 Eadie, p.51.
20 Eadie, pp.45–46.
21 Eadie, pp.52–53.
22 Eadie, pp.80–81.
23 Eadie, p.57.
24 Eadic, p.58.
25 Eadic, p.55.
26 Eadie, pp.56–57.
27 Eadie, p.59.
28 Eadic, p.64.
29 Eadie, p.67.
30 Eadie, p.71.
31 Eadie, p.99.
32 Eadie, p.90.
33 Eadie, pp.103–104
34 Eadic, p.127.
35 Eadie, p.31.
36 Eadie, p.82.
37 Eadie, p.41.
38 Eadie, p.45.
39 Eadie, p.61.
40 Eadie, p.109.
41 John Ankerberg and John Weldon, *Cult Watch—What You Need to Know about Spiritual Deception,* (Eugene, OR: Harvest House Publishers, 1991), p.11.
42 Ankerberg and Weldon, p.25.
43 Eadie, p.48.
44 Eadie, pp.51–52.
45 Eadie, pp.52–53.

Chapter 15
 1 Dannion Brinkley, *Saved by the Light,* (New York: Villard Books, 1994), p.25.
 2 Brinkley, p.26.
 3 Brinkley, p.72.
 4 Brinkley, pp.46–47.
 5 Brinkley, pp.59–60.
 6 Brinkley, p.153.
 7 Brinkley, p.159.
 8 Brinkley, p.160.

 9 Reader's Digest, *Life Beyond Death*, p.23.
10 Time-Life Books, *Mysteries of the Unknown: Psychic Powers*, (Alexandria, VA: Time-Life Books, 1987), p.88.
11 Taylor, p.177.
12 Stephan Hoeller, *The Gnostic Jung and the Seven Sermons of the Dead*, (Wheaton, IL: Theosophical Publishing House, 1982), p.4.
13 Melvin Morse with Paul Perry, *Closer to the Light—Learning from the Near-Death Experienes of Children*, (New York: Ivy Books, 1990), pp.4–7.
14 Morse, p.7.
15 Morse, p.124.
16 Reader's Digest, *Life Beyond Death*, p.29.
17 Marrs, p.96.
18 Paul Pearsall, *Making Miracles*, (New York: Prentice Hall Press, 1991), p.i.
19 Pearsall, pp.2–3.
20 Pearsall, p.5.
21 Pearsall, p.18.
22 Pearsall, p.214.
23 Pearsall, p.243.
24 Goldman, *Angel Voices*, pp.88–89.
25 Goldman, p.87.
26 Guiley, pp.109–110.
27 Guiley, pp.109–111.
28 Rawlings, *To Hell and Back*, p.164

Chapter 16
 1 Rebecca Springer, *Within the Gates*, (Dallas, TX: Christ for the Nations, 1971), p.3.
 2 Goldman, *Angel Voices*, p.140.
 3 *U. S. News and World Report*, 25 (March 1991), p.57.
 4 Rawlings, p.70.
 5 Burnham, *A Book of Angels*, p.143.
 6 Rawlings, pp.81–83.
 7 Rawlings, p.11.
 8 Rawlings, p.73.
 9 Reader's Digest, *Life Beyond Death*, p.27.
10 Mary K. Baxter, *A Divine Revelation of Hell*, (Springdale, PA: Whitaker House, 1993), p.42.
11 Baxter, p.45.
12 Baxter, p.155.
13 Baxter, p.113.
14 Baxter, p.119.
15 Baxter, p.113.
16 Baxter, p.191.
17 Baxter, p.88.

Chapter 17

1 Charles and Frances Hunter, *Angels on Assignment,* (Houston, TX: Hunter Books, 1979), pp.58-59.
2 Hunter, p.52.
3 Hunter, p.70.
4 Joan Wester Anderson, *Where Angels Walk,* (New York: Ballantine Books, 1992), pp.233-234.
5 Shedd, p.14.
6 Guiley, pp.117-118.
7 Eileen Elias Freeman, *Touched by Angels,* (New York: Warner Books, 1993), p.23.

Chapter 18

1 Rawlings, *To Hell and Back,* pp.138-139.
2 Joseph Carr, *The Lucifer Connection,* (Lafayette, LA: Huntington House, Inc., 1987), p.63.
3 Guiley, pp.81-82.
4 Guiley, pp.61-62.
5 Guiley, p.14.
6 Jeffrey Iverson, *In Search of the Dead—A Scientific Investigation of Evidence for Life After Death,* (San Francisco, CA: Harper Collins, 1992), p.88.
7 Taylor, pp.92-93.
8 Burnham, *A Book of Angels,* p.57.
9 Stephen Arterburn and Jack Felton, *Faith that Hurts, Faith that Heals,* (Nashville, TN: Thomas Nelson Publishers, 1992), p.268.
10 George Barna, *The Frog in the Kettle,* (Ventura, CA: Regal Books, 1990), p.118.
11 George Gallup, Jr., and Sarah Jones, *100 Questions and Answers: Religion in America,* (Princeton, NJ: Princeton Religion Research Center, 1989), p.188.
12 Barna, p.114.

Bibliography

Mortimore J. Adler, *The Angels and Us*, New York: Collier Books, 1982.

**John Ankerberg and John Weldon, *Cult Watch—What You Need to Know about Spiritual Deception*, Eugene, Oregon: Harvest House Publishers, 1991.

Joan Wester Anderson, *Where Angels Walk*, New York: Ballantine Books, 1992.

Stephen Arterburn and Jack Felton, *Faith that Hurts, Faith that Heals*, Nashville, Tennessee: Thomas Nelson Publishers, 1992.

George Barna, *The Frog in the Kettle*, Ventura, California: Regal Books, 1990.

**Will Baron, *Deceived by the New Age*, Boise, Idaho: Pacific Press Publishing Association, 1990.

Mary K. Baxter, *A Divine Revelation of Hell*, Springdale, Pennsylvania: Whitaker House, 1993.

Bookselling This Week, May 16, 1994.

Dannion Brinkley, *Saved by the Light*, New York: Villard Books, 1994.

Sophy Burnham, *A Book of Angels—Reflections on Angels Past and Present and True Stories of How They Touch Our Lives*, New York: Ballantine Books, 1990.

Sophy Burnham, *Angel Letters*, New York: Ballantine, 1991.

Joseph Carr, *The Lucifer Connection*, Lafayette, Louisiana: Huntington House, Inc., 1987.

David Connolly, *In Search of Angels—A Celestial Sourcebook for Beginning Your Journey*, New York: Perigree Books, 1993.

Constance Cumbey, *The Hidden Dangers of the Rainbow*, Shreveport, Louisiana: Huntington House, Inc., 1983.

Alma Daniel, Timothy Wyllie, and Andrew Ramer, *Ask Your Angels*, New York: Ballantine Books, 1992.

*C. Fred Dickason, *Angels Elect & Evil*, Chicago, Illinois: Moody Press, 1975.

Larry Dossey, *Healing Words—The Power of Prayer and the Practice of Medicine*, San Francisco, California: Harper Collins, 1993.

Betty J. Eadie, *Embraced by the Light*, Placerville, California: Gold Leaf Press, 1992.

Peter Elkind, *The Curse of the Black Lords*, Texas Monthly, May 1990.

Don Fearheiley, *Angels Among Us*, New York: Avon Books, 1993.

Eileen Elias Freeman, *Touched by Angels*, New York: Warner Books, 1993.

George Gallup, Jr., and Sarah Jones, *100 Questions and Answers: Religion in America*, Princeton, New Jersey: Princeton Religion Research Center, 1989.

Kenneth O. Gangel, *Unwrap Your Spiritual Gifts*, Wheaton, Illinois: Victor Books, 1983.

Karen Goldman, *The Angel Book,* New York: Simon & Schuster, 1992.

Karen Goldman, *Angel Voices,* New York: Simon & Schuster, 1993.

*Billy Graham, *Angels: God's Secret Agents,* New York: Doubleday & Company, Inc., 1975.

Nancy Gray, *The Angelic Army,* Tulsa, Oklahoma: Harrison House, 1993.

Ingrid Groller, *Do You Believe in the Supernatural?* Parents, October 1989.

Rosemary Ellen Guiley, *Angels of Mercy,* New York: Pocket Books, 1994.

Gail Harvey, *On the Wings of Angels,* New York: Gramercy Books, 1993.

Marilyn Hickey, *Angels All Around — The Present-day Ministry of Angels,* Denver, Colorado: Marilyn Hickey Ministries, 1991.

Marilyn Hickey, *Activate Your Heavenly Force,* Charisma, September 1993.

Stephan Hoeller, *The Gnostic Jung and the Seven Sermons to the Dead,* Wheaton, Ilinois: Theosophical Publishing House, 1982.

Charles and Frances Hunter, *Angels on Assignment,* Houston, Texas: Hunter Books, 1979.

Jeffrey Iverson, *In Search of the Dead—A Scientific Investigation of Evidence for Life After Death,* San Francisco, California: Harper Collins, 1992.

**Paul A. Kienel, *Handbook for Christian Living—A Resource Manual for Applying God's Truth in a Mixed-Up World,* Nashville, Tennessee: Thomas Nelson Publishers, 1991

**Berit Kjos, *Your Child & the New Age,* Wheaton, Illinois: Victor Books, 1990.

Jane Mersky Leder, *Psychics at Work,* McCall's, October 1987.

C. S. Lewis, *Mere Christianity*, London: Collins Clear-Type Press, 1952.

C. S. Lewis, *The Screwtape Letters,* New York: MacMillan Co., 1961.

Morris B. Margolies, *A Gathering of Angels—Angels in Jewish Life and Literature,* New York: Ballantine Books, 1994.

**Texe Marrs, *Dark Secrets of the New Age—Satan's Plan for a One-World Religion,* Westchester, Ilinois: Crossway Books, 1987.

Daisy Maryles, *Behind the Bestsellers,* Publisher's Weekly, June 20, 1994.

**Josh McDowell and Don Steward, *Understanding the Occult—Handbook of Today's Religions,* San Bernardino, California: Here's Life Publishers, Inc., 1982.

Melvin Morse, *Transformed by the Light — the Powerful Effect of Near-Death Experiences on People's Lives,* New York: Ivy Books, 1992.

Melvin Morse with Paul Perry, *Closer to the Light—Learning from the Near-Death Experiences of Children,* New York: Ivy Books, 1990.

Paul Pearsall, *Making Miracles,* New York: Prentice Hall Press, 1991.

Phil Phillips & Joan Hake Robie, *Halloween and Satanism,* Lancaster, Pennsylvania: Starburst, Inc. 1987.

John Randolph Price, *The Angels Within Us—A Spiritual Guide to the Twenty-Two Angels that Govern Our Lives,* New York: Fawcett Columbine, 1993.

Maurice Rawlings, *Beyond Death's Door,* Nashville, Tennessee: Thomas Nelson, Inc., 1978.

Maurice S. Rawlings, *To Hell and Back,* Nashville, Tennessee: Thomas Nelson Publishers, 1993.

Reader's Digest, *Quest for the Unknown—Life Beyond Death,* Pleasantville, New York: The Reader's Digest Association, Inc., 1992.

Charlie W. Shedd, *Brush of an Angel's Wing,* Ann Arbor, Michigan: Servant Publications, 1994.

David Spangler, *Reflections of the Christ,* Scotland: Findhorn, 1977.

Rebecca Springer, *Within the Gates,* Dallas, Texas: Christ for the Nations, 1971.

Lester Sumrall, *The Reality of Angels,* South Bend, Indiana: LeSEA Publishing Company, Inc. (no date).

Terry Lynn Taylor, *Creating with the Angels—An Angel-Guided Journey into Creativity,* Tiburon, California: H. J. Kramer, Inc., 1993.

Time-Life Books, *Mysteries of the Unknown: Mystic Places,* Alexandria, Virginia.: Time-Life Books, 1987.

Time-Life Books, *Mysteries of the Unknown: Psychic Powers,* Alexandria, Virginia.: Time-Life Books, 1987.

Kelsey Tyler, *There's an Angel on Your Shoulder: Angel Encounters in Everyday Life,* New York: Berkley Books, 1994.

U.S. News and World Report, (25) March 1991.

Ian Wilson, *The After Death Experience—The Physics of the Non-Physical,* New York: William Morrow and Company, Inc., 1987.

*Recommended as comprehensive books about angels from an authentic Christian perspective.

**Recommended books to consult regarding the New Age philosophy and the occult.

A Personal Note From the Author

Now that you have read this book . . . .

For over eleven years I have been fighting for your children, and millions of parents, grandparents, pastors and teachers have been influenced by this ministry. Although my ministry may be new to you, much of the increased awareness we see today on the affect of toys and media on children are fruit from the seed I planted as a young man.

At age four I gave my heart to the Lord, and at age fifteen I was called into the ministry. I have never strayed from that calling and have always considered it an honor and privilege to serve the Lord in full-time ministry.

My wife Cynthia serves in the ministry with me as well as home schools our four children. We have dedicated our lives to confronting issues that affect children and challenging parents to train and command their children.

One of my most recent books, *Helping Your Children Walk With God,* reveals the heart of this ministry. It is one of the most Important books I have ever written and every parent and grandparent who desires that their children know God in a deeper way needs this book.

This 260 page book is available for your donation of any size to our ministry. Please make your checks payable to Child Affects. Send to Child Affects, P.O. Box 68, Rockwall, Texas 75087. Your gift is tax deductible.

Thank you in advance for your generous donation to help me continue this fight for your children.

For the Children,
Phil Phillips

Phil Phillips is available for speaking engagements, parent training workshops and interviews. If your church or organization is interested in scheduling Phil Phillips write to:

Child Affects
Phil Phillips, Director
P.O. Box 68
Rockwall, Texas 75087
Telephone (817) 430-1774

Other Books by Starburst Publishers

(Partial listing—full list available on request)

Angels, Angels, Angels —Phil Phillips

Subtitled—*Embraced by The Light...or...Embraced by The Darkness?* Discovering the truth about Angels, Near-Death Experiences and other Spiritual Awakenings. Also, why the sudden interest in angels in this day and age? Can we trust what we read in books like *Embraced By The Light?*

(trade paper) ISBN 0914984659 **$10.95**

Dinosaurs, The Bible, Barney & Beyond —Phil Phillips

In-depth look at Evolution, Creation Science, and Dinosaurs in the media and toys. Reader learns why Barney, the oversized purple dinosaur, has become a pal to millions of children, and what kind of role model is Barney.

(trade paper) ISBN 0914984594 **$9.95**

Turmoil In The Toy Box —Phil Phillips

A shocking exposè of the toy and cartoon industry—unmasks the New Age, Occult, Violent, and Satanic influences that have invaded the once innocent toy box. Over 175,000 in print.

(trade paper) ISBN 0914984047 **$9.95**

Halloween And Satanism —Phil Phillips and Joan Hake Robie

This book traces the origins of Halloween and gives the true meaning behind this celebration of "fun and games." Jack-O-Lanterns, Cats, Bats, and Ghosts are much more than costumes and window decorations. In this book you will discover that involvement in any form of the occult will bring you more than "good fortune." It will lead you deeper and deeper into the Satanic realm, which ultimately leads to death. Over 90,000 in print.

(trade paper) ISBN 091498411X **$9.95**

Horror And Violence—The Deadly Duo In The Media —Phil Phillips and Joan Hake Robie

Americans are hooked on violence! Muggings, kidnappings, rape and murders are commonplace via your TV set. This book not only brings you up-to-date on what is happenig in the media in general, but also will help you and your children survive with integrity in a complex media environment.

(trade paper) ISBN 0914984160 **$9.95**

The Truth About Dungeons & Dragons —Joan Hake Robie

A close look at the fascinating yet dangerous game of Dungeons and Dragons. What it is about. Why it holds such fascination for certain people, especially young, well-educated and gifted people.

(trade paper) ISBN 0914984373 **$5.95**
(audio cassette) ISBN 091498425X **$7.95**

Teenage Mutant Ninja Turtles Exposed! —Joan Hake Robie

Looks closely at the national popularity of Teenage Mutant Ninja Turtles. Tells what they teach and how this "turtle" philosophy affects children (and adults) mentally, emotionally, socially, morally, and spiritually. The book gives the answer to what we can do about the problem.

(trade paper) ISBN 0914984314 **$5.95**

Beyond The River —Gilbert Morris & Bobby Funderburk

The first novel of *The Far Fields* series, **Beyond the River** makes for intriguing reading with high spiritual warfare impact. Set in the future and in the mode of *Brave New World* and *1984*, **Beyond The River** presents a world that is ruined by modern social and spiritual trends. This anti-utopian novel offers an excellent opportunity to speak to the issues of the New Age and "politically-correct" doctrines that are sweeping the country.

(trade paper) ISBN 0914984519 **$8.95**

TemperaMysticism —Shirley Ann Miller

Subtitled—*Exploding The Temperament Theory*. Former Astrologer reveals how Christians (including some well-respected leaders) are being lured into the occult by practicing the Temperaments (Sanguine, Choleric, Phlegmatic, and Melancholy) and other New Age personality typologies.

(trade paper) ISBN 0914984306 **$8.95**

Political Correctness Exposed —Marvin Sprouse

Subtitled—*A Piranha in Your Bathtub*. Explores the history of Political Correctness, how it originated, who keeps it alive today, and more importantly, how to combat Political Correctness. Contains 25 of the most frequently told Politically Correct lies.

(trade paper) ISBN 0914984624 **$9.95**

Reverse The Curse In Your Life —Joan Hake Robie

A handy "guidebook" for those who wish to avoid Satan's snares. Includes Biblical Curses, Forbidden Practices, Warfare Prayers, and much more. This book is the result of author Joan Hake Robie's over ten years of research on the subject of the occult, demons, and Satanism.

(trade paper) ISBN 0914984241 **$7.95**

Books by Starburst Publishers—cont'd.

The Rock Report
—Fletcher A. Brothers

An "uncensored" look into today's Rock Music scene—provides the reader with the necessary information and illustrations to make intelligent decisions about rock music and its influence on the mind.

(trade paper) ISBN 0914984136 **$6.95**

A Woman's Guide To Spiritual Power
—Nancy L. Dorner

Subtitled: *Through Scriptural Prayer.* Do your prayers seem to go "against a brick wall?" Does God sometimes seem far away or non-existent? If your answer is "Yes," *You* are not alone. Prayer must be the cornerstone of your relationship to God. "This book is a powerful tool for anyone who is serious about prayer and discipleship."—Florence Littauer

(trade paper) ISBN 0914984470 **$9.95**

The World's Oldest Health Plan
—Kathleen O'Bannon Baldinger

Subtitled: *Health, Nutrition and Healing from the Bible.* Offers a complete health plan for body, mind and spirit, just as Jesus did. It includes programs for diet, exercise and mental health. Contains foods and recipes to lower cholesterol and blood pressure, improve the immune system and other bodily functions, reduce stress, reduce or cure constipation, eliminate insomnia, reduce forgetfulness, confusion and anger, increase circulation and thinking ability, eliminate "yeast" problems, improve digestion, and much more.

(trade paper-opens flat) ISBN 0914984578 **$14.95**

Purrables
—Alma Barkman

Subtitled: *Words of Wisdom From the World of a Cat.* This book was derived from the antics of the family cat, Sir Purrcival van Mouser. The author has taken anecdotal material used in a weekly humor column and combined it with Scriptural truths from the book of *Proverbs. Purrables* is an inspirational self-help book, with a very unique slant. Sir Purrcival van Mouser draws the reader into consideration of spiritual truths as they apply to everyday living. The humorous behavior of the cat is used to draw a parallel with our own experience or attitude, and the application is summarized by an appropriate proverb. *Purrables* especially appeals to anyone who loves a cat and would therefore enjoy reading truth from a different *purr*spective.

(trade paper) ISBN 0914984535 **$6.95**